W9-BUL-692

THE METAPHOR OF CELEBRITY

Canadian Poetry and the Public, 1955–1980

The Metaphor of Celebrity

Canadian Poetry and the Public, 1955–1980

JOEL DESHAYE

UNIVERSITY OF TORONTO PRESS
Toronto Buffalo London

Toronto Buffalo London
www.utppublishing.com
Printed in Canada

ISBN 978-1-4426-4661-2

Printed on acid-free, 100% post-consumer recycled paper with vegetable-based inks.

Library and Archives Canada Cataloguing in Publication

Deshaye, Joel, 1977–
The metaphor of celebrity : Canadian poetry and the public, 1955–1980 / Joel Deshaye.

Includes bibliographical references and index.
ISBN 978-1-4426-4661-2 (bound)

1. Canadian poetry – 20th century – History and criticism. 2. Poets, Canadian – Public relations. 3. Poetry – Social aspects. 4. Authors and readers – Canada – History – 20th century. 5. Influence (Literary, artistic, etc.) – History – 20th century. 6. Identity (Psychology). I. Title.

PS8153.D47 2013   C811′.509   C2013-903482-X

University of Toronto Press acknowledges the financial assistance to its publishing program of the Canada Council for the Arts and the Ontario Arts Council.

This book has been published with the help of a grant from the Canadian Federation for the Humanities and Social Sciences, through the Awards to Scholarly Publications Program, using funds provided by the Social Sciences and Humanities Research Council of Canada.

University of Toronto Press acknowledges the financial support of the Government of Canada through the Canada Book Fund for its publishing activities.

Contents

THE METAPHOR OF CELEBRITY

Canadian Poetry and the Public, 1955–1980

Introduction

> I am ashamed to ask for your money. Not that you have not paid more for less. You have. You do. But I need it to keep my different lives apart. Otherwise I will be crushed when they join, and I will end my life in art, which a terror will not let me do.
>
> – Leonard Cohen

This book is about poets imagining celebrity when they are not thinking much about money. Although the following chapters help to measure the celebrity of various poets, and although their recognition in public can to some extent be understood in terms of commodities and other such things, my focus is on other issues. Celebrity does move cash; it is transactional, but it is also a cultural phenomenon that obviously depends upon fantasies of more intimate exchanges, and of changing clothes and dressing up to be someone different. Celebrities and fans are involved with each other in such imitation and identification. Their imaginary relationships can define who they are and want to be – sometimes with ironic results, as when the poets in this book write about themselves as if they were more widely recognized celebrities. These poets were stars *and* fans, neither altogether star-struck nor hopelessly narcissistic, and their works encourage a critical understanding of celebrity and its effects on individuals and society.

The poets in this book – Irving Layton, Leonard Cohen, Michael Ondaatje, and Gwendolyn MacEwen – often write about the experience of celebrity and the effects of stardom. Over and over, they imply that an identity crisis can result from their widespread recognition and the public's intense scrutiny of them. As celebrities attempt to manage the public's desire to know them, they seem to become confused about the difference between their private selves and various personas – what Cohen calls his "different lives" in the foregoing epigraph from *Death of a Lady's Man* (1978). The metaphors of identity crisis in the poetry in the following chapters almost always involve the risky interaction of these different lives, or selves, with the public. When the public causes those selves to fuse or "join," as Cohen writes in the epigraph, stars experience what I call the metaphor of celebrity: *privacy is publicity*. Because of this metaphor, celebrity is much more literary than we might expect. It is inseparable from literary culture, and it makes visible some of literature's main themes, such as identity. It is also an experience that people familiar with metaphor can help to explain. And often the explanation is in further metaphors, as when Ondaatje's 1973 poem "Heron Rex" describes celebrity as "a razor in the body."

In discovering a specific metaphor of celebrity, this book asks a fundamental question about the influence of literary thinking in popular culture, and it reasserts the importance of knowledge derived partly from literature even in the context of phenomena that tend not to be associated with supposedly elite forms of art. The discipline of literary studies is not alone in suggesting that metaphor exists, or happens, outside poems and beyond the written word.[1] Linguistics, language philosophy, and psychoanalysis (e.g., in the work of Roman Jakobson, Paul Ricoeur, and Diana Fuss) also recognize metaphor's importance to cognition and feeling. Even neuroscientists are involved, scanning the brain to see how metaphor elicits measurable cognitive events that help literature to seem alive (Paul). My interest is in both the expressive potential of metaphor and its emotional, imaginative, and irrational function in identity formation. The metaphor of celebrity – *privacy is publicity* – is one way of understanding identity formation, self-promotion, and invasions of privacy as enacted and experienced by celebrities and, to some extent, all of us. Metaphor involves the public in everyone's identity formation, especially that of celebrities, because their identities are so often defined according to their publicity, their condition of being very public figures. The following chapters support this argument by invoking examples of what might be called "metaphorical thinking" or "thinking through metaphor," though neither of these phrases adequately describes the real and sometimes unconscious effect of metaphor on our experiences of becoming ourselves.

Although Layton, Cohen, Ondaatje, and MacEwen in the 1960s and 1970s were celebrities who used metaphor and the public to their advantage, they struggled with both of these aspects of their writing, and in general their ambivalence toward both is ultimately more negative than positive. On the one hand, in Ondaatje's "Letters & Other Worlds" (1973), the speaker tells the story of his letter-writing father's "instant fame" (24) and subsequent retreat into privacy, where he dies "without metaphor" (26) in his head. On the other hand, as much as Ondaatje is suggesting that metaphor is vital because it involves people in the publics of family and community, he is also implying that – for star authors – the public's expectations and judgments elicit a fear that can ruin a writer's ability to control metaphor and enjoy the privacy of writing. In various texts by these four poets, one of the author's most important tools becomes a weapon used against him or her. Literary celebrity becomes an existential crisis involving metaphor and the public.

In calling this book *The Metaphor of Celebrity*, I am drawing attention to a metaphor that is less an expression than a state of being. A star whose *privacy is publicity* is someone whose private life has become interesting to the public and has begun to serve as an advertisement. In the popular culture of movies, this metaphor is in the tabloids and magazines, in photographs and interviews. In the usually less popular culture of literature, it is in autobiographical details revealed, altered, or invented in poems and stories. To accept it as metaphor helps us to understand how language and art connect our inner and outer worlds – not merely pragmatically but also with all the wonder and confusion involved when two concepts become at least temporarily indistinguishable. For celebrities, the potential collision of those worlds is both an opportunity for publicity and a multifaceted risk. One aspect of the risk is the invasion of privacy by the paparazzi, fans, or intrusive biographers or critics. These members of the public transmit images, responses, and reviews to stars and thereby help to define the stars, even to themselves and against their better judgment. Unlike some logical statements, metaphors can be inverted: *publicity* can begin to define one's *privacy*. Imagine if a lyric poem or the lyrics of a popular song began not inside, with personal emotions, but with collective feeling and generically determined moods; in fact, genres ensure that this is often the case. The audience's expectations begin to influence the author's sense of autonomy and selfhood. For star poets, this is a cause for introspection that is often acted out in public.

The demands of celebrity on the self began to interest poets at a time when authors in Canada and elsewhere were gaining publicity through the converging media of television and radio. In the nationalistic 1960s and 1970s in Montreal and Toronto, people in government, the media, and the arts communities were promoting these cities as national centres charged with developing Canadian culture throughout the land. Although the distances, languages, and cultures would never be fully bridged, readers could feel involved in the nation's artistic rally by purchasing books that were helped into print by new governmental funds, and, by supporting poets, readers could associate themselves with newly public figures. They had a stake but not a share in those careers. The return on their investment was partly an assurance that they had contributed to the arts, and partly the status of owning something trendy. In the 1960s, poetry seemed at times almost as vital as music; actually, Cohen and other writers sometimes thought of those two arts as interchangeable, just as some critics assume that any form of art that uses metaphor is poetry (thereby dismissing literal poetry as something categorically different, e.g., verse) – whether music, cinema, or literature. For a while, through poetry and celebrity together, metaphor gained unusual publicity, though we hardly recognized it as such. A private experience of imagination and identification had gone public for better or worse.

The authors in this book, and my arguments about them, combine to reveal something about celebrity and metaphor that is not restricted to national, historical, or even traditionally literary contexts, though such contexts help us to gauge the reality, fantasy, and criticism in each author's representations. My analysis focuses on poetic texts written and performed by celebrities during what I call the era of celebrity in Canadian poetry – around 1955 to 1980. This era, though relatively brief, was in the course of Canadian literature in English a dramatic change. By the beginning of the 1960s, poetry was extraordinarily popular. Favourable conditions in the publishing industry, recent convergences of other media, and Layton's example and selective encouragement helped to make celebrity available to poets. Canadian poets experienced stardom and wrote about it; eventually, however, as the interests of writers, publishers, and the public changed, Canadian poetry lost prominence relative to novels – leading the poet James Reaney to reflect in 1984 that "as poets, we've fought the novel and lost" (qtd. in Rae 5).

As the 1960s elapsed, the publishing industry in Canada was rapidly changing. Initially, leaders in the industry used their new funding (resulting from the recommendations of the Massey Commission in 1951) to print books by a wide range of authors. Poetry was cheap partly because there were so few pages in each book compared to the many pages in a novel. When some poets emerged as more successful than others, and when a sufficient market had developed for publishers to take bigger risks, many poets began writing novels, and publishers accepted them. Although the total market increased, poetry became much less prominent than novels by the mid-1970s. By the end of the 1970s, no new poets who could be called celebrities were emerging in Canada. Poets who wanted to maintain or heighten their celebrity needed to become known as novelists, as Ondaatje and Margaret Atwood did, or musicians – though Cohen is the only Canadian author-turned-musician to have enjoyed such mainstream success. Cohen had the option of music when his novels did not satisfy his ambition; MacEwen's two novels appeared too soon (the second, *King of Egypt, King of Dreams*, was published in 1971) to win her further recognition. She did not continue her attempts to write novels when novels were evidently more popular than poetry – a case, perhaps, of bad luck in the timing. The realization that poetry had lost its status was disappointing to many poets, Layton and MacEwen arguably among them (though Layton's strategy was, even from the start, to rail against the philistines, as if literature were not and had never been a success in Canada). This context of shifting taste was an influence on the tone of their poetry; stardom became a false hope for poets.

Partly for this reason, MacEwen, Ondaatje, Cohen, and Layton wrote about their status not only to promote themselves, and sometimes each other, but also to critique celebrity. Except for novelists such as Mordecai Richler in *The Incomparable Atuk* (1963) and Atwood, who tended not to write about celebrity in her poetry, these four poets are mostly alone in imagining the experiences of Canadian poets who were celebrities through the exhilarating and then disappointing transition from the 1960s to the late 1970s. They either exemplified celebrity during this era or had enough experience of it to be especially astute critics. They almost always represent it as harmful – partly because it was a real strain and partly because their successes and status were restricted in degree (literature being less equipped to support celebrity than other types of art, such as music or cinema, especially in Canada). The resulting works form an unofficial collection that can be understood as a historical commentary on the era of celebrity in Canadian poetry.

This commentary focused on two features of stardom that have been identified in recent studies, such as those by John Frow and Loren Glass: its pretence of religious significance and, in the field of poetry, its problematic masculinity. Layton and Cohen exaggerated these two features but not always as obvious parody; on occasion, they were simply grandstanding. One of my arguments, however, is that such grandstanding can initiate or be the catalyst for subsequent expressions and experiences of the metaphor of celebrity – a metaphor that makes the identities of these poets difficult to separate from pseudo-religious and parodically masculine personas. Because Ondaatje and MacEwen experienced stardom of lesser degree than Layton and Cohen during the era of celebrity in Canadian poetry, their critique is somewhat more objective and less implicated in religion and masculinity. Layton's critique was lacking because of his enthusiasm for the potential of celebrity in the field of poetry, but it was original; he was the first. Cohen, having experienced a much higher degree of celebrity than the rest, defined its extreme possibilities by representing celebrity as slavery; Ondaatje and MacEwen later responded to both men by indirectly representing themselves as celebrities who had ambiguous sexual orientations and were sometimes secular – or flawed as religious characters – whereas Layton and Cohen, as social critics, questioned masculinity much less obviously and maintained religious interests despite their generally secular attitudes.

Religiosity and masculinity were some of Layton and Cohen's titular concerns but were not always under examination. Loosely book-ending the era of celebrity in Canadian poetry were Layton's *A Red Carpet for the Sun* in 1959 and Cohen's *Death of a Lady's Man* in 1978; the first can be understood as an introduction and the second as a conclusion to that era. Among other meanings, the "red carpet" in Layton's title refers to what might be called the royal treatment that he received upon being published by a commercial press for the first time. The title also boldly and rather vaingloriously implies that Layton is not only the "sun" but also the *son* of God, which he suggests more explicitly in his memoir *Waiting for the Messiah* (1985). Layton's religious pretence was closely related to the problematic masculinity of his public persona, though Cohen seemed to announce the end of that masculinity – along with the era of celebrity in Canadian poetry – by calling his book *Death of a Lady's Man* and symbolically retiring from stardom, temporarily, into the practice of Buddhism. As the definitive figures of that era, Layton and Cohen became known, and notorious, for their masculinity and religious pretence. Although they were often parodying themselves, they were also flagrantly promoting themselves, and other poets articulated the critique more clearly and from new perspectives.

Ondaatje and MacEwen expressed their opinions about celebrity by writing ostensibly about others, not themselves, and thereby gained a critical distance from celebrity. They were celebrities of lesser degree than Layton and Cohen during the era of celebrity in Canadian poetry, though Ondaatje later became more widely recognized than Layton. Ondaatje's *The Collected Works of Billy the Kid* (1970) exposes the violence of traditional masculine roles and the bias toward heterosexual men in the culture of literary celebrity. His representation of Billy as a ghost, in my view, shows him to be distancing himself from celebrity's religious pretence by depicting a secular paranormal figure rather than one of religion. He also clarifies the differences between stardom and other types of recognition, such as legend. MacEwen's interest was especially in myth, but she also exposed the heteronormativity of literary celebrity (at least in Canada) and the violence of masculinity in *The T.E. Lawrence Poems* (1982). Like Ondaatje's Billy, her Lawrence is less dogmatically religious; he is, rather, more mystical – but also problematically imperial. Nevertheless, her Lawrence's mysticism allows him to distance himself from customs and traditions that give religion and celebrity power. MacEwen's own experience of celebrity was similar to Ondaatje's until his success in the 1980s and 1990s, but she chose not to continue writing novels. For that reason, among others, her celebrity was considerably restricted. Another reason for the limit of her celebrity was that she was a woman in a field, as Atwood and others have suggested, that was dominated by men; her critique of stardom is especially personal because of this discrimination, yet it is especially objective because *The T.E. Lawrence Poems* appeared after the end of the era of celebrity in Canadian poetry.

The themes of masculinity and religion also gave these four poets much of the symbolism that helps them to express negative opinions of the public. As Michael Warner has shown throughout his recent work, publics are seldom unitary and cohesive, but they can be imagined as one normative body: "the." Although the symbols are various in the poems of the following chapters, the public is almost always demonized, sometimes as literally as possible. For Layton, the star poet is a prophet whose audience, when he has one, comprises demons, gnats, and hunters that assault, confine, and emasculate him. For Cohen, the star poet is a masochist who gives up masculine dominance for enslavement by photographers and the public more generally. For Ondaatje, celebrities are men both ostracized and hunted, even figuratively raped (as in the case of his Billy the Kid, led by his captors through the desert) by symbols of the public such as the sun (notably a star). For MacEwen, they are martyrs pursued by demons both religious and psychological. So frustrated by the culture of stardom as they obviously were at times, these poets represented celebrity as a status negotiated with the public in a Faustian bargain – the devil granting success in exchange for the soul, the private self.

The first chapter of this book expands upon this introduction, beginning with my argument about the metaphor of celebrity and what catalyses it: a sequence made up of the would-be celebrity's grandstanding, his or her creation of various personas to negotiate with the public's demands, and the public's invasion of the celebrity's privacy. The chapter also explains the connections between the metaphor of celebrity, the problematic masculinity that other scholars have noticed in poets who are celebrities, and the pretence of religious significance that has also been noticed in celebrity more generally. It finally joins the debate about the terms *celebrity* and *fame* in the historical context of the twentieth century and its media, arguing that the difference between these terms is important to authors, while acknowledging the ideological assumptions involved in using those terms differently or as synonyms.

The second chapter is very different from the first in its critical methods; it is more specific to the history of Canadian literature, and it attempts to quantify the celebrity that characterized an era in Canadian poetry that began around 1955, peaked around the late 1960s, and ended around 1980. As my statistical research into the topicality of these poets in some magazines and newspapers and on national radio and television suggests, celebrity in Canadian poetry was a multi mass media phenomenon for a few poets during a general boom in publishing for everyone else. But it was also involved in the changing relationship between the popular literary forms of poetry and the novel. Poetry became less prominent than the novel for reasons such as Layton's relative overexposure and the opportunities that poetry created for novelists (who were often also poets) and their publishers.

Layton was prototypical, and he changed how poets and poetry influenced culture. In chapter 3, my argument is that Layton was Canada's first star poet, one whose recognition was established through his notorious persona in the spectacular medium of television, in public discourse, and in poetry from the mid-1950s until the 1970s. Layton established the terms of reference (viz., masculinity and religiosity) for the next generation of poets who were celebrities. He did so by adopting and adapting Friedrich Nietzsche's prophetic character Zarathustra, who supplied some of the ideology and symbolism related to Layton's religious pretension. Although Layton was enthusiastic about the potential of celebrity, his initial ambition was for fame; celebrity distracted him, led to his typecasting, and partly ruined his potential – consequences that he anticipated remarkably early in his career. He eventually realized that the typecasting that stars sometimes experience tends to limit their freedoms of expression and self-definition, yet he compulsively promoted himself until his celebrity faded as a result of his overexposure and the changing values of the 1960s and 1970s.

An overview and analysis of Layton's appearances on television and radio are the basis of chapter 4, a shorter transitional chapter, which argues that he wanted to be seen and heard through those media so that he could popularize, through controversy, an art associated with a small number of intellectuals. From the mid-1950s to 1960, he was involved in debates on both televised and radio versions of *Fighting Words* with panellists of various political orientations, and on other programs beyond the 1960s. Numerous authors, notably including Miriam Waddington and Morley Callaghan, argued with Layton about various topics, the focus being (in this chapter) on high and low cultures, mass media, and celebrity. Layton's contrarian attitude in some of these debates suggests that he believed controversy itself would be self-promotional; he sometimes played the devil's advocate even if that role led him to seem hypocritical in the context of his performances in other debates, interviews, and his writing. He agreed with others, however, when their opinions were favourable to the arts or critical of the cultural factors that discourage the public from reading poetry and literature in general. Cynical about the likelihood of reconciling popular and literary cultures, he nevertheless helped to draw attention to poets as broadly relevant critics and public figures.

Cohen, the subject of chapter 5, was Layton's protégé and began to exceed his mentor's celebrity around the time that the film *Ladies and Gentlemen ... Mr. Leonard Cohen* introduced him to national audiences in 1965. By 1968, he was the unsurpassed star poet in the history of Canadian literature, thanks partly to the international success of his music, which had a spin-off effect on his literary career until the early 1970s (and sporadically after the mid-1980s). Another shorter chapter that focuses on media other than print, this chapter introduces some of Cohen's main concerns through his music – not to suggest that his music is more important to this book than his poetry is, but to acknowledge that modern audiences probably first hear of Cohen through his songs. Parallel to his more traditionally literary texts, his albums from the 1960s and 1970s also commented on celebrity, often by relying on his preferred metaphors of saints and martyrs to invoke the religious pretence of celebrity. Cohen's favourite musical persona was, perhaps, that of the mysterious stranger – a figure sometimes recognizable but sometimes so anonymous that he is unfamiliar even to himself. This chapter follows the development of that persona through his albums from the 1960s and 1970s.

As chapter 6 argues, although Cohen won accolades for his early love poetry, he began writing increasingly negative poetry as his literary celebrity neared its peak. Cohen represented his extreme success by suggesting that celebrity is slavery – an interpretation supported by his fascination with martyrdom and his subtle, ironic critique of masculinity. Adapting psychoanalytic and psychological theories of masochism and sadomasochism, this chapter argues that Cohen's metaphor of celebrity as slavery is a response to Layton's idealization of freedom, which was not sustainable under the circumstances of a high degree of celebrity. At the conclusion of this chapter, I suggest that Cohen turned from representations of sadomasochism and began to rethink masculinity and the religious pretence in the context of the historical fade of celebrity in Canadian poetry at the end of the 1970s.

One of the most insightful studies of Cohen's work continues to be Ondaatje's *Leonard Cohen* (1970), which is the first major sign of Ondaatje's interest in stardom. Chapter 7 demonstrates that Ondaatje first became widely known for *The Collected Works of Billy the Kid* (1970), though his literary celebrity was not comparable to that of Layton or Cohen during the era of celebrity in Canadian poetry. Ondaatje arguably represents the Wild West's infamous gunslinger Billy the Kid as a celebrity and as a ghost. Focusing (as much as possible) on the uncanniness of Billy's ghostliness and invisibility, I show how various symbols in the book suggest that Billy wants to avoid the public's gaze and its normative influence on sexuality and masculinity. He wants to be a legend to avoid that influence of stardom. By questioning heterosexual masculinity and offering a secular alternative to the comparatively religious personas of

Layton and Cohen, and by often choosing non-Canadian characters (in addition to Billy) to represent as stars, Ondaatje initiates a commentary on the era of celebrity in Canadian poetry that has greater critical distance than the parodies by Layton and Cohen.

Chapter 8 extends the argument from the previous chapter with an analysis of the development of Ondaatje's representations of celebrity after *The Collected Works of Billy the Kid*. Focusing on *Rat Jelly* (1973) and *Secular Love* (1984), which includes the long poem *Tin Roof* (first published in 1982), I argue that Ondaatje's sensual style and his related focus on bodies should be understood in the context of his celebrity and an implicit conflict between bodies and images. His ambivalent identifications with Hollywood stars, and his phenomenological representations of the body, help to explain concepts of privacy and publicity that are major aspects of both stardom and publicity in general, including the publicity of writing.

Similarly, in her poetry, MacEwen identifies with public figures. Chapter 9 shows how MacEwen developed the figure of the magician as a representation, among other things, of celebrity. I look briefly at MacEwen's novel *Julian the Magician* (1963) and show how her poetic sensibilities were engaged, in prose as in poetry, in her questioning of celebrity and its religious pretence. The figure of the magician appears also in various poems and other guises in *The Rising Fire* (1963) and *A Breakfast for Barbarians* (1966). MacEwen reveals her interest in performance in these poems, which culminates in her arguably classic poem "Manzini: Escape Artist." Therein, the escape artist is an extension of the magician, another figure more relevant than ever in the context of her celebrity and its limitations.

By the time she wrote *The T.E. Lawrence Poems*, the era of celebrity in Canadian poetry had recently passed, and women had tended not to experience a high degree of celebrity in poetry. In my final chapter, I argue that *The T.E. Lawrence Poems* is an apt, sophisticated rejoinder to that exclusion. MacEwen's impersonation of Lawrence is her most significant attempt at grandstanding, which can be better understood in her context as *passing*, given the postcolonial strategies of that book. Following theories from postcolonial and gender studies, I argue that MacEwen concludes her various observations about celebrity by attempting to pass as Lawrence so that she can expose the public's expectations about the sexuality of male celebrities. She also sympathizes with Lawrence by imagining his struggles with postcolonial guilt, masculinity, and his difficult quest for spiritual enlightenment. This chapter includes the most biographical and potentially controversial of my interpretations of the aforementioned poets, but they are justified in part by evidence that suggests MacEwen was thinking not only personally but also fatalistically about the consequences of stardom for identity.

The conclusion of this study partly responds to this question: if the era of celebrity in Canadian poetry was exclusive to a small number of poets, why did they represent it so negatively? To answer this question, I look at some examples of poetry and other star texts since the year 2000 to see what has changed in mass media and on the national scene.

Because of the small number of poets who could be called celebrities in the Canadian context, and because of the brevity of their historical presence as celebrities, I can offer a fairly thorough historical account and interpretation of celebrity in Canadian poetry, and I include the perspectives of some of those who knew it best. In this study, I also offer new arguments, based on the metaphor of celebrity and various other metaphors of identity crisis, about how celebrities can be changed by their status, success, and experience.

1 The Metaphor of Celebrity

> There are ways of going
> physically mad, physically
> mad when you perfect the mind
> where you sacrifice yourself for the race
> when you are the representative when you allow
> yourself to be paraded in the cages
> celebrity a razor in the body
>
> – Michael Ondaatje

In these lines from "Heron Rex," Michael Ondaatje shares some of his disturbing thoughts about celebrity. He represents it as "a razor" that gives a star the means of conducting a suicidal "sacrifice" of mind and body. Coming from his book *Rat Jelly* (1973), these lines imply that the "race" exalted by the sacrifice is also a "rat race" for celebrity – a competition for wealth, power, and prestige that reduces individuals to the status of rodents in "cages." He suggests furthermore that celebrity cuts through the public-private interface of "the body" into "the mind," threatening to reveal the private self to the public. Even when celebrities willingly give out details of their private lives for self-promotion, their exposed selves tend to be redefined by the public, or for the public, which cannot fail to be imagined as something greater than the individual. When privacy is publicity, privacy ceases to exist as such. Publicity thereby grows.[1] As a metaphor according to the formula "this *is* that" (Frye 11, his emphasis), *privacy is publicity* helps to explain one of celebrity's defining functions and experiences: the invasion of privacy that can result in a star's identity crisis. Although stardom depends on a complex system of media and various aspects of culture, it also involves variations on this metaphor. It is literary, and writers are therefore some of its best "representative[s]" and its best critics.

My argument about celebrity's literary status is less about the shared privileges of celebrity and literature, and more about celebrity's metaphoric, and thus literary, function. Among the existing theories of metaphor is the idea that metaphor is not only a literary device but also an aspect of perception and cognition (not "merely" imagination). We often forget that literature and other arts do not simply produce objects and cultural events. Art involves thinking and performing that can change us personally. It becomes especially meaningful when we attempt to determine if we are being true to ourselves, and if our identities realign as we imitate art, other artifices, and other people. The partial and sometimes total indistinguishability of categories associated with identity is partly the result of metaphor at their basis. For the sake of understanding our own confusion, we can try to "think through metaphor" – to solve the problem of metaphor (which is rarely neutral, though not always negative) but also to speak self-consciously in metaphor so that we can appreciate its cognitive function in identity formation. Because it is so visibly public, celebrity is the phenomenon that best illustrates this function, which can be seen in every star's life and, less obviously, in all our lives.

There are two related metaphors that are generic to celebrity (and then there are the many other specific metaphors that artists create in their work, such as the razor in Ondaatje's aforementioned poem). The first is more obviously performative than the one I call *the* metaphor of celebrity. Most of the poets in this study wrote about themselves as if they were more widely recognized than they were in reality, or they wrote as if they were other celebrities of higher degree. I call this self-aggrandizement "grandstanding" to suggest that their self-promotion and identity formation depend on metaphor: "a process ... by means of which one thing is made to *stand in* for another thing" (Punter 2, my emphasis). When Ondaatje displays a photograph of himself as a boy in a cowboy costume at the end of *The Collected Works of Billy the Kid* (1970), to some extent he "stand[s] in" for Billy, a man whose celebrity was greater than his own emerging reputation in 1970. The *Oxford English Dictionary* defines the verb *grandstanding* as "perform[ing] with an eye to the applause of the spectators in the grandstand," but I also mean it as standing in for someone more grand – a bigger man or even a god (someone "larger than life"). This supplementary definition calls attention to the metaphoricity of performance and helps to explain the pretence of religious significance, the exaggerated sexuality, the delusions of grandeur, and even the likely disappointment that often seem to constitute the identities of celebrities; it also helps to explain their sometimes enthusiastic sense of potential identity formation as they experiment with different personas, different selves.[2]

The adoption of any public persona is in itself metaphoric; in doing so, a person in effect says, "I am someone else" (a syntax equivalent to Northrop Frye's "this *is* that").[3] We all have personas that developed through metaphor and are involved in our identities, but they are less noticeable than the personas of stars, because their publicity (their condition of being public) is much more visible. We develop our personas through identification with others and by other means. Identification is a feeling of affinity or similarity – a sense that an otherwise different person could relate to you, be a model for you, even stand in for you. Diana Fuss argues that identity formation is metaphoric because metaphor, "*the substitution of the one for the other*" (5, her emphasis), enables identification and the social mingling of privacy and publicity. Fans relate to celebrities through identification more obviously than we all relate to others, again because the star-fan relationship is so visible – for example, when the audience at a concert sings along with the musicians, thereby identifying with them (and each other) and sharing emotion, including emotions that the lyricist(s) might have felt in writing the song. In less public relationships, we privately affirm to ourselves that someone else is notably like us or our ideals, and we adjust our personas so that we may belong with them. Or we might learn that lovers sometimes attempt to remove their masks, their personas, and join with each other so intimately that they feel as one. Metaphor is thereby an aspect of human relationships in general.[4]

Stars exemplify self-other relationships through their personas, which are comparatively distinct because of their work in the limelight and because of public interest in them. A star has multiple selves on a continuum between privacy and publicity. "'Everybody wants to be Cary Grant,' said Cary Grant. 'Even I want to be Cary Grant'" (Cowen 4). His joking acknowledgment of his grandstanding and his recognition of the appeal of his public persona suggest that he was coping well enough with his celebrity at the time. Like Grant, any star has a real, private self that cannot be known through literature or other public media. No private self can be known in such media because private information, once divulged, becomes public by definition. After this self, there are various personas, including the one that we could refer to as the *private persona*, which is a decoy or token offered to the audience to appease its demand for access to the celebrity's private life. Then there is the public persona, which is the obvious performer – the bigger man – whose allegiance is ultimately with the audience, a guarantor of celebrity. In our daily lives, for example, these personas are active when we reveal a little of our privacy to help others feel closer to us, or when we assert our confidence in jobs we have not yet won. In the lives of celebrities, grandstanding is especially the role of the public persona, but the private persona engages in it, too, whenever celebrities exaggerate their own status by referring to their private lives as evidence, real or imagined, of being widely recognized.

The second metaphor that is generic to celebrity often develops from grandstanding, but it is not secondary in importance; rather, it is the essential metaphor that results in personal consequences for celebrities, and by understanding it as a metaphor we can appreciate the subtle depreciation of the private self that occurs when celebrities behave as if they were more widely recognized than they are – when they ambitiously associate themselves with others or perform as future, more successful versions of themselves.[5] When the public's interest in the celebrity's private life overcomes the decoy of the private persona, and when success depends on the revelation of biography, the personas must come closer to the private self, and then this metaphor of celebrity – *privacy is publicity* – has a detrimental effect: the public asserts control over the star all along the continuum of his or her identity.[6] Personas are confused; selves fuse. The result is identity crisis – especially if celebrities resort to looking for knowledge of themselves in the audience that seems to know them, as if they were saying, "Tell me who I am because I don't know." The French actor Jean Gabin once said, "People say ... I'm the same in real life as I am in my movies, and that's why they like me'" (qtd. in Boorstin 159); A.D. Hope wrote of Irving Layton that "[n]o poet I have met is so like his books" (102). Although the biographical fallacy is not usually considered to be the author's problem (rather, it is an interpretive problem), it can harmfully affect how celebrities understand themselves.[7]

Their "identity confusion" (Rojek 11), when it becomes fusion in the metaphor of celebrity, is the ultimate transfer of power to the public that defines them. This metaphor is essential to stardom because, unlike grandstanding, it is arguably involved in all cases. Not all celebrities are involved in grandstanding, because not all of them have careers in performance; some are just lucky or unlucky enough to be starkly exposed under the temporary examination of the mass media – for reasons often as banal as the number of hamburgers they have eaten during their lifetimes or the silliness of their names. All celebrities, however, must deal with the risk of exposed privacy, whether they are using their own biographies self-promotionally or whether a journalist or fan uncovers and widely shares the details of their private lives. When privacy is publicity, metaphor is helping to change a star's sense of identity, but it is also helping to form our assumptions about our privilege of access to others and our own limits as selves.

Metaphors propose irrational and impossible dualities, but the metaphor of celebrity is at least temporarily unilateral in its effect on identity. It is not a balanced equation – this *is equal to* that. It is an equation that demonstrates the enormity of publicity in contrast with privacy.[8] The poets in this book implicitly wonder, "What if my privacy becomes interesting to the public and serves to advertise me?" The threat of the metaphor of celebrity is more obvious if the question is reversed: "What if publicity *is* my privacy?" You can look out on the world of crowded streets, nearly ubiquitous logos, advertisements, "reality TV," video screens, and wireless communication devices, and see yourself literally or figuratively reflected in them. To say, "*That* is privacy," or "*That* is what constitutes my private self," is to realize the potential of the metaphor of celebrity. One of the cultural ramifications of identity formation in an era of celebrity is that we are at risk of understanding ourselves merely as combinations of branded things we own, objects we desire, images, recorded memories, actions outside ourselves, and public relationships. What of suppressed or repressed drives, of untold stories, of dreams and activities and things not meant for others? These secrets are aspects of our identities, but they can seem minimally important compared to publicity. When an anonymous young woman knocked down at a 2011 riot was photographed kissing her boyfriend on the street behind the crowd, they were later identified by the social media, and then the traditional media, throughout the world. Brian Stelter wrote in response that "[t]he collective intelligence" of billions of online minds "makes the public sphere more public than ever before" (par. 5). As in the epigraph to this chapter, the representations of stardom in Canadian poetry tend to be negative, partly because stardom magnifies publicity and involves the cultural depreciation of the value of privacy and the related sense of self.

Our fascination with celebrity is partly the result of our sympathetic understanding, conscious or not, that celebrities are the epitome of our own relationships with the public. They perform the extreme versions of our own desire to be someone different, to be desired as sex symbols, to be loved, and to be heard and acknowledged in the public realm. Celebrities are also subject to a degree of humiliation that we recognize, in its narrower scope, in our dealings with others. Whenever we wish that a private moment had remained so, and when the condition of being public is difficult, we can look to stars who have often experienced worse. Such identification is metaphoric, and celebrity can help metaphor to be more evident to us.

Although identification is very personal, it is also political; it affects how we behave with others, who are always to some extent public, at least relative to the private self. The metaphor of celebrity essentially involves an initial, contested, and finally untenable distinction between the private and public realms – which have been, however, separated and guarded for sociopolitical reasons. Because the public-private dichotomy was historically gendered to exclude women from the public sphere and to restrict their influence to the comparative privacy, and marginality, of the domestic sphere, feminist scholars have tended to decry the effects of accepting the public as a singular, dominant category (Warner 32–3). Contrary to that thinking, the poets in this book tend to represent the public not exactly as singular but as singularly dominant and deserving of resistance, and this helps to valorize the private self and its realm in the context of the bigger and generally more influential public.

In *Publics and Counterpublics* (2002), Michael Warner argues that the public is "an imaginary convergence point" (55) in society, though in reality that "point" is not singular; it is composed of many groups of people who are not always united (and not necessarily present, unlike the audience). It is therefore like a nation: an "imagined community," in Benedict Anderson's phrase, but without the national connotations.[9] As with nations, however, we should recognize the importance of imagining the public: "People do not always distinguish even between *the* public and *a* public, though in certain contexts the difference can matter a great deal. *The* public ... is thought to include everyone within the field in question" (Warner 65, his emphasis). Poets who write to promote themselves are imagining a readership and by extension a public, but the traits attributed to it often imply that it is *the* public, which does not exist only as it is represented by them – as a homogeneously negative social entity that affirms cultural ideals as norms. Nevertheless, that public, imagined as "the," is also expected to enforce certain "norms" and "deep and unwritten rules" (Warner 25) that can impinge upon privacy.

The private self is imagined, too, and its relationship with the public is a concern for celebrities. The private self might not exist before social relationships are formed, and it might simply not even exist – but a person has a sense of self, regardless of its origin, that affects motivation, reasoning, and the perception of quality of life. Although current debates about social networking technologies raise questions about the value of privacy in the twenty-first century, the twentieth-century poets in the following chapters imagine the private self as an ideal worth guarding from the public.[10] Not long after the peak of his 1960s celebrity, Leonard Cohen wrote: "This is a threat / Do you know what a threat is / I have no private life" (*Energy* 62). Despite the potential critical or philosophical objections to the private self as a model of subjectivity, celebrities often perform as if they need recourse to such an ideal because of the "threat," experienced as the metaphor of celebrity, of the public's interest in them.

Metaphor itself is both private and public, and often worrisome in both cases. It is evident in the newspapers, for example, when politicians and journalists describe politics as a "fight" and a "battle" conducted by parties in "war rooms." Politicians choose these military metaphors over terms of diplomacy and thereby manipulate opinion. David Punter argues that "[a]ll public life sustains itself through metaphors" (46). Recently, Paul Krugman in the *New York Times* noticed the common, implicit metaphors that describe the economy as a stalled car or sick person: "The idea that the economic engine is going to catch or the patient rise from his sickbed any day now encourages policy makers to settle for sloppy, short-term measures when the economy really needs well-designed, sustained support" (par. 4). Such public metaphors influence our thinking, subliminally or otherwise; George Lakoff and Mark Turner argue that metaphors can reveal "hidden aspects of one's own mind and one's own culture" (214). They can mislead us. Whereas similes are true (because there are almost always similarities between different things), metaphors are false (Davidson, "What" 39, 41). They are convenient but often illogical as thought and as expression. In public, metaphor can be a serious threat, which is how the poets in this book characterize celebrity and, implicitly, metaphor.

In private, however, that falsity can be understood as fantasy or wishful thinking.[11] However public metaphor can be, and however negative, it can enable and extend individual creativity and fulfilment because it does not initially seem to close down possibility. As many teachers of literature know, it encourages discussion and negotiation of interpretations, though compared with symbolism it is usually more definite and dramatic. Metaphor is also involved when stars tensely negotiate their personas – their fantastic, make-believe selves – with the public. If metaphor were a person (and, indeed, personification is a type of metaphor), it would be someone highly resourceful and adaptable – and yet someone whose desires are conflicting, who wants incompatible things. Eli Mandel states that metaphor "is not only identity, but analogy; not only the fusion of opposites, but particularization" (*Irving* 26). In *The Rule of Metaphor* (1975), Paul Ricoeur makes a similar statement, that metaphor involves "a tension between identity and difference" (4). Although Ricoeur and Mandel suggest that metaphor is never an easy compromise,[12] their common term is "identity," and this is the trouble – at least when we consider it to be involved not only in language but also in selfhood.

I hope not to complicate celebrity unnecessarily with this argument about metaphor. The aforementioned metaphoric processes and effects – grandstanding and the fusion of selves – might seem to describe a conceit (which, in literary studies, is an elaborate metaphor); however, my intention is not to create metaphor but to explain what is already metaphoric. Indeed, "[a]ny statement concerning anything whatsoever that goes on, metaphor included, will have been produced *not without* metaphor" (Derrida 50, his emphasis).

But rather than simply exaggerate the metaphoricity of language, my argument about grandstanding accounts for the literariness of identity formation and self-promotion as both begin to go wrong for celebrities, and it joins the three main parts of my argument about celebrity: that it involves metaphor, that it is problematically masculine for poets (and sometimes for other writers), and that it also involves a pretence of grandeur or religious significance.

Together, exaggerated sexuality and a degree of religiosity – from subtle to dramatic – help to consolidate a star's social power, though the poets in this book represent that power as ultimately reversible. Because metaphor is more obviously involved in sexuality than it is in religion (being that, for example, it can promote a feeling of oneness in sexual relationships and, in another sense, fuse the private and public realms to redouble the influence of sexual norms), I will focus on the latter, to show that metaphor and celebrity do some of the same things: they both elicit feelings of spiritual connection and empathy between writers and readers, or stars and fans. When scholarly interest in metaphor revived in the 1960s and 1970s, critics from various fields reached a tacit agreement: that metaphor is illogical (Frye 11), that it depends on subjective effects such as feelings (Davidson, "What" 45; Ricoeur, "Metaphorical" 144), and that its subjectivity helps to create a sense of "intimacy" (Cohen, "Metaphor" 9) between writers and readers – or, I would add, stars and fans. Obviously, given the erotic representations of so many celebrities, this "intimacy" is potentially sexual, and sexual intercourse and romantic love do sometimes create feelings of oneness that can be described as metaphoric.

More than on sexual metaphor, literary celebrity depends on religious metaphor, partly because of the separation in space and time that exists between authors and readers, a separation that precludes the sexual tension of bodies that are close to each other. Metaphor can create a "mystical sense of union" (Crocker 62) and transcendence that defies space and time. In the context of increasing secularism, Karsten Harries suggests that "lacking faith, modern man seeks refuge in an unreal, aesthetic environment of his own making" (82) – the world of metaphor. He concludes: "All metaphor that is more than an abbreviation for more proper [i.e., literal] speech gestures toward what transcends language. Thus metaphor implies lack. God knows neither transcendence nor metaphor – nor would man, if he were truly godlike" (Harries 84). In other words, those who have faith have no need for transcendence or metaphor because God is there, unspoken, not needing His work to be simulated in language. In contrast with these faithful people are those "modern" people who need metaphor to compensate for an absent god. Therefore, any type of stardom (and perhaps especially literary celebrity, because it involves the aforementioned separation) can be compelling because its metaphor fulfils the social function of creating a feeling of belonging ("a mystical sense of union") and compensating for that absent god. People need others to engage in grandstanding and thereby supply the culture with the bigger men or gods that are lacking: the heroes of politics, sports, music, or literature.

Most celebrities, however, and literary celebrities especially, probably understand that they are not religiously significant, despite the public's supposed devotion to them. Any adequately self-reflective poets engaged in grandstanding – pretending to be God or a god or merely someone grander – must understand themselves to be fundamentally insufficient as people and as writers. Language, always lacking (partly because the word is not the thing), cannot give them the power to transform beyond certain limits common to all human beings. Furthermore, if the religious pretence has a sanction, in the sense of a limit, it is that hardly anyone really believes the pretence; celebrities are not literally considered sacred in most cases (Frow 201, 204). Celebrity as we know it depends partly on the assumption that religious belief weakened during the general trend toward a secular society in the Western world in the latter half of the twentieth century. Although John Frow argues that "the secularization thesis ... is plainly wrong" (207) because religion thrives in many places of the world – including later twentieth-century North America – he claims that it sometimes exists in "mutant religious forms" (208), such as the worship of celebrity.

Lynn McCutcheon et al. can refer to fans as "celebrity worshippers" (*passim*), but fans are not often devoted to a star in the long term. The phenomenon of the "one-hit wonder" is evidence of this and of the public's seemingly unreasonable expectations. Fans rarely remain devoted to stars, and sometimes their devotion is ironic. As I wrote in a 2009 article, "the 'cult of personality' is sometimes as much a sardonic indulgence in spiritual kitsch as it is an uncritical deification of celebrities and their ways of life" (80). The irony of this religious function is often reflected in texts written by literary celebrities who had religious personas, such as Layton's prophet and Cohen's saint. In some cases, however, a star seems so committed to his or her art and work that it is painful to accept the religious function as only a pretence – though the pain might also be nostalgia for a status that never truly existed. An imbalance in devotion is a bigger problem for celebrities than for fans, because fans can easily find more stars to follow, whereas a star cannot always hold the public's attention.

One of the powers of the public is to shun former stars or ignore those who want some type of recognition for the first time; another is to increase someone's visibility until intimacy becomes invasive. Fans want a personal connection with celebrities rather than a public character, even though the public character – and all of the images and performances associated with it – is what attracts them. They want what Richard Dyer calls, in *Stars* (1979), the "unmediated personality" (17) that seems to be revealed in close-ups in films. In *Star Authors* (2000), Joe Moran has a similar argument, that "the audience's relation with the star is a compulsive search for the 'real' – an attempt to distinguish between the 'authentic' and the 'superficial' in the star's personality" (62). This "search" sometimes results in the invasion of a star's privacy.

Although the balance of power between celebrities and the public constantly shifts (Marshall 183) – which is to be expected, given the fusion and confusion of the terms *public* and *private* – the metaphor of celebrity ensures that power eventually reverts to the public. Because the audience is an aspect of the star's public,[13] and yet because the star is individually more public and therefore helps to represent the public to the audience, both the star and the audience have eyes on the public. Fans are usually understood to be the public because as a multitude they cannot be the singular, private self that a given celebrity represents; however, from the perspective of the fan, the celebrity tends to reinforce social norms, *public* norms. Rarely does anyone seem to represent privacy, and, lacking representation, privacy lacks power. Although the private self can be made public, rarely can anything public be made private (except in the very different sense of the privatization of public goods). Relative to the individual, the public does not need to negotiate with the outside influences that make the private self vulnerable. It is already outside. The representations of celebrity in the poetry examined in the following chapters almost always focus on the star as an individual beholden to the public's normative influences, which might be more serious when the star's private self is not aligned with sexual norms. Thus, Ondaatje writes in this chapter's epigraph that as a celebrity "you sacrifice yourself for the race / when you are the representative when you allow / yourself to be paraded in the cages." He suggests that celebrities "allow" themselves "to be paraded in the cages" where the public can see them, control them, and exploit them. The star is willing – despite the consequences – to be vulnerable to an audience that seems to have much more power.

The balance of power is especially fascinating when the star is also an audience of other stars – or of someone comparatively public or grand. When a celebrity realizes how small he or she is compared to the audience, the audience can "cut" the celebrity "down to size" (which is another way of interpreting the razor in this chapter's epigraph), and the celebrity becomes the audience of a much more impressive entity: the audience. At an event such as the Academy Awards in Hollywood, the star power of the audience is always greater than that of the celebrities on stage, because the audience has more once, future, and present celebrities. When Ondaatje writes about Billy the Kid and Gwendolyn MacEwen writes about Lawrence of Arabia, they are thinking about their own celebrity in relation to more widely recognized people, while they are also imagining themselves *as* those other people. As fans, and as authors, they gain control over fictional versions of historical figures. They invade the privacy of other celebrities through identification and imagined intimacy with them, and their doing so helps them to appreciate the potential risk that they face in becoming more and more public.

How compelling could the related feelings of intimacy, invasion, confusion, and crisis be, and how real could they – and metaphor – seem? When *privacy is publicity*, what was once secret is now shared, and the distinctions between self and other become less obvious and might even seem to disappear. Even if celebrities videotape themselves having sex in their bedrooms, or have their garbage stolen, or are exposed as drug addicts, there is much that remains private in their lives. If nothing else, they still have their thoughts. Literary celebrities, however (and others, such as actors), make their thoughts and feelings public through their work. What happens to the identities of celebrities when what they do in their minds is reflected upon them by a public that assumes those works and thoughts are authentic, or that seems to accept them as such even if the acceptance is ironic? Many celebrities manage to keep their distance. Others, however, became writers or actors to learn about themselves or perhaps to sublimate their drives and feelings. In those cases, when the sense of intimacy extends to the audience, metaphor can seem so convincingly real that, from the star's perspective, it *is* real.

This experiential reality is illogical, and it can be feigned so that celebrity continues to seem important as an area of inquiry that focuses on individual stars – and it can thereby help celebrity to remain disproportionately important in our culture. To some extent, the poets in this book – and this book itself – are guilty of potentially increasing sympathy for celebrities who are faking or exaggerating their troubles. Celebrity is predisposed to draw attention. Besides its spectacularity, it has the rhetorical advantages of significant emotive potential and a logical circularity that is not easily detected. In his essay about the social function of metaphor, J. Christopher Crocker anticipates the circularity of this logic; he argues that "rhetorical devices" used to express social values can "too easily become tautological self-fulfilling prophecies" (66). Indirectly or otherwise, various critics all provide evidence that a major problem of celebrity is its tautological tendency, which also corroborates my argument about its metaphoricity. Having little that is objectively real to point to, metaphor and celebrity point to themselves.

Yet self-reflexivity and self-reflection are similar processes with different outcomes, and both working together produce an ironic mix. Grandstanding is self-reflexively self-promotional, but it is also a tactic of calling attention to differences in status. It is ironic: a self-promotional complaint that might fail as both promotion and complaint. Stars might convince the audience of their total exposure to the public, including that audience, and thereby create intimacy or its illusion. They might also convince themselves, however erroneously, that they are now defined by the public (which is the threat of typecasting). And yet they might also retain a critical distance that allows them to understand the metaphor of celebrity without succumbing to it themselves. This could be an advantage of literary celebrity over other types, though the dual role that star authors often play as celebrities and fans of more widely recognized stars complicates the issue: they are not bystanders. They are involved. While invoking traditional sources of power such as religion and masculinity to promote themselves to higher degrees of celebrity – thereby to redress the imbalance of power between cultures of celebrity – poets might forget that those traditions are historically interdependent sources of the public's own influence over its membership, including celebrities. Although a knowledge of metaphor can help writers to question both celebrity in general and their own indulgence in it, these poets have something to gain – such as further recognition – in critique. Their opinions on the potential gains and losses resulting from their celebrity tend to be ironic and negative – another indication, perhaps, of literariness, of a culture associated with literature that is not as popular as it once was.

The relationship between literariness and irony is beyond the scope of this book, but the nationally specific ironies in the grandstanding of Canadian star poets are not, given the significance of nationality in some of their performances. These ironies help to introduce those of literary celebrity in general. They are ironies, especially, of relative status – of who is more widely recognized and in what contexts. They help us to realize that grandstanding tends to involve a contextual, often historical, irony related to the varieties of public recognition, such as celebrity and fame – a distinction that is valuable to the poets in the following chapters.

Regardless of the type, the scope of public recognition in Canada is narrow, partly because of the country's small population relative to its own size and its neighbouring countries. As a result, Canadian celebrity is often promoted to these other countries without being marked as Canadian. The poets in this book invoke non-Canadian models of celebrity or fame to promote themselves, theoretically, to readers in Britain and the United States, where celebrity is much more culturally and economically significant, thanks in part to lucrative film industries and a more active tabloid press. In doing so, they imply that Canada cannot or will not sustain literary celebrity of high degree. The example of Ondaatje writing about himself as if he were Billy the Kid calls attention to their similarities, but they are obviously not the same. Their important difference in the context of this chapter is not their separation in time and space or their incommensurable ethnic heritage; it is that one of them was more widely known than the other. These poets understood that, as writers and Canadians, they were unlikely to achieve success comparable to that of internationally well-recognized figures, and they were therefore seemingly unable to enjoy the power of their celebrity without reservation. They promoted themselves through metaphor not as Canadians but as stars.

The irony is that this self-promotion involves a lot of self-deprecation. Ondaatje, MacEwen, Cohen, and Layton deprecated themselves by implicitly comparing themselves to people of greater renown, even as they attempted, with varying degrees of seriousness, to emulate those people and gain recognition in public. Wryly but also grimly acknowledging that imitation can be the result of attempted emulation, MacEwen indirectly describes herself in *The T.E. Lawrence Poems* (1982) as a "monkey" (66). These poets were admitting the unlikelihood of ever becoming truly grand. Their grandstanding implies that they were living vicariously or felt inferior to the celebrities of higher degree.

The insights of the poets in this book can help to explain the behaviour of aspiring stars in many other contexts, even if as Canadians they were especially sensitive to the degree of their public recognition. Louis Dudek argued that Layton was "[a]s a celebrity ... a purely typical Canadian product, a blow-up of our national inferiority complex" ("Layton" 92), and Desmond Pacey wrote in his review of Layton's *The Swinging Flesh* (1961) that "[Layton's] arrogance is so arrogant that it becomes a form of humility ... as if he were saying, 'You know that I know that I couldn't possibly be as good as I pretend to be'" (119). This hypothetical "national inferiority complex" raises the question of whether Canadians are unusually qualified to say something about celebrity. Indeed, Ondaatje's and MacEwen's choices of non-Canadians raise yet another question: "Why are Canadians not good enough to be stars?" Although there are reasons to doubt "the notion of a specifically Canadian approach" (York, *Literary* 3) to celebrity, the grandstanding of these poets reveals that nationality is an aspect of their criticism of celebrity, which they promote – but sceptically, to say the least – according to models adapted from other countries. One explanation for the insightfulness of these poets on the topic of stardom is that their nationality corresponds with a perception of inferiority that writers anywhere, not only in Canada, have to deal with when attempting to promote themselves in a market that is more conducive to the success of other forms of entertainment, such as movies, music, and sports. *Literary* celebrity?! *Canadian* celebrity?! Canadians share with authors the difficulty of succeeding relative to more populous countries and more popular arts.

The few women who engaged in grandstanding in Canadian poetry did so with a keen awareness of the same problem but in a sexual context that might apply to the national. MacEwen's grandstanding is important partly because her stardom was of lesser degree than that of Layton and Cohen (and obviously the historical Lawrence) during the era of celebrity in Canadian poetry. Her grandstanding reveals the differing degrees of celebrity that were available to male and female poets. Celebrity now seems evenly distributed among the sexes, but literary celebrity has not always been a currency available to women, especially poets, in Canada or elsewhere. In *Women, Celebrity, & Literary Culture between the Wars* (2007), Faye Hammill argues that many women in various countries in the 1920s and 1930s became celebrities despite "various forms of hostility toward women's writing" (21); however, with the exception of Dorothy Parker, none of them was popular as a poet. In the United States and Britain, the scarcity of female star poets was partly the result of "the restrictive promotional system of introducing, editing, and anthologizing" (Jaffe 165), which men controlled. Rarely were women seen to have "muscled in" (Jaffe 165) to cliques formed by men and for men. Loren Glass explains this exclusivity partly in terms of a "hypermasculine public posturing" that "can be understood as a symptomatic response to the feminized, and feminizing, literary marketplace" (18). Although female writers of prose (rarely of poetry) were unusually successful in "the mass cultural public sphere" (Glass 18), some male writers had contempt for that success even as they established their own similar brands of popular writing – and these conditions also existed in the field of Canadian poetry in the 1960s and 1970s. It might be overly provocative to suggest that star poets in Canada wrote mostly about male foreign stars in response to a "literary marketplace" "feminized" as Canadian, but some of the tactics of star poets in Canada reflect a desire to participate internationally in celebrity, just as women have had to be insistent, creative, and sometimes controversial to participate in public discourse along with men.

So MacEwen's Lawrence can be understood as a symbol of gender trouble in addition to national troubles, and of course he is a metaphor. When a man says to himself, "I can be anything I want," he expresses a desire to actualize metaphor that is irrational enough for himself but more so for women in a discriminatory culture. Why was MacEwen not a celebrity of higher degree? She could have chosen any number of other personas: Margaret Atwood chose the comparatively obscure Susanna Moodie, Canadian pioneer; MacEwen thought Pierre Trudeau at the time of "Trudeaumania" was good for Canada (Sullivan 233) – but she selected one of the most globally recognized men of the twentieth century: "I am Lawrence," in effect. With that decision alone, she draws attention to the near absence of female poets that Atwood also noticed at almost the same time ("Introduction" xxix). Despite MacEwen's admiration of Lawrence, in its historical context her choice of him can be interpreted not only as ironic but also as partly critical, a choice directed at Lawrence and maybe by extension at other foreign stars.

The grandstanding of these poets is therefore tactical without always being self-promotional, and, although their identifications with more widely known people involve a degree of idolization and potential disappointment, they might also be relieved not to become them, whether as persons or citizens. Ondaatje's Billy the Kid and MacEwen's Lawrence of Arabia are victims of their celebrity. MacEwen, Ondaatje, Cohen, and Layton – all poets who experienced some degree of celebrity (from national to international levels) – usually represent celebrity as an experience of unwanted scrutiny and restriction on freedoms of expression, self-definition, movement, and sexual behaviour. The stars they write about are alienated, trapped, broken-down, assaulted, disillusioned, even suicidal, largely because they have experienced the worst of the metaphor of celebrity; they are not appealing in the sense that someone might want to be one of them – a tragic American or Briton. Calling them "grand" is ironic; their religious pretension and the advantages of their masculinity do little to make them magnificent, imposing, or powerful – except maybe in contrast with Canadians.

The irony of grandstanding for Canadian poets – which Mordecai Richler once indirectly described through a character in *The Incomparable Atuk* (1963) who claims to be "world-famous ... all over Canada" (40) – reflects some of the other ironies of literary celebrity that some scholars have begun to notice. In recent studies, however, literary celebrity has not been adequately defined except as a biographical category for authors who are also celebrities, and scholars have not yet agreed on a general definition of celebrity (Turner 4) or how it could ever be specifically literary. In *Literary Celebrity in Canada* (2007), Lorraine York refers to "the ideological ironies of the very concept of literary celebrity" (13) and concludes that it remains "a contradiction in terms" (170). Celebrity in general is used for the hawking of everything from kitsch to glitz and things much more serious; it helps to motivate a fan's desire for information about the private lives of those relative few who embody it. Literary celebrities usually seem unprepared, however, to make the sacrifice of privacy that Ondaatje alludes to in the foregoing epigraph; so do many actors, but their work is more public. Although culture, materials, and economy enable the production of a text and its transfer into the public realm, that text is usually written in private by the author, though collaboration and editing can also involve other people. Glamour and charismatic facilitation of the promotion of the text are not often among the author's social graces; promotion tends to be scorned as a detriment to art. Because of these "contradiction[s]," York argues that "we need a theory of literary celebrity that does not need to divide the celebrity author into the high-culture personality artist and the crass-minded potboiling best-seller hack" (*Literary* 21). We might then understand the impression of the discrepancy between the private affair of writing literature and the text's public role in enabling celebrity.

My explanation of the metaphor of celebrity helps to answer York's call for a less divisive understanding of literary celebrity. There is of course a separation between the literary-private and the celebrity-public,[14] but my claim that privacy and publicity can fuse extends to the reconciliation of the literary and popular cultures of the 1960s. In *Modernism Is the Literature of Celebrity* (2011), Jonathan Goldman claims that celebrity is a "missing link" (2) between these cultures, and he thereby agrees with York and others such as Moran in *Star Authors*. But my argument also diverges from theirs, and I want to join in the cultural debate that their work involves. York's recent *Literary Celebrity in Canada* is the first book to examine celebrity in Canadian literature in terms of public personas, advertising, and economics, often from a Bourdieuian perspective that disagrees with elite assumptions about the products of different cultures. I have followed her example in many of my critical methods, including the analysis of artistic representations of celebrity, which are comparatively prominent in my thinking. Both York and Moran begin with literature and publicity in the late nineteenth century (in the United States, in Moran's case), focusing afterward on star authors who are known today mainly for prose fiction – such as Atwood and Ondaatje, in York's case.

The Metaphor of Celebrity differs from these books by York and Moran partly in its emphasis on the implicit competition between poetry and prose in literary history. By also focusing on poetry and on celebrity after the Second World War, this book demonstrates how the art best known for metaphor both negatively represented and promoted stardom *through metaphor* when television and radio, for the first time, were increasing the potential for the public recognition of authors. To help in explaining and minimizing the separation between popular and literary cultures, I have been showing how knowledge derived from literary studies and related fields can be perhaps unexpectedly useful in fields usually understood through sociological, historical, and related methods. I also mean, however, to avoid overly minimizing the separation between those cultures, because literature and literary studies would suffer a crisis of their own (with repercussions for popular culture, which sometimes depends on literature for its movies) if they were ignored in favour of other popular culture and its study.

The ideological debate about literary celebrity might be usefully simplified if we better understood how celebrity and "the literary," or literariness, are similarly exclusive. Celebrity is "[t]he condition of being much extolled or talked about" but not in the "good sense" of *fame* (*OED*). Resisting that pejorative connotation, Moran attempts "to challenge the way the emergence of literary celebrity is most commonly explained" (1), which is that the "commercial mass media" (1) that support the system of celebrity have conspired to debase literariness. His opinion seems to be not that celebrity is especially bad but that literariness has never been especially good. Celebrity is as problematically exclusive as literariness. Distinguished by "the characteristics of that kind of written composition which has value on account of its qualities of form" (*OED*), the literary is associated in the *OED* with the artistic refinement, elegance, and taste of "polite learning." It is exclusive in the same way that celebrity can make a person known as "the" (e.g., "Are you *the* Leonard Cohen?").

The elite assumptions about exclusivity, taste, and quality codified in many texts besides the *OED* must be tested. Under analysis, literary celebrity does not become any simpler. It is revealed as a category produced and negotiated by media, class, individuality, race, creativity, sexuality, audience, commerce, nationality, and many other aspects of culture. It is so complicated that it sometimes elicits "ambivalence" (Moran 7) and "uneas[e]" (York, *Literary* 4) not only in scholars but also in authors who embody celebrity, invest in it, question it, and make it literary (in another way) through representations in their texts. York also shows, however, that literary celebrities represent their status with persistent negativity (*Literary* 42). One of this book's main questions is why literary celebrities might offer such a comparatively negative opinion when they have the privilege of enjoying such exclusivity.

One answer is that authors who become celebrities are actually hoping and working for a type of recognition that retains an elite status (such as legend, which is considered in the first Ondaatje chapter, or fame, which is considered in the next few pages of this chapter and especially in the first Layton chapter). Most people, including many scholars, use the terms *fame* and *celebrity* interchangeably. Although they are almost synonymous in the *OED*, their difference is significant to our knowledge of grandstanding and other types of promotion, metaphoric or material or otherwise. *Stardom* and *celebrity* are better synonyms because they connote the entertainment and culture industries (which often include literature, despite its pretensions), including the mass media.

Understanding the debate about literary celebrity, therefore, requires considerably more attention to the distinctions between celebrity and fame.

Fame, for example, is "[r]eputation derived from great achievements" (*OED*), whereas celebrity need not derive from any achievement whatsoever. In the widely quoted early study *The Image* (1961), Daniel J. Boorstin insists that "[t]he celebrity is a person who is known for his well-knownness" (57). Boorstin's tautology is meant to suggest that the popular media can produce celebrities simply by reproducing images of people: "the most familiar is the most familiar" (61). Perhaps the best proof that celebrities are not necessarily known for their "great achievements" is that their names are "worth more than [their] services. For an endorsement the use of a name is frequently all that is wanted" (Boorstin 220). Granted, celebrity can be the product of someone's "apprenticeship" and other "work" (York, *Literary* 40), but it is not made by such work alone – and sometimes not at all. An individual's deeds are an optional aspect of celebrity, which depends first and foremost on a point of interest for the popular media (a look, a name, but not necessarily a wilful action, performance, or text) and, for authors, a related network of mentors, cliques, agents, editors, publishers, marketers, granting agencies, patrons and their awards, readers, and academics. Although famous people are also involved in this system, the critical acclaim for what they have done will not soon be withdrawn – but they sometimes have no way of knowing, initially, whether they are celebrities or *en route* to fame.

The duration of widespread recognition is another important difference, though not all critics bother with it, between fame and celebrity. Boorstin argues that "[celebrities] can be produced and displaced in rapid succession" (74). Celebrity is quick to come and quick to go. The etymological evidence for this claim is the Latin word *celere*, which is associated with both the English *celerity*, meaning "swiftness," and *celebrity* (Rojek 9). York has suggested that duration is "slightly beside the point" and that the "effects" (*Literary* 26) of fame or celebrity are more important – but what if the effects depend on the duration? Some authors who seek fame get celebrity instead. Some of them never know the difference, but some of them have to deal with disappointment after the comparatively intense experience of celebrity. What Andy Warhol calls "fifteen minutes of fame" is celebrity, and so is what Ondaatje calls "instant fame" (24) in his poem "Letters & Other Worlds" (1973).[15] Time is relative in Warhol's distinction, of course, and in *What Price Fame?* (2000) Tyler Cowen argues that "Warhol did not recognize that short-term celebrity and long-run fame are largely complements rather than substitutes" (77). I agree; fame complements celebrity as an enticement for ambitious people, and celebrity complements fame by drawing attention to failure, burnout, and disasters that can prevent someone's memorable accomplishment.[16] Cowen also suggests that "short-term celebrity is based on commercial factors far more than is long-term fame" (79), and yet that institutions such as the Hall of Fame can extend the profitability of celebrities by giving them another chance of becoming famous – and continuing to generate sales and incomes in excess of the cost of promotion.

On the topic of profitability and the different ethical connotations of fame and celebrity, David Schmid argues that, in America, "the concept of 'fame' has evolved in ways that not only allow for the existence of criminal celebrities such as the serial killer but also make the serial killer the exemplary modern celebrity" (297). His essay on the subject has an initial emphasis on the profits of the "murderabilia industry" (295), which thrives on mementos collected after the arrest of a serial killer. Schmid contends that "[o]nce fame is characterized *primarily* by visibility rather than achievement, however, it no longer makes sense to distinguish between good and bad forms of fame" (298, his emphasis), such as notoriety, celebrity, prestige, iconicity, or infamy. His example of the serial killer helps to reveal the ethical problem of the old adage that any publicity is good publicity. The adage is wrong, in my opinion. I can see only a commercial value in the categorical breakdown involved in the widespread visibility-as-publicity of serial killers. This value is suspect on its own, and so a less empirical and more culturally and historically sensitive definition of fame – one that connotes good work and not only successful marketing – is relatively appealing to me, though I realize that "good works" are not defined in the arts and academia without considerable scepticism and resistance, and though I do not usually think of myself as a conservative.

I recognize, however, that I can be described as such based on my role in conserving a traditional definition of fame (and returning attention to authors and to a literary abstraction such as metaphor). The poets in this book also seem to be conscious of important differences between types of recognition, partly because authors are often sensitive to the unlikelihood of remaining in print and generating an income without canonical recognition (i.e., literary fame), and many of them often hope that their work will have some value for posterity.[17] In *The Frenzy of Renown* (1986), Leo Braudy refers to "our current urge to distinguish fame from celebrity" (281). Cowen labels critics who feel such an urge as "gatekeeper critics" (77) who attempt to reserve fame for those who supposedly ought to be remembered for a deed or something made. These are the critics who establish canons in literature and other fields. My own work is not intended to help canonize or sustain the canonicity of widely recognized authors, though this is a potential result. Part of my argument, instead, is that having no clear definition helps celebrity (even capitalism more generally) to do its work of quickly raising and suddenly letting fall its stars according to whatever standards of topicality are in fashion. A too-complete acceptance of postmodernism's destabilization of historical definitions ultimately serves a wasteful culture of novelty and disposability, which celebrity promotes. The result can be that empirical valuations and evaluations of art supplant less objective measures, thereby reducing the value of cultural activities, including criticism and artworks that are not often profitable. Many canonized writers never were celebrities or were never very profitable. Many of them developed their own voices and continued to speak in them despite changes in period style. For others, maintaining public interest or surviving celebrity long enough to be selected by "gatekeeper critics" might, in itself, be an achievement – of endurance – worthy of fame.

Preserving distinctions between the terms is valuable, and considering them in different historical contexts can also help to explain why authors have a special interest in the consequences of stardom. Although some critics have suggested that even eighteenth-century authors such as Samuel Johnson, Laurence Sterne, and Frances Burney had careers that were affected by celebrity (English and Frow 40), Boorstin suggests that the terminological change began in the nineteenth century as the popular media developed in technical sophistication, from the inventions of dry-plate photography in 1873 and the phonograph in 1877, through Thomas Edison's refinement of radio leading to his patent in 1891, to widespread radio broadcasts in the 1920s and the establishment of commercial television by 1941 (13). Tom Mole, in *Byron's Romantic Celebrity* (2007), demonstrates that celebrity is as old as the first inexpensive newspapers and cheap books: "[By around 1850] [c]elebrity was no longer something you had, but something you were. By the end of the Romantic period, one could meaningfully speak of a celebrity or a star [a term first recorded in the *OED* in 1824] as a special kind of person with a distinct kind of public profile" (xii). Mole also states that "[i]t was also in the Romantic period that celebrity first came to be understood as a distinctively inferior variety of fame" (xii).

When Boorstin first published *The Image* in 1961, he was already arguing – perhaps too insistently – that the distinction Mole observes was on the verge of collapse; the popular media of the twentieth century were to blame. Despite convincing evidence from Mole and York that celebrity as we know it originated in the nineteenth century, "overwhelmingly the standard view" (Turner 10) is that celebrity fits most snugly in the twentieth century. York reasonably cautions other critics about thinking that "the costs of sudden fame ... increase the closer one approaches the present historical moment" (*Literary* 24), but the "standard view" gains credibility because of questions about the state of meaning itself in the twentieth century. If the cultural phenomenon of celebrity can be measured in part by the replication of names, voices, and images, then the convergence of media made possible by cinema and television greatly increased the potential scope of celebrity. "There had been nothing to compare with [television]" (Cashmore 259), writes Ellis Cashmore in *Celebrity / Culture* (2006). Not until the Internet became available did the mass media gain a new dimension of equal significance.

The scope of celebrity's effects changed with the times. The "age of simulation" (Baudrillard 43) that began with the World Wars and with the sudden excess of information produced by radio, cinema, and television was, and is, a difficult time for interpretation. What, now, is "real"? The "degrading" of fame into celebrity is an example of "the vertigo of interpretation" (Baudrillard 16), especially because *fame* historically referred to achievements that were real. Arguably, celebrity is still far less real than fame, because celebrity seldom refers to anything but its own image; it tends to produce an excess of itself. After Mole asks what "cultural problems" (xiv) celebrity might solve, he answers that celebrity has been not solving but "palliat[ing]" "information overload and alienation caused by celebrity culture" (155). This tautology (celebrity "palliat[ing]" the result of celebrity) and the one proposed by Boorstin (being "known for ... well-knownness") suggest that celebrity is related to the proliferation of meaningless information, which is one way to define tautology.[18] The "information overload" unquestionably became more intense during and after the World Wars; it did not necessarily change celebrity in kind, but it certainly changed it in degree.

Who would notice such a change, and who would consider it to be negative? Besides scholars, one answer is certainly authors who are celebrities. Writers are purveyors of information and meaning. Although information is abundant, its abundance has contributed to a crisis of meaning. Authors in cultures of celebrity might perceive themselves to be threatened by that culture, and those who are celebrities are likely to be affected more directly. More than other types of celebrities (such as musicians, politicians, and athletes – though there are many exceptions among them), authors are generally not averse to self-reflection. They often write about what they know through experience, observation, or study. In doing so, literary celebrities – at least in Canada – have created a stereotype of celebrity as a "destroyer" (York, *Literary* 42) that the poets in the following chapters almost constantly affirm.[19]

Despite the commercial success of many authors – Mazo de la Roche sold more than eleven million books from her Jalna series in her lifetime (York, *Literary* 64); John Grisham sold sixty million books in the 1990s ("Grisham" par. 1–2, 4); J.K. Rowling is a billionaire because of her Harry Potter series and has more money than the Queen of England (English and Frow 41) – many of them persist in slandering the same cultural phenomenon that could make them rich or richer. Moran argues that "literary celebrities cannot simply be reduced to their exchange value – they are complex cultural signifiers who are repositories for all kinds of meanings, the most significant of which is perhaps the nostalgia for some kind of transcendent, anti-economic, creative element in a secular, debased, commercialized culture" (9). York has criticized Boorstin for indulging in the nostalgia that Moran mentions (*Literary* 8). Maybe unintentionally, Moran's Boorstinian emphasis here is on "signifiers," "meanings," and "significan[ce]" – aspects of language and knowledge that are seriously complicated by popular media in the twentieth century and the foreseeable twenty-first-century future. Moran rather vividly argues that "the contemporary star system, far from being a closed shop populated by mutual log-rollers and backscratchers and number-crunching accountants, is an evolving organism which is not immune to intense self-scrutiny and soul-searching about its more malign aspects" (35). Literary celebrities tend to represent celebrity negatively because they understand, experientially, the problems that affect what they do. They are self-reflective, not only self-reflexive.

In this chapter, my intention has been to explain relationships between celebrity, fame, and literariness, partly by arguing about celebrity's extraordinary dependence on metaphor, and partly by reflecting upon a terminological debate. The poets in the following chapters seem to respect traditional definitions in implying their disappointment with celebrity and their ambitions for something more permanent and illustrious. I would define literary celebrity as a generally less popular type of stardom often characterized by both the canonical dreams and the negative opinions that its stars have for it – opinions deriving in part from an intuitive or conscious understanding of the metaphoric basis of all stardom in the context of "overloaded" media. But the metaphor of celebrity – as a phenomenon rather than a direct expression from writers – needs no literary context. It applies in general to stardom, whenever privacy is publicity for those involved, or whenever privacy is at risk of becoming so.

Besides race, sex, class, age, upbringing, and the ways of thinking and feeling that lead to enlightenment, suicide, or marriage, perhaps nothing has more influence on the identity of a celebrity than celebrity itself. The religious pretence of stardom gains new significance in relation to the metaphor of celebrity, which helps to articulate theories of the private self in relation to the public and its social norm, and which is especially understandable by writers who know both metaphor and celebrity first-hand. Although stardom itself is obviously not inherently masculine, it is associated historically with practices of exclusion that tended to restrict literary celebrity to small groups of men, especially in the case of poets. It is also historically specific – a result of twentieth-century modernity's crisis of meaning, which writers felt keenly. As it is expressed in language, celebrity is an opportunity for writers to test the limits of the feelings they can communicate and how close they can come to others and to understanding themselves. As it is experienced through metaphor, celebrity is a threat to identity that elicits confusion and misgivings about the coherence – even sanity – of the individual. In the epigraph that began this chapter, Ondaatje imagines the experience of going "physically / mad when you perfect the mind" by representing celebrity. The following chapters will begin to explain how celebrities who were poets were also coping with the challenge of understanding celebrity. The next chapter is both a brief history of the era of celebrity in Canadian poetry and a test of some of the theoretical claims about celebrity made here and elsewhere.

2 The Era of Celebrity in Canadian Poetry

Many people have difficulty believing that celebrity could ever be relevant to Canadian poetry or its history. Their incredulity is mostly due to the obscurity of Canadian poetry today and to legitimate, unanswered scepticism about the type and scope of recognition that Canadian poets have experienced. Information that can help to explain this recognition is not easy to find or validate, but in this chapter I work toward a better understanding of the extent to which some Canadian poets were widely recognized around the years 1955 to 1980, which span what I call the era of celebrity in Canadian poetry. Existing scholarship and new evidence from various magazines, a national newspaper (the *Globe and Mail*), and the national radio and television archives suggest that the stardom of poets in Canada, despite its narrow scope and historical brevity, was significant in the production of texts, in the development of forms of literature in Canada, and in the careers of some poets. It was also significant enough, as the following chapters will show, that authors such as Gwendolyn MacEwen, Michael Ondaatje, Leonard Cohen, and Irving Layton all wrote about it, symbolically or with relative directness.

My argument in this chapter has three purposes: first, to establish that there *was* an era of celebrity in Canadian poetry and, through an overview of that era, to establish approximately its beginning (1955), peak (1964 to 1970), and ending (1980); second, to consider data that help to determine, however incompletely, the scope of the celebrity experienced by poets in Canada during that era; and third, to contend that the scope of their celebrity was affected by the changing relationship between poetry and the novel, which as art forms were affected by celebrity in the 1960s and 1970s. The era of celebrity in Canadian poetry defined twentieth-century post-war Canadian literary celebrity until novelists regained their historical prominence (not necessarily in the canon, where novelists seem not to have been as consistently recognized) compared to poets starting in the 1970s. Some of these novelists were poets first and had become novelists partly because their celebrity and the era in general were opportunities for them and their publishers. Considering the relationship between forms of art and degrees of celebrity, I compare the relative status of six different poets who could be described as celebrities: Layton, Cohen, Ondaatje, MacEwen, and, for additional comparison, Margaret Atwood and Al Purdy, who have been otherwise excluded from the central chapters of this study because they did not write about celebrity in their poetry.

Measured by appearances on television, book sales, and topicality in magazines, the successes of each of these writers were different for many reasons, including the timing of their publications, the degree of their commitment to poetry, their conformity to the public's expectations of them, and their multiple talents, though as poets they were in my opinion equal at their best. Layton's mastery of prose should be evident to anyone reading his prefaces and letters, but his short stories and plays were less eloquent, and he did not persist with his attempts to supplement his poetry, and even expand his stardom, by writing in other forms; Cohen became a novelist but achieved his highest degree of celebrity as a popular musician; Ondaatje directed short films in the early 1970s and, after the era of celebrity in Canadian poetry, became internationally successful as a novelist; MacEwen experienced celebrity that was limited partly because she was a female writer committed to poetry in a field dominated by men when the novel was becoming a more fashionable literary form. The story of their relationship with the public begins again here, at the start of the era of celebrity in Canadian poetry.

Celebrity was not unknown to Canadian literature before the mid-1950s, though it was different then from what it became after the mid-1950s, when Layton became the first Canadian poet to exploit television. In *Literary Celebrity in Canada* (2007), Lorraine York shows that the late nineteenth- and early twentieth-century mass market of books, newspapers, and public readings was sufficient for the creation of celebrity, or at least its unmistakeable prototype, for writers such as Pauline Johnson, Stephen Leacock, Mazo de la Roche, and Lucy Maud Montgomery. These writers were internationally recognized, their books often sold in great numbers, and they generally needed to be shrewd negotiators when dealing with their publishers and the public. Using the term *fame* but probably also meaning celebrity, York argues that "[f]ame ... is a much more powerful force in the history of Canadian literature than has been suspected, and its possessors have not been blasé about or unaffected by its workings in their careers and lives" (*Literary* 34). Notably, of the four writers in York's chapter on turn-of-the-century celebrity, only one (Johnson) was recognized mainly as a poet.[1] The other three were successful mainly as writers of prose, especially fiction and often novels.

Similarly, in *The Confederation Group of Canadian Poets, 1880–1897* (2004), D.M.R. Bentley explains that poets such as Bliss Carman, Charles G.D. Roberts, Archibald Lampman, and Johnson had their photographs in magazines and were widely known – even notorious – in the newspapers (273, 276), but they were unable to sustain their status because of competition from prose fiction (282–3). Although celebrity usually makes "literary and dramatic form ... irrelevant" (Boorstin 158) by drawing attention to the star's image – thereby enabling cross marketing and spin-offs regardless of the commodity's form – literary celebrity in Canada from at least as early as the end of the nineteenth century through the first half of the twentieth century tended to include writers of prose fiction but few poets.

In the mid-1950s, this situation changed, rapidly and temporarily; until then, poetry only rarely emerged from literary circles and academia into the public realm. The "national tours" (Solecki, "Introduction" xv) of Carman in the 1920s and E.J. Pratt in the 1940s were precursors to, and not inaugurations of, the era of celebrity in Canadian poetry. In 1954, Robert A. Currie wrote that Bliss Carman was known to every Canadian only because "captive schoolchildren" (149) were forced to read his work. Also in 1954, Louis Dudek could claim that "[p]oetry today is not a popular art; Canadian poetry is even less known than English poetry in general" ("State" 153). From a considerably more retrospective position in 1993, Dudek said that "[t]here was no competition for recognition, nobody wanted to be known more than anyone else ... there was no ambition of that kind among poets because no recognition was possible. This was from 1940 to 1955, let's say ... There was no audience for poetry and there were no prizes and no success" ("Committed" 7). Although he predicted that "poetry, not prose, ... will in the end prove to be the successful literary medium of this century," Dudek called poetry immediately prior to 1954 an "almost secret activity (so far as the public is concerned)" ("State" 153). Poets and their works tended to remain out of sight.[2]

Even as Currie and Dudek were writing, however, celebrity was about to become a factor in Canadian poetry – partly because of Layton's sudden success, involving a 1956 appearance on television, and partly because of a culture of youth associable with Beat culture that wanted to use poetry to effect various "social changes" (Davey, *Canadian* 12). Once in 1956, again in 1958, and three times in 1960, Layton was seen on CBC TV, especially its *Fighting Words* program; he was debating with others, not reading his poetry, but his presence introduced television audiences to him as a poet and indicated that television producers could accept a poet as a commentator not only on art but also on society.[3] By appearing on television, Layton was also introducing himself to younger audiences. "Irving Layton converted a whole generation to poetry," said Cohen (qtd. in Cameron 367). Dudek said, with little of Cohen's enthusiasm and at least some disdain for celebrity, that for Canadian poets in the mid-1950s to the 1960s

> [s]uccess came only with a kind of youth that created hero-celebrities who were idolized. They were screaming for Frankie – Frank Sinatra – and for Elvis and for Leonard Cohen, which is really an offshoot of the same idea, isn't it? It's a minor whirlpool of the main sociological wave in which people are going nuts about some particular individual entertainer. It's a very harmful business that has nothing to do with poetry in the long run ... It's the culture of entertainment that came with television.[4] ("Committed" 7–8)

Although celebrity in poetry was perhaps only "a minor whirlpool of the main sociological wave," it was remarkable that celebrity had become a factor in poetry even to that extent. Poets in general were not regularly on television – such experiences were the exception – but television and the culture of youth (in which Cohen was becoming iconic) had emerged simultaneously with an enthusiasm that, for several years at least, did not spare poetry.

Although national television and film agencies (the Canadian Broadcasting Corporation and the National Film Board) documented and helped to produce a Canadian model of literary celebrity in the two decades after the Second World War, they were only the most visual of several media involved. In his contribution to the third volume of *Literary History of Canada* (1976), George Woodcock argues that very few poets were able or lucky enough to be successfully promoted by television and film (288–9). Instead, poets were brought to the attention of the public through a combination of other media and venues: radio broadcasts by the CBC, audio recordings on vinyl records and cassette tapes available for purchase and borrowing from libraries, and frequent public readings (Woodcock 287–9). Dudek and Michael Gnarowski state that "[b]y the end of the 1950s, poetry and news of poetry began to appear regularly in the popular media, in the metropolitan daily and weekly press, in magazines like *Maclean's* and *Time*, as well as on radio and television" (232). In this welcoming environment, new poets began appearing "in almost uncountable numbers" (Pacey, "Writer" 494) as the 1950s turned into the 1960s. Woodcock makes note of some remarkable statistics: "[i]n 1959, 24 books of English verse were published in Canada," but "[r]ound about 1963 the growth in publication was sharply evident, and in 1970 more than 120 books of verse were published, a five-fold increase" (284). This increase was the result of little magazines and small presses adding their influence to the publishing industry. Partly because audiences had so many options for reading, listening to, and seeing authorial readings and recitals of poetry, Canadian literature was suddenly changed by what Dudek called "[t]he great boom of young poets" ("Poetry" 117). The single most obvious sign of the change was the NFB's *Ladies and Gentlemen ... Mr. Leonard Cohen* (1965), which suggested – even before the official start of Cohen's career as a singer-songwriter – that Cohen would be the pre-eminent poet of his generation.

In the same retrospective essay on the 1960s, however, Dudek was already predicting – less than a decade after the boom began – that poetry's popular foundation would soon "collapse" ("Poetry" 117). Similarly, Purdy said on CBC Radio's *Anthology* on 21 December 1968 that "poetry seems to be the most thriving of all the arts but also the most doomed." Purdy and Dudek were correct, though the foundation of poetry shifted instead of collapsing. It was a relative doom. Compared to other arts and diversions, the prominence of poetry was in decline by the early 1970s, a decade that marked the end of "star-making" (Messenger 944) in Canadian poetry. Remarkably, medium-sized[5] Canadian publishers had nothing but poetry on their lists in 1964, yet poetry represented only 33% of their output in 1972 (Broten 36) because they were beginning to publish prose fiction and other forms.[6] Large Canadian publishers reserved about 19% of their output for poetry during the years 1963 to 1972, while prose fiction grew from 39% to 45% (Broten 36). By that measure, the era of celebrity in Canadian poetry peaked around 1964, barely a decade after it started – but there are other measures. While poetry in book form was in relative decline, the established star poets on radio and television and in newspapers gained increasing attention on occasion afterward, as high and low cultures diverged. If there was good reason to be fatalistic, as Purdy and Dudek were, it was that the traditional ways of reaching audiences were changing and that poetry's special new status was evidently not going to last.

The relative decline of poetry was possible because, during the era of celebrity in Canadian poetry, the market and industry had sufficiently developed so that medium-sized publishers could risk printing longer books – novels – by authors who had established themselves as successful poets. Notably, throughout the middle years of the era, large publishers were releasing more novels than books of poetry. The boom was somewhat countercultural: smaller companies and lesser-known authors profited, not only big companies and big names;[7] it was helped by the medium-sized publishers until they began following the model of the large publishers and thereby boosted the novel's relative popularity. Atwood and Ondaatje profited from that transition much more than Cohen and MacEwen, whose novels appeared a little too early. The total number of books of poetry, however, increased at the same rate as prose fiction (Broten 17), meaning that the number of books of poetry in print was still rising despite its relative decline. Poetry was doing well in absolute terms but not in comparison with other forms.[8]

Poets and academics alike noticed the implicit competition between poets and writers who wrote in other forms or not mainly in poetry. The competition seemed so overwhelming that Rosemary Sullivan claimed that, by the 1980s, "poetry was dying" (385); at that time, no new poets who could be called "celebrities" were emerging in Canada (Hošek 939–40). Similarly, in 1984, James Reaney said that "as poets, we've fought the novel and lost" (qtd. in Rae 5). Frank Davey, paraphrasing David Solway, stated that poetry had "entered into a direct and suicidal competition with prose fiction" (*Canadian* 79). Furthermore, Laurie Ricou argued that, in the early 1980s, "[p]oetry continued to suffer, in comparison with prose fiction, by the very slight amount of criticism devoted to it" (7); he also implied that poetry became difficult to understand because its writers had been newly influenced by postmodernist theory and, I would add, were often established in academia and promoted canons more than celebrity.[9]

What is missing from this overview of the era of celebrity in Canadian poetry is information that would explain how widespread the boom really was, and how the degree of celebrity differed from poet to poet during that era. Gerald Lynch argues that more needs to be said about "the extent of [each writer's] celebrity" (88) in comparative studies. Unfortunately, this is not easy to measure. Considering one possible measurement, Daniel J. Boorstin argues in *The Image* (1961) that "[t]he factual basis for calling any book a best seller is not so much a statistic as an amalgam including a small ingredient of fact along with much larger ingredients of hope, intention, frustration, ballyhoo, and pure hokum" (165). He explains that publishers rarely reveal the sales figures that support the claim that a given book is a "best seller" (Boorstin 166). Publishers are likely to release sales figures when such figures are impressive enough to be promotional; the absence of sales figures for a given author implies that the publisher did not expect to promote or sustain anyone's celebrity by releasing them. Regardless, such figures do not accurately reflect "sales to readers" (Boorstin 166), partly because books are often ordered by stores and later returned to the publishers – or they are bought, kept, but never actually read. Furthermore, some of the bestselling authors in the world are "more read than read about" (Moran 6); they are not necessarily celebrities, in the same way that literary celebrities are often more "read about" than "read." Nevertheless, studies of celebrity are not aided by this lack of information; they are only made more general.

Some sales figures for Layton, Cohen, Odaatje, and MacEwen are readily available, but comparing them cannot be entirely accurate because markets change over time, and not all of these records are from the same era. They do, however, provide an indication of the relative success of these writers, and I will include some figures for Purdy and Atwood for further comparison. Although MacEwen's biographer provides various information about MacEwen's income at different times in her life – it was never high – there seems to be little information about the sales of her books. In 1961, MacEwen wrote to Milton Acorn to claim that, at a reading from her chapbooks, she had the "best reception ever – sold 50 books!! Am being treated like a national celebrity by these people" (Sullivan 126). Although Sullivan offers anecdotes that suggest MacEwen later earned a lot of money from her publishers (261) – but died broke (404) – she also quotes MacEwen, who correctly anticipated that her second novel would be consigned to "oblivion" (qtd. in Sullivan 288) despite favourable reviews. In terms of sales, MacEwen was probably the least successful of these six writers. For reasons that I will soon explain, Cohen was hardly comparable; his *Selected Poems: 1956–1968* (1968) was notable for selling 200,000 copies in the first three months (Ondaatje, *Leonard* 5) and for selling 700,000 copies by 1978 in the United States alone (Amiel, "Leonard" 56).

In contrast, this is what Purdy said about his own *Selected Poems* (1972): "I think I once got $500 as an advance on a book of poetry and it has taken six years for my *Selected Poems* to sell 10,000 copies" (qtd. in Amiel, "Poetry" 50). He wryly noted in the same interview that his A-frame house in Ameliasburgh still did not have plumbing. Layton, meanwhile, "had sold 7,500 copies" (Cameron 369) of *A Red Carpet for the Sun* by 1964. In terms of sales throughout an approximately equal number of years, Purdy's book was more popular than Layton's.

None of these sales figures, however, compares with what Atwood and Ondaatje later achieved with their fiction in prose. York's research suggests that, at some bookstores, Atwood's novels had been selling in the same range as those of Danielle Steel and John Grisham[10] (*Literary* 111); York also puts Ondaatje's *The English Patient* (1992) in that range. *The English Patient*, promoted by the film based on it, sold 1.3 million copies in paperback (York, *Literary* 124), and more in hardcover, in the decade following its publication. In contrast, in the 1980s a book of poetry was considered a success if it sold five hundred copies (Sullivan 385). All these writers were more successful than average but in very different degree; they cannot be ranked precisely because comprehensive sales figures are not available, though Atwood and Cohen were almost certainly the most successful after 1980, followed by Ondaatje. Notably, these three were the writers to switch, substantially, from poetry to other forms.

Somewhat more valid and detailed sets of data about the relative success of these writers are available through the *Globe and Mail*, the *Canadian Periodical Index*, and the CBC's radio and television archives, which I have surveyed for insights into the era of celebrity in Canadian poetry (see the appendix).[11] The databases of both the in-house CBC Radio archives and the more publicly available digital archives of television (online) enabled me to search for appearances of any writer. These "appearances" involved the recorded presence of the writer in the studio or broadcasts that focused on a given writer's work and image. Unlike other searches that were possible in the *Globe and Mail*, searches through the CBC returned not every mention of an author but, instead, broadcasts that were comparatively promotional for the author.

I want sufficient emphasis on this caveat about these searches and their results: celebrity cannot be measured only quantitatively, because cultural events are subjective in effect; however, qualitative responses to celebrity are likely to be exaggerated, making almost anyone seem like the most famous person in the world if the circumstances are conducive to generating excitement.[12] The rationale for the following numbers is to ensure there is a fair analysis while also recognizing the real, though limited, success of this group of poets beyond and in the literary field ordinarily assumed to be incapable of supporting stardom.

Movies and music remain the primary vehicles of stardom in North America, but of the poets in this book only Cohen had a career in music, and he was the only one to have been promoted by a film early in his career. Television, therefore, seems to be the first medium to think about comparatively in this chapter. In the early to mid-1950s, Canada's adoption of television was faster than any other country in the world (McKay 65; "Canadian Broadcasting Corporation"). In Toronto and Montreal, the number of TVs in use increased almost exponentially in 1953 and 1954, to more than 700,000 (Nash 242). In 1955, Robert Weaver estimated that between 50% and 70% of Canadians watched television or listened to the radio, usually the former, every night in Toronto, Vancouver, and Montreal (104–5). By 1975, almost seven million Canadian households had television, and the broadcasters (including the CBC, its affiliates, and privately owned corporations) provided service in English to 91% of the total Canadian population; the CBC was broadcasting coast to coast (McKay 70, 76, 78). According to the archival sales representatives at CBC TV, the best historical database of CBC TV broadcasts is searchable through the publicly available CBC Archive Sales website.

My searches there reveal that Layton and Atwood had the biggest presence on CBC TV during the era of celebrity in Canadian poetry, though their appearances were hardly regular (see Table 1). Layton appeared around thirty times in twenty-five years, with small peaks in 1960, 1967, 1973, and 1978. Atwood appeared eighteen times: once in 1967 and then in gradually increasing numbers throughout the 1970s. Cohen appeared only eleven times, six of them between 1965 and 1967 – a sign of attention to his controversial *Flowers for Hitler* (1964) and his early music, and possibly a sign of the CBC's reduced access to him when he was touring and living outside Canada. Purdy, Ondaatje, and MacEwen almost never appeared on television.[13] The appearances of Layton, Atwood, and Cohen sometimes coincided with the publication of their books (especially their prose texts, when applicable) or their winning of literary prizes. Without a chart of their book sales over the years, we cannot know to what extent the presence of these poets on television widened their readership, but we can assume it did not hurt; millions of Canadians would have seen them, many would have remembered their names, and some would have purchased their books out of curiosity. It also would have excited the core readership and called attention to poetry and the boom in that era – affirming its popular relevance – while the new medium was broadcasting into more and more households.

At a time when listening to radio broadcasts was much more central to the day-to-day experience of the media than it is now, these poets appeared far more frequently on CBC Radio than on CBC TV (see Table 2). The value as publicity of a small number of appearances on television (which has the advantage of broadcasting images, which are usually more memorable than spoken texts) compared to a greater number on radio is impossible for me to determine, but for these poets the two media were probably of equal value. Layton's TV appearances peaked at five in one year (1978), but he attained a peak of ten on radio in 1959 and again in 1975; all of the other poets had a similarly higher ratio of appearances on radio.

Again, Layton and Atwood were more present than the others between 1955 and 1980. Layton appeared 138 times, Atwood 135, Cohen 118 (not counting broadcasts of his songs on musical programs on CBC Radio or popular music stations, which would most likely prove him to be far more recognizable than the others), Purdy a surprising 94 (implying his much greater willingness to be heard than seen), Ondaatje 34, and MacEwen 14. The four most popular of these writers appeared on radio an average of four or five times per year during that era. If you listened to CBC Radio daily, you might have heard Layton, Atwood, Cohen, or Purdy speak a couple of times per year – not often, but they had the advantage of being associated with national shows whose producers or hosts were themselves well known (e.g., Weaver's *Anthology*, Don Harron's *Morningside*, and *This Is Robert Fulford*). The group in general also appeared on a wide variety of other programs, with the exception of MacEwen, who appeared mostly on *Anthology*. As a group, their appearances clustered in the mid-1960s to the early 1970s, when Cohen was most popular. Before and after those years, there was no general popularity for these writers; Layton and Atwood, respectively, were clear favourites.

Radio and television were promotional for literature in the 1960s and 1970s, though the medium of print did more to establish the name recognition of these poets. The *Globe and Mail* now offers a website – *The Globe and Mail: Canada's Heritage from 1844* – that allows users to search for an exact phrase, such as "Irving Layton," in every page of its newspaper in any range of years.[14] The actual pages can then be viewed as scanned images. The *Globe and Mail* began declaring itself a national newspaper shortly after the beginning of the twentieth century ("Globe") but has a reputation for favouring the Toronto area; nevertheless, it is adequate as an indication of celebrity of relatively high degree,[15] as are records from CBC's radio and television networks, which often solicited participation from listeners and viewers across the country.

Similarly, the standard prefatory remark from the editors of the *Canadian Periodical Index* is that it is an "adequate" indication of who published what and about whom in a sample of Canadian periodicals – little magazines, popular magazines, and scholarly journals. The *CPI*'s omissions can be partly compensated for with the use of other indices, but because a thorough accounting of other indices, newspapers, and media could be a book-length study in itself, my argument is partly restricted to the *CPI* on the assumptions that "adequate" is still useful and that its editors in the Canadian Library Association and the National Library of Canada were fair in deciding what to include. Because American publications are not included, the *CPI* restricts me – acceptably, given the scope of my argument – to Canadian literary celebrity.

My method of surveying the *Globe and Mail* and the *CPI* comes from "Time and Literary Fame" (1985), in which Karl Erik Rosengren develops an argument about what he calls the "mentions technique," which entails counting how often an author is mentioned in reviews as a way of determining the "topicality" (159) of authors in comparison with each other. Applying such a technique to a given historical period in the *CPI* allows me to compare the name recognition of four poets corresponding to the following chapters – Layton, Cohen, Ondaatje, and MacEwen – with others whom I have otherwise excluded, such as Atwood and Purdy. Although the *CPI* is not the *Celebrity Register* (1959) to which Boorstin refers, it can be used for a similar purpose. The *Celebrity Register*'s compilers claim that "'it's impossible to list accurately the success or value of men; but you *can* judge a man as a celebrity – all you have to do is weigh his press clippings" (qtd. in Boorstin 58). By counting the number of publications *by* each author (mainly poems, stories, reviews, and articles) and the number of publications *about* each author (including portraits of them) in the *CPI*, I am offering one way of measuring the "mentions" and "press clippings" of Canadian literary celebrity. When it is relevant to do so, I remark upon the different promotional value of a publication being *by* or *about* an author (not only in the *CPI* but in the *Globe and Mail*, too), and upon the qualitative differences between individual publications (e.g., the popular *Saturday Night* compared to the scholarly *Canadian Literature*) as vehicles of celebrity or other types of recognition.

The *Globe and Mail* was widely circulated and well read, and Layton and Atwood often appeared in it. During the historical period in this survey – the years 1955 to 1980, which correspond with the general range established as the era of celebrity in Canadian poetry earlier in this chapter – the pages of the *Globe and Mail* contained the name Margaret Atwood more often than any of the other poets from this chapter (see Table 3). Each page was counted as one mention regardless of how many times the name was repeated on that page.[16] In those twenty-five years, Atwood was mentioned 263 times (but only once when she won the Governor General's Award for poetry in 1966, and only once more until the 1970s, when she was recognized more often and more consistently than either Layton or Cohen – her prose, not her poetry, being the attraction); Layton was mentioned 226 times, compared with 206 mentions of Cohen, 42 of Purdy, 35 of Ondaatje, and 12 of MacEwen. Of the poets considered in the next eight chapters, Layton and Cohen were the only ones who had any significant degree of celebrity in the *Globe and Mail*.

Layton, however, was not simply being mentioned by journalists. After a spike in his topicality in the *Globe and Mail* in the mid-1960s, his name appeared in the paper much more often in the 1970s – partly because he began to write controversial letters to the editor (around eleven of them from 1970 to 1980) on topics such as premarital sex, sexual or violent movies – such as *Last Tango in Paris* (1973) and *Apocalypse Now* (1979) – religion, and politics. His letters provoked responses from the public and, occasionally, a further letter from him. His books and readings were advertised more often than those of other poets, too. His name recognition was not the result of spontaneous interest in him; he promoted himself in public. Despite his efforts, his book sales began to decline in the early 1970s (Cameron 425). The commercial value of even Layton's poetry was affected by the changing trends in literature. Even into the late 1970s when the era of celebrity in Canadian poetry was coming to an end, he was gaining name recognition – a possibility only for authors whose celebrity was already established – but without improving his profitability or the status of the field of poetry in general.

The data from the *Globe and Mail* also offer some insights into the development of Layton's celebrity in relation to where he lived. Layton first attracted attention when he was living in Montreal. Although my overall argument is that the era of celebrity in Canadian poetry began in the mid-1950s and that Layton's celebrity peaked shortly before Cohen symbolically inherited Layton's celebrity in the mid-1960s, the *Globe and Mail* mentioned Layton only four times in 1959 (the year that he won the Governor General's Award), never in 1960, and only twenty-two times between 1961 and 1965 compared to higher five-year averages later. The newspaper's lesser interest in him before the 1960s suggests that his celebrity was not populist in the 1950s, despite his appearances on television; however, the *Globe and Mail* might simply have been slow to recognize an emerging celebrity from Montreal who had not yet moved to Toronto. He moved there in 1969 and immediately raised his profile in that city. Because the *Globe and Mail* was and is published in Toronto, no one should be surprised that Layton and Atwood appeared so often in that newspaper; they both lived there, though neither of them were there for most of the 1960s. The lack of corresponding attention to MacEwen – who lived more consistently in Toronto – suggests that journalists did not readily understand her as politically engaged and as worthy of national attention as Atwood and Layton were.[17] Despite the *Globe and Mail*'s supposedly national scope, in Layton's case his celebrity in that newspaper seemed to be partly determined by a combination of his temporary local residency and his political engagements in the editorial pages.

Similarly, the appearance of Cohen's name in the *Globe and Mail* would have been much less frequent if his poetry and novels had been his only way of drawing attention to himself. Despite his early popularity, Cohen was almost entirely ignored until 1966, when he was mentioned seven times; Cohen's national celebrity was confirmed again in that year by his successful readings and performances in Alberta (Bouchard R3). After 1969, there were three years in which Cohen was mentioned more than twenty times in the *Globe and Mail*. In 1969, he was mentioned twenty-seven times; his recent album and his *Selected Poems* account for some of that attention. In 1970, he was mentioned twenty-six times, and in 1973, his name recognition peaked in the *Globe and Mail* at thirty-nine mentions. Only Atwood ever exceeded that number (with forty) in a single year (1980) during the era of celebrity in Canadian poetry. As with Layton, Cohen's presence in the *Globe and Mail* depended relatively little on his poetry. In the early 1970s, Cohen's name often appeared in the newspaper because of a musical, *Sisters of Mercy*, and a ballet, *The Shining People of Leonard Cohen*, which were based on his music. Ondaatje's mentions in the newspaper were often related to spin-offs (adaptations for the stage) of his books, too, but the sexual content of Cohen's spin-offs attracted much more attention.

Ondaatje was mentioned in the *Globe and Mail* one-sixth as often as Layton, and MacEwen one-fifth as often as Cohen. Ondaatje and MacEwen were topical mainly in the early to mid-1970s. Their lesser degree of celebrity compared to Layton and Cohen can be partly explained by their later start; Layton and Cohen were two and one generations older, respectively, and had been nationally recognized before the 1970s. Although many other factors contributed to the varying celebrity of these poets, even half a decade seems to have made a difference in the lesser degree of celebrity experienced by Ondaatje and MacEwen. The timing of the careers of these four writers was a factor, as I will argue with other evidence later in this chapter.

The *Globe and Mail* is only one indication of celebrity, and it reveals that Layton, Atwood, and Cohen were being mentioned relatively often in that newspaper in their peak years; another, broader indication is the *CPI*, which shows, as is to be expected from an index of periodicals rather than dailies, that these writers were not as commonly written about in magazines and journals (see Table 4). First, some remarks on the coverage of the *CPI*. From the years 1948 to 1959, the *CPI* indexed ninety-nine periodicals without stating whether all ninety-nine periodicals were indexed in all of those years, though they were probably not.[18] Starting in 1960, the *CPI* indexed seventy-one periodicals. In 1965, the number was eighty-five and, after minor fluctuation, it remained at eighty-five in 1970. In 1975, the number had increased by only two, but in the next five years the number increased to 131. This relatively sudden change after 1975 could account for the semblance of increasing topicality of these literary celebrities.[19] Their topicality *was* increasing, in some cases, after 1975 (as it was for Layton and Atwood in the *Globe and Mail*, and Atwood in other media), but only Purdy and Atwood were evidently searching for a broader range of magazines that would accept their work, and only one – *Quill & Quire* – made enough mentions of any one writer to be significant in her promotion after 1975.[20] Accordingly, the most reliable and significant information from the *CPI* generally pertains to before 1975 and to the magazines that mentioned these writers more than a few times – the general trends, not the outliers.

The thirty-four periodicals that included work by and about Layton, Purdy, Cohen, Atwood, MacEwen, and Ondaatje were not only literary magazines and journals; however, only eleven of the thirty-four periodicals made frequent mention of those writers and all of them were literary magazines except *Saturday Night*, *Maclean's*, and *Chatelaine*. These three magazines had a less academic audience and provide indications of popularity beyond the realm of literariness. Because they were not literary magazines for which poetry was a priority, my initial focus here is on publications *about* the authors. Until and including 1970, Cohen was mentioned the most: four times in *Maclean's*, three times in *Saturday Night*, and once in *Chatelaine*. These numbers are low, given his phenomenal success as a popular musician in the late 1960s; Cohen was perhaps of more interest to international music magazines than to popular Canadian magazines.[21] None of the other writers appeared in all three of these magazines before 1971. After 1970, Atwood was mentioned the most: eight times in *Maclean's* and six times in both *Saturday Night* and *Chatelaine*. In general, these writers were not being mentioned often, though they were being featured in the popular magazines more often than in the literary magazines (where they tended to publish their own works instead of being written about by others). Remarkably, in the popular magazines, their celebrity barely registered in terms of mentions – but their celebrity registered in other ways, especially on radio and in the newspapers.[22]

Although *Saturday Night*, *Maclean's*, and *Chatelaine* were not literary magazines, publications *by* these authors were actually more common than publications *about* them in those magazines. Ondaatje, MacEwen, and Cohen hardly ever appeared as authors in these magazines during the era of celebrity in Canadian poetry. In contrast, these magazines published twenty-nine works by Purdy (especially in *Saturday Night* and to a lesser extent *Maclean's*), twenty-one by Atwood (with several appearances in all three), and eleven by Layton.[23] Their works appeared in these popular magazines far less frequently, of course, than they appeared in literary magazines such as *Canadian Forum*, the *Tamarack Review*, *Queen's Quarterly*, *Alphabet*, *Fiddlehead*, *Delta*, and *Canadian Poetry*. With the exception of Cohen, these writers were more successful and maybe more interested in promoting themselves *as writers* in literary rather than popular magazines; nevertheless, Purdy, Atwood, and Layton were also surprisingly effective in placing their work in *Saturday Night*, *Maclean's*, and *Chatelaine*, thereby bringing themselves to the public as both creative writers and social critics – not merely as "arts and culture" news.

Canadian Forum, the *Tamarack Review*, *Queen's Quarterly*, *Alphabet*, *Fiddlehead*, *Delta*, and *Canadian Poetry* often contained works by and about these writers, and the single most important vehicle for the work of all these writers – except Cohen, who rarely published in periodicals (at least in Canada) – was *Canadian Forum*. It published over a hundred poems by Layton and slightly more by Purdy. Between 1955 and 1980, Atwood published forty-eight works in *Canadian Forum*; there were twenty-six from Ondaatje and twenty-two from MacEwen, but none from Cohen. The *Tamarack Review* was the next best vehicle for their work: it published fifty-one works by Layton, thirty-eight by Purdy, twenty-three by Atwood, eight by MacEwen, five by

Cohen, and one by Ondaatje. These literary magazines were, of course, more likely than the popular magazines to publish works by these writers; Layton, Atwood, and Purdy were the most prolific therein. If my estimate is correct and the era of celebrity in Canadian poetry peaked around the late 1960s, no one should be surprised to learn that Cohen was written about more than any of the others until 1970; Cohen was the definitive figure of the second half of the boom, partly because of *Ladies and Gentlemen ... Mr. Leonard Cohen* and the cultural event of his phenomenally bestselling *Selected Poems*. Before 1971, Cohen was written about fourteen times compared to eight for Layton, five for Purdy, two for MacEwen, and one each for Atwood and Ondaatje. According to the *CPI*, he attracted the most attention between 1965 and 1970, largely in *Maclean's* and *Canadian Literature* – both popular and scholarly periodicals, indicating together his crossover appeal.

A question about this appeal remains. If Cohen could sell so many more books than the others in the 1960s and 1970s, why was he not proportionally as topical on radio and television and in print? Layton, Atwood, and sometimes Purdy were equal to his popularity and usually surpassed it in media other than books and music. Perhaps his literary celebrity should be questioned because it peaked thanks to his music, and York justifies her exclusion of Cohen from her book with that reason (*Literary* 7); she is correct to suggest that his literary celebrity emerged from another field (in almost the same way, I would add, that Atwood's celebrity in poetry emerged from the field of prose – one difference being that the words in Cohen's songs are usually heard before they are seen). But my explanation of the discrepancy is that Cohen was most successful in the most individualistically commodifiable media. A fan of music will buy a musician's book but is unlikely to subscribe to a magazine or newspaper because a star's name appears in it. Magazines and newspapers are not exclusively focused on any one star, and so they are not commodities that can give their buyers a sense of ownership or star-specific prestige (though such publications can supply a more general sense of prestige). Cohen therefore worked toward publicity that would raise his individual profile and sales. For this reason and others, Cohen was alienated from the small community of literary celebrities in Canada, and in terms of engagement in that community, Layton and Atwood were more current.

The *CPI*'s accounting of popular and literary periodicals suggests that, as the subjects of writing by others, Layton and especially Atwood were the most popular overall of the six writers considered in this chapter. Whereas Cohen was written about more than any of the others until 1970, Atwood got more attention than him after 1970, when the possibility of celebrity in Canadian poetry was fading. She was written about sixty-nine times, compared to twenty-three for Layton, sixteen for Purdy and Ondaatje, fourteen for Cohen, and seven for MacEwen. Much of the increased interest in Atwood came from academic articles in *Canadian Literature* and others in *Maclean's*, *Quill & Quire*, *Saturday Night*, and *Chatelaine*. These were the periodicals whose editors seemed most interested in promoting Canadian writers, especially Atwood – whose talent as a poet, novelist, and critic, along with her savvy feminism and nationalism, helped to make her appealing.

And now to sum up. Atwood and Layton were the most popular stars across the media during the era of celebrity in Canadian poetry. If being written about were the only indication of celebrity, Atwood would be unmatched in this group, followed in descending order by Layton, Purdy, Cohen, MacEwen, and Ondaatje; if a writer's sheer volume of publication in periodicals were the only indication, Purdy would be unmatched, followed by Layton, Atwood, MacEwen, Ondaatje, and Cohen. When the *Globe and Mail* is also considered, along with the CBC archives, the two clear winners are always Layton and Atwood. For Layton, 1959–60, 1967, and 1973 were years that could have seemed like overexposure to him and to those in literary circles who were unaccustomed to such concurrent spikes in publicity in the various media. Behind Layton and Atwood were Cohen and Purdy. Purdy was rarely mentioned in the newspaper, and Cohen rarely published in the periodicals, but their frequent appearances on radio put them in the middle of the rank – except, of course, when book sales are also considered, in which case Cohen should be understood as the most popular but certainly not the most engaged in the literary field of popular culture. Ondaatje and MacEwen alternate in the rankings and are therefore about equal. According to the *CPI* during the era of celebrity in Canadian poetry, Atwood and Purdy were among the most popular of these literary celebrities, yet I have generally excluded them from this study. Obviously, their exclusion must be explained.

Although Atwood is Canada's most consistently and widely recognized author, there are reasons to focus elsewhere in a study about stardom in Canadian poetry. Mainly, celebrity is not *in* her poetry; she writes about it elsewhere. York effectively locates Atwood's "meta-commentary on her own celebrity" (*Literary* 100) in her fiction, interviews, and on her website. Although she writes about subjects of photography and about people with audiences in some of her books of poetry, her theme is usually subjectivity but not stardom. In contrast, Layton and Cohen wrote about each other as celebrities, Ondaatje wrote about Cohen and Billy the Kid, and MacEwen wrote about Lawrence of Arabia; Atwood wrote about Susanna Moodie, who was comparatively obscure despite being the "best known of Canada's early pioneers" (Staines x). Furthermore, Atwood became "a 'known' poet" (Cooke 142) with the poems of *The Circle Game* (1966), but her fame or celebrity came less from poetry than from the fiction and scholarship of *Surfacing* (1972) and *Survival* (1972) (Cooke 200, 214). *The Circle Game* won the Governor General's Award but did not gain her a mention in the *CPI*, at least not in the subsequent three years; she did not attract significant attention until 1972, when her prose became popular. She appeared on CBC Radio (but rarely on television during this era) twenty-eight times between 1964 and 1971; in the next eight years, she appeared 107 times – an increase owing, again, partly to her output in prose and her relative success in that form. Although Ondaatje's peak of celebrity is the result of his novel *The English Patient* and the film based on it, he represented celebrity in his poetry of the 1970s. For whatever reason, Atwood did not.

It was never a topic of Purdy's poetry, either, nor of his only novel, *A Splinter in the Heart* (1990). As Purdy implies in his memoir *Reaching for the Beaufort Sea* (1993), one reason that he ignored the topic is that he did not feel affected by celebrity: "Prizes and flattery don't have much effect on me, or so I think" (281), though he also claims that he felt "inhibit[ed]" (279) by the presence of the camera when he was filmed at the ceremony for his Governor General's Award in 1986. In the 1960s and afterward, Purdy became a mentor to many poets who reflected on being welcomed into his home in Ameliasburgh, but he did not welcome the cameras in the same way. The NFB film *Al Purdy: "A Sensitive Man"* (1988) shows that he indulged in clowning for the cameras only at a distance, never in close-up, and he is occasionally defensive and irritable in response to direct questions about his poetry. Except when on stage, his manner is awkward and partly confirms Sam Solecki's observation that he is "wholly indifferent to fashion" (*Last* 217). Notwithstanding his determination to publish a lot of poetry, he never aspired to fame through celebrity as Layton, Cohen, Ondaatje, and MacEwen seemed to do. He stated that "[s]ome writers – and I think of Irving Layton especially – yearn to have their work live on into the future. That kind of immortality, which probably amounts to fifty or a hundred years at most, is not attractive to me. I shall not be around then to enjoy such possible fame" (Purdy, *Reaching* 281). His public persona is an interesting topic for further research, but because he was not self-promotional in the same way as these other writers – mainly because he did not write poems about celebrity – I have not included him in the next chapters.

The *CPI* reveals that some of the six aforementioned writers were highly popular as writers in literary magazines and were of interest in popular magazines; nevertheless, the *CPI* and the CBC archives seem to corroborate

Dudek's aforementioned observation that literary celebrity in Canada during the 1960s and 1970s was "a minor whirlpool." In a recent interview with Jian Ghomeshi on CBC Radio, Cohen said this of having a career as a poet in Canada in the mid-1960s: "That [the term *career*] hardly begins to describe the modesty of the enterprise in Canada at that time." During the era of celebrity in Canadian poetry, the peak of Cohen's topicality in the *CPI* was in 1978 and 1979, when he was written about five times in both years; Atwood's peak was when she was written about sixteen times in 1977, which is an average of 1.3 mentions per month – hardly what might be called a media frenzy (though a survey that included more newspapers would undoubtedly increase these numbers). The era of celebrity in Canadian poetry was important to Canadian literature, but its whirlpool might not have been pulling in much of the general public – except indirectly, when Layton was generating editorial controversies unrelated to poetry or when Cohen was appealing to audiences through music.

Cohen's celebrity as a poet reached its peak during that era immediately after he released his first album, *Songs of Leonard Cohen* (1967); the remarkable boost that the album gave his *Selected Poems* is a perfect example of celebrity's spinning-off between forms. Cohen used one medium to promote another. After his relative lack of success with his first novel *The Favourite Game* (1963), his first opportunity for cross marketing was with the aforementioned *Ladies and Gentlemen... Mr. Leonard Cohen,* which was filmed in 1964 when he was on tour with Layton, Earle Birney, and Phyllis Gotlieb. Its timing was convenient; it immediately followed *The Favourite Game* and his third book of poetry, *Flowers for Hitler*, though it was probably initially conceived to promote or record McClelland and Stewart's book-promotion strategy.[24] When Cohen reached the peak of his literary celebrity with his bestselling *Selected Poems,* his success was not owing strictly to his poetry – and not mainly to his controversial second novel, *Beautiful Losers* (1966) – but to his music. In 1978, Barbara Amiel wrote in *Maclean's*: "In 1967 Cohen released his first album, *Songs of Leonard Cohen,* and a cult of international dimensions was established" ("Leonard" 56). She states that by 1978 his books had been translated into eleven languages; he had sold over two million books (not only poetry but also his two novels) and over nine million albums. With the exception of his mid-1970s slump (when he was not publishing new books anyway), his career in music was the main reason that he could sell so much poetry.

Cohen's success in the era of celebrity in Canadian poetry and its aftermath is not the same as that of most other writers, and this discrepancy also raises the question of how celebrity might have been involved in promoting one literary form at the relative expense of another. This question is important because, in theory, celebrity is formally neutral. The earlier quotation from Boorstin – that celebrity makes "literary and dramatic form ... irrelevant" – suggests that celebrity exists outside those forms in the realm of images. Partly because images are nearly ubiquitous in society, celebrity is transferable and therefore useful in cross marketing; it functions as what Aaron Jaffe calls, in *Modernism and the Culture of Celebrity* (2005), an *imprimatur*: a literary brand signified by a "textual signature" (3) or "stylistic stamp" (20). Initially, Cohen's example seems to prove Boorstin and Jaffe correct; because of Cohen's success as a singer-songwriter, he could have sold suits, sunglasses, bananas, or anything else remotely related to his image.[25] He sold poetry, novels, and music, but his celebrity was theoretically transferable to products not associated with the activities in which he was engaged.

Why did the imprimaturs of Layton, Ondaatje, and MacEwen function differently? Why did these three writers have less success than Cohen during the era of celebrity in Canadian poetry? Obviously, the main reason is that they were not popular musicians, as Cohen was. Their choices of artistic forms affected their success; various aforementioned numbers and the tables in the appendix demonstrate that books of poetry were partially but not consistently linked with their success, which was greater when other artistic forms – music or prose – were later involved. Other possibilities should be mentioned but cannot be proven here, given this chapter's scope: Layton was too old to compete as a star with younger poets and yet promoted himself until he was overexposed, thereby contributing to his literary celebrity's fade even as he gained exposure on television and radio; Ondaatje was especially private and less willing than Cohen to negotiate with the public when he was younger (and often enough since then); MacEwen remained mostly committed to poetry, and she might have been limited in her celebrity because she was a woman working in a field that was traditionally more welcoming to men. The next chapters consider some of these possibilities.

This chapter is focused partly on the relative cost to poetry after the rise of the novel in Canada, but that relative cost is greater to the poets who chose to remain committed mostly to poetry; some of them resented the novel. The form associated with a given writer is an aspect of how that writer defines himself or herself, as the previous quotation from Reaney suggests: "as poets, we've fought the novel and lost." Layton briefly tried to follow Cohen into other forms by collaborating with him on plays that were almost never produced (Cameron 313–14) and intending to write a novel as Cohen had (Layton, *Wild* 181), but he admitted that "[s]ome poets there are who can switch from one form to the other ... but I'm simply not one of them" (qtd. in Cameron 400). Although MacEwen said, "I don't call myself a poet, I call myself a writer" (qtd. in Sullivan 193), she remained mostly committed to poetry partly because her novel *King of Egypt, King of Dreams* (1971) did not bring her financial security; she subsisted on a small income from poetry readings and verse plays she wrote for CBC Radio (specifically for Weaver's *Anthology*; he had also been the editor of the *Tamarack Review*) (Sullivan 191, 324). Layton is the only one of them to admit, eventually, a commitment to a single form. MacEwen wrote in several but did not return to the most popular. Whether Layton and MacEwen resented the novel is a matter for speculation, and I suspect they did.

Unlike Layton and MacEwen, Cohen and Ondaatje deftly mixed these forms and others. Cohen has said, "All of my writing has guitars behind it, even the novels" (qtd. in Nadel 175), and Ondaatje has said that he prefers the term *artisan* (Rae 93) to *poet* – presumably also to *novelist* and *filmmaker*, which is the least-known of his occupations despite or because of the unassuming ingenuity of *The Sons of Captain Poetry* (1970) and *The Clinton Special* (1974). In *From Cohen to Carson* (2008), Ian Rae examines similarities in the works of Cohen and Ondaatje; their experimentation helped to develop what Rae and Gary Geddes refer to as the poet's novel in Canada. Calling *genre* what I call *form*, Rae argues that "[w]orking within this cross-genre context has allowed me to dispel the notion that poets who turn to the novel betray their allegiance to poetry" (5). Rae suggests that the impression of conflict between forms is unnecessary: "the strength of the novel in Canada, in particular the critical acclaim brought to it by poets, is also evidence of the vitality of the long poem" (6). If poetry survived its "dying" days reborn as the novel then two problems that have concerned me lose their salience: what one form can do for celebrity that another cannot; what celebrity can do for a form.

The reception of a work of art depends so much on its form, however (e.g., on what one form can do well that another cannot), that the distinctness of forms remains an important premise of my argument in this chapter. Even if an artist or a critic believes that formal distinctions are unimportant compared to the value of the creative process or of art in general, form matters to the public – as does genre. In given historical periods, some forms were more conducive to celebrity than others, and celebrity had effects on the development of some forms. A writer's commitment to a form evidently affected his or her success. The poet's novel in Canada developed partly because authors brought poetic techniques and concepts to the novel, and partly because changes in the publishing industry and market encouraged poets to write novels – thereby motivating the allegations of "betray[al]" that Rae dismisses.

Notably, the presence of celebrities in the field of poetry in Canada in the 1960s was another reason for the rise of the poet's novel – not only because it helped to establish successful new authors and publishers who could then afford the time and materials to produce novels, but also because it motivated resistance against typecasting and overexposure. The small number of writers that I have identified as potential celebrities in this chapter – only six – could not be expanded much. Jaffe's argument throughout his book is that modernist poets who were celebrities worked together to maintain a small and exclusive group. In *What Price Fame?* (2000), Tyler Cowen argues that having such a small coterie of potentially overexposed celebrities can be worse for a genre (or form, I would add) than having many celebrities. Cowen calls this potential abundance the "superstars model" (107) of fame – a flawed model that predicts that having more superstars (i.e., the overexposed) in a genre (e.g., tennis on television) results in more popularity for that genre. Layton experienced the consequences of this model; he realized that he was overexposed in the literary field of popular culture and said, in 1965, that "[t]he last thing I want to see happen to me is to be taken captive by my own image" (qtd. in Cameron 373). His public persona subsequently changed in character, mellowing a little.

My guess is that some poets who were celebrities in Canada – especially Cohen and Ondaatje – intuitively understood that, to solve the problem of overexposure and profit from the historical see-sawing of the relative popularity of poetry and the novel, they needed to broaden the field of celebrity by complicating the distinctions between forms. But this complication can also be understood as a tactic not only of self-promotion but also of avoiding, subverting, or co-opting the consistent products and typecasting that the public seems to want. It is a tactic of both artistic and commercial success.

Although the poet's novel in Canada is the result of creative experimentation, it is arguably also the result of celebrity that was overexposing not only poets but also the form of poetry itself. Dudek accurately predicted that celebrity in Canadian poetry would be a harmful fad; others might have been equally astute, or were listening to sceptics such as Dudek, and wanted alternatives. Cohen obviously wanted alternatives. He not only helped Layton to define the beginning of the era of celebrity of Canadian poetry but also led the change that ended it, at least symbolically, as Rae implies by starting *From Cohen to Carson* with him.

Cohen would probably disagree with my theory about the overexposure of poetry in Canada, and his experience in the 1960s helps to explain what was happening. His first novel, *The Favourite Game*, "had sold approximately two hundred copies in Canada and one thousand in the United States" (Nadel 142). His second novel, *Beautiful Losers*, also had "marginal sales, selling only one thousand copies in Canada and three hundred in the U.S." (Nadel 142). In *Various Positions* (1996), Ira Nadel argues that Cohen turned to music because "he couldn't earn a decent, or even an indecent, living as a writer" (141). The publication of his novels in the mid-1960s was too early for them to profit fully from the growth of the Canadian prose fiction market. Although Cohen's timing was impeccable at the beginning of his career as a musician, he was too early in becoming a novelist. He had made almost the same suggestion in a letter to his sister after he did not win the Governor General's Award for his poems in *The Spice-box of Earth* (1961): "I'm now running three and a half years ahead of enlightened poetic taste and the time-lag is increasing daily" (qtd. in Nadel 109). Ironically, the cliché about being ahead of his time might have been more accurate than he could have realized at that time. MacEwen's first novel, *Julian the Magician* (1963), seems to have suffered from the same problem of arriving precociously early; even *King of Egypt, King of Dreams* might have appeared too soon in 1971. Although I have no sales figures for the novels by Atwood and Ondaatje in the 1970s, I would not be surprised if they were generally higher than those of earlier examples of the poet's novel. Regardless, Ondaatje and Atwood are unquestionably more canonical than Cohen and MacEwen as novelists, and one reason for their recognition is that they were lucky to have come later, when novels were more popular in relation to poetry than they had been earlier.

The timing was, proverbially, everything: the changing popularity of literary forms coincided with emerging and mutually supportive popular media that made celebrity temporarily possible for ambitious poets. The era of celebrity in Canadian poetry, which I have defined as approximately 1955 to 1980, started partly because Layton so vigorously promoted himself, including on television, and thereby helped to attract attention to poetry. Canada's publishers also helped; its medium-sized companies focused until (and during) 1964 mainly on poetry, and even one of the large companies, McClelland and Stewart, was promoting poetry with unusual abandon (as with Cohen, Layton, Birney, and Gotlieb's tour). Many other new poets were emerging in this era, and, though they were not stars, they helped to generate an excitement about poetry that has not since been apparent in Canada.

The era was brief: only twenty-five years, and for only around five or ten years in the 1960s was poetry truly a *cause célèbre*. The presence of Ondaatje, MacEwen, Layton, Cohen, Atwood, and Purdy in the popular magazines was not common, though some of them were publishing many poems in literary magazines and were appearing fairly often in the *Globe and Mail*. As the data in this chapter suggest, Layton, Cohen, Atwood, and Purdy were the most popular. Because Ondaatje and MacEwen were less recognized, their commentary on celebrity is especially objective (and especially interesting, given that they imagined high degrees of celebrity as so invasive and destructive). Their markedly lesser stardom during the era of celebrity in Canadian poetry reveals that cultural factors and the limited Canadian resources for the promotion of literary celebrity restricted the stardom of poets in Canada to an exclusive group. There were few poets who were celebrities in Canada in the 1960s and 1970s – and they were not widely recognized outside of the field of literature – but that was their era, and they began immediately to imagine its opportunities, consequences, and how they – and their field by extension – would be changed by the celebrity that was now available to them.

3 Becoming "Too Public" in the Poetry of Irving Layton

Celebrity for Irving Layton was a serious problem; how to get it, what to do with it, and how to avoid its typecasting effect were questions that he raised in his poetry from the mid-1950s at least until the end of the 1970s. In those years, which I defined in chapter 2 as the era of celebrity in Canadian poetry, Layton emerged as the first star poet in Canada. According to his biographer Elspeth Cameron, "[p]artly because of Irving Layton, poets and poetry in Canada became 'news'" (368). Later poets variously modified and rejected his model of celebrity but tacitly accepted the terms of reference that he had helped to establish. Problematic masculinity in poets (Glass 18; Jaffe 165) and religious pretension in general (Frow 201, 204; Turner 6–7) were historical tendencies of literary celebrity; Layton accepted them too readily, and inflicted too many abuses with them (e.g., sexist poems), but he also resisted their detrimental effect on his identity. He wondered about the uses and limitations of celebrity and ultimately decided that becoming too public would endanger what he valued most about himself as a poet.

Of the highest importance to Layton were his freedoms of expression and self-definition, which are closely related because poets can to some extent define themselves through their expression – and when Layton felt that celebrity was limiting those freedoms, he reacted against the public. Brian Trehearne has remarked in "'Scanned and Scorned': Freedom and Fame in Layton" (1992) that "[i]n the same decade [the 1950s] that saw him develop the figure of the 'murdered selves' as a response to his own earlier poetry, Layton began the assault on his Canadian readership that reverberates in his reputation to this day" (142). Layton's emphasis on multiple "selves" instead of one self was a response to celebrity's typecasting effect, as was his simultaneously self-protective and self-promotional "assault" on his audience. Jonathan Goldman argues that "celebrity makes the self contingent; identity depends on an audience for its continued existence, turning the individual into a stereotype, condemned to perform itself until death" (1). Seeking to avoid this fate, Layton was interested in defining and redefining himself through multiple artistic rebirths, even if the audience would figuratively kill him every time. Trehearne states that Layton began "to conceive literary reputation – that is, wide audience approval [e.g., stardom] – as a kind of death knell for true creativity" (142). Consequently, Layton almost always represented his audience negatively and had to "shock" (Trehearne 143) his audience more and more as it became less sensitive to his offences. His situation became less conducive to "true creativity" as his audience began to expect the (gradually less electric) "shock." Contrary to the likely intention of his tactics, he was typecast. A crucial theme in Layton's poetry is his struggle to maintain his freedoms of expression and self-definition in spite of his celebrity – a struggle against typecasting that, because of his celebrity, he could not win.

A paradox of my argument about Layton's celebrity is that he wanted to know how to transform it into *fame*, and yet fame, to some extent, is fixity. Whereas celebrity is quick to come and quick to go (Rojek 9), fame lasts longer (Cowen 77) partly because it is "[r]eputation derived from great achievements" (*OED*); celebrity need not derive from any achievement whatsoever. Layton wanted achievement; he claimed that he hoped some of his poems would be granted "a permanent place" (*Tall Man*) in literature, but "permanen[ce]" is contrary to the desire for flux that he expressed in his poems. Given stardom's ephemerality, Layton should have expected it to grant him freedom in flux but not permanence through greatness. Much of Layton's trouble with celebrity was probably the result of his concern about what he might gain and lose from it. Layton wanted fame but was tempted by and embroiled in stardom, which seemed not only to motivate him but also to frustrate, worry, and otherwise preoccupy him for several years.

No one would be surprised, then, to learn that Layton's "assault" on his public became more intense as his celebrity became more widespread. Not only was his career definitive for the next generation of poets who were interested in celebrity, but it was also partly defined by his celebrity. It had three phases that this chapter examines: first, his early anticipation and experience of celebrity, in the mid-1950s, when he was writing his major poems and imagining how his ideal poet would fare in the context of celebrity; second, the peak of his celebrity and its immediate aftermath, from 1959 to the culmination of his desperation in *The Laughing Rooster* (1964), when he rarely published major poems because he was attempting various strategies that might sustain his already fading stardom; and third, his gradual acceptance of being overexposed and then *passé* after 1965, when he could write poems such as "Shakespeare" (1971), which represents his celebrity and his potential fame with much less angst. From the mid-1970s onward, Layton's poetry finally mellowed and matured in tone – a change arguably made possible not only because he was in his sixties but also because he was relieved of some of the earlier pressures of his stardom and had achieved some recognition as a famous poet. He changed only when he felt reasonably secure in his reputation after the difficult dénouement of his stardom.

Although Layton had been writing poetry throughout the 1940s, the first phase of his stardom began in the mid-1950s, when radio, film, and television helped make literary celebrity possible beyond its previous confinement to books, newspapers, and poetry readings. Layton was the first Canadian poet, and one of the few, to be known through television. His appearances on CBC TV's *Fighting Words* debate show from 1956 to 1958 and again during its 1982 revival (Allan) were important instances of his celebrity extending to the general public. The 1950s and 1960s were a time when Canadian television was dominated by the Canadian Broadcasting Corporation (CBC), whose programming was indirectly paid for by a federal government increasingly committed to supporting the arts, following the recommendations of the Massey Commission in 1951. From 1952 to 1962, the CBC had a monopoly on network broadcasting and by 1962 was broadcasting into over 85% of Canadian homes ("Television"). Wynne Francis's claim that Layton "became a public figure known to millions of Canadians whether or not they had ever read his poems" (*Irving* 4) therefore deserves some credence. The historical circumstances in Canada were conducive to literary celebrity's emergence from print into the other media that would define post-war celebrity.

Besides his television appearances, Layton was a highly prolific writer whose one hundred-plus journal publications, typically annual or biannual book publications, frequent readings, numerous editorials in newspapers, and several teaching jobs – including many years at Sir George Williams (through its transition from college to university) in Montreal and York University in Toronto – helped to make him widely recognized. Sam Solecki argues that Layton was "the most popular and controversial poet in Canada" from the "early 1950s to the mid-1970s" (xv). If we separate those characteristics, Layton was no longer the most popular by the mid-to-late 1960s when Leonard Cohen surpassed his celebrity and Al Purdy equalled his popularity – but Layton did epitomize the combination. Solecki further explains Layton's early to mid-career:

> A critical buzz and often hostile reviews accompanied the publication of each of his collections of poetry, while his public readings attracted capacity audiences

> often in the hundreds. He was a star attraction ... Though his popularity was based on the fact that he was writing original poems of remarkable profundity and power ... he also had a reputation beyond poetry circles as an often abrasive and polemical commentator on culture and society. Thus even if you knew nothing else about Layton, you probably knew from his combative letters to newspapers and from the television program *Fighting Words* that he was the *enfant terrible* of Canadian literature. ("Introduction" xv)

Solecki and Francis seem to concur that Layton was a celebrity in the 1950s and 1960s because he was better known for his personality than his poetry. Their observation corroborates Daniel J. Boorstin's claim in *The Image* (1961) that "[t]he great significance of the star system for literary and dramatic form was simply that the star came to dominate the form and make it irrelevant" (158). My suspicion is that Layton's performance as an "*enfant terrible*" was tenacious into his fifties because he was frustrated that his poetry was "irrelevant" to his celebrity. Nevertheless, he had accepted that his stardom would involve self-promotion beyond poetry.

Until then (c. 1955) – for ten years after his first book – Layton had to cope with writing in obscurity despite improvements in the arts market in Canada. After a "renaissance" (Pacey, "Writer" 493) in Canadian literature in the 1940s, post-war cultural nationalism lost no ground; it encouraged the establishment of new magazines even before the recommendations in the report of the Massey Commission were acted upon by the federal government later in the 1950s. Nevertheless, the earlier "renaissance" did not mean that Layton could easily publish his work. *Here and Now* (1945) appeared thanks to his affiliations with *First Statement* magazine, where he was on the editorial board; he helped to finance *Here and Now* himself, as he did with his next fourteen books (Francis, *Irving* 4). In the eleven years after *Here and Now*, he published ten new titles that attest more to his determination as a writer than to opportunities in the market. Eli Mandel observed that "Layton, in a burst of somewhat bitter enthusiasm, had stood in a park handing out free (and unsalable) copies of his *The Long Pea-shooter* [1954]" (*Irving* 13). Between 1952 and the end of the 1950s, his books sustained "an average loss of $200 apiece" (Callwood 109). He persisted, and when the market and his audience grew, he ignored what has been called "the archly modernist preoccupation with undersupply" (Jaffe 106) and gained a temporary advantage over less prolific poets.

Layton suggests in *The Long Pea-shooter* that he had been recently thinking about the relationship between sales figures and celebrity or fame. His "bitter enthusiasm" in giving his books to passers-by implies not only resentment but also disdain for markets in general – a sign of his Marxism when it was beginning to mean less to him (Cameron 207). He was starting to realize that widespread recognition was not likely to be the result of poetry on its own. In the "Prologue to the Long Pea-shooter" from 1954, he sardonically advises poets,

> Resolve before ink you try
> That your books may not remaindered lie;
> Think only of kudos and a name
> And failing greatness, acquire fame (10)

Each line here is a syllable short of making each pair into a heroic couplet. Their shortness accentuates Layton's disillusionment, which is evident in his ironic advice about establishing "a name" even "before [putting] ink" to paper. In other words, he thinks that if he had "fame" his reputation would precede him and even make his poetry unnecessary. His use of the word *fame* really means *celebrity* – a status that needs no "greatness." If Layton's ideal in this poem is greatness despite what appears to be his cynicism, he suggests that he actually wanted fame: lasting recognition derived from his accomplishments as a poet, not as a huckster. Impatient for fame, however, he accepted celebrity and its capitalist economics.

He would soon be admired for his poetry but would also immediately exploit that admiration to sell more books, which suggests that he understood celebrity as a means to some other end, such as fame – or financial gain. Layton achieved recognition when *In the Midst of My Fever* (1954) garnered "his first major and favorable critical reviews" (Mandel, *Irving* 13), notably from Northrop Frye. The next year was even more important for him; although he seems to have published no more than two poems outside of his books (as indicated in the *Canadian Periodical Index*), his *The Blue Propeller* (1955) had been successful enough to warrant a second edition in the same year. In October 1955, only around a year after being unable to sell *The Long Pea-shooter*, he wrote to Jonathan Williams, an American publisher:

> At the moment, in this country at least, there's a BOOM IN LAYTON; how long it will last I don't know. But I really think that such a book [as the one he had proposed to Williams] will find an interested public waiting for it. ... Now suppose I could give you a lump sum of $200.00 wd [*sic*] you be interested in turning out such a book for me before the end of March? (*Wild* 63; his emphasis)

He also guaranteed Williams against any financial loss incurred by the publication of the book (*Wild* 64). The so-called "BOOM" was an example of his grandstanding: an exaggeration of his celebrity for the purpose of self-promotion; Layton later wrote to Desmond Pacey that publishing with Williams "meant sinking over $600 which not only we hadn't got but which we couldn't even borrow. Madness!" (*Wild* 84). Williams accepted the book and it became *The Improved Binoculars* (1956), which also had a second edition. Its success was somewhat owing to a scandal – the likes of which Layton later made a habit of exploiting as promotion.

A tendency to publish controversial material was already evident in Layton's career. *The Blue Propeller* was demeaning to women, other poets, academics, puritans, and Canada itself, among other targets. According to Francis Mansbridge, the editor of Layton's selected letters, "[i]nitially Ryerson Press in Toronto was to co-publish [*The Improved Binoculars*] along with Jonathan Williams' American Jargon Press. When William Carlos Williams agreed to write the introduction, success seemed assured, but Ryerson's last-minute refusal to distribute the book because of alleged obscenity was only an apparent defeat" (*Wild* 4). He states that Layton "was not surprised when Ryerson decided not to distribute his book, but was in fact delighted when their withdrawal occasioned a controversy that he saw as potentially beneficial to the book's success" (*Wild* x); "he was not far wrong in his assessment of its effects" (*Wild* 80). Mandel argues that Ryerson's refusal occasioned "a minor *cause célèbre* ... Whether it was the scandal or the enthusiastic blurb by William Carlos Williams or the poems themselves, the book went into a second edition with some 30 new poems added to the original 87, and the Layton phenomenon had truly begun" (*Irving* 13). Like most instances of celebrity in Canadian poetry, it was "minor" compared to celebrity in other fields, but it helped Layton to profit from the growing market for poetry. His poems began appearing more and more frequently in magazines and journals: eight times in 1956, eighteen times in 1958, and peaking at twenty-two times in 1960 (according to the *CPI*; see chapter 2). The serendipity of the distribution scandal was never really repeated during the era of celebrity in Canadian poetry, but Layton got the message: lacking controversy, create it.[1]

Even some of his first published poems indirectly suggest that Layton foresaw himself as a salesman of scandal – perhaps news – as when the analogous character of the "Newsboy" introduces *Here and Now* (1945). A short poem, it arguably represents the newsboy as a poet selling headlines to the public. "Newsboy" is written in the third person and does not refer to the biographical Layton, who had, however, been a pedlar and a delivery boy as a teenager (Cameron 41, 55). Instead, the newsboy is associated with celebrity through the headlines, and the speaker perceives in him the masculinity and religiosity that would soon become associated with Layton's performance as a celebrity. The newsboy has "last-edition omniscience" (n.p.) that gives him the knowledge that he can sell, in newspapers, "to the gods and geldings" (n.p.). Layton, here, associates knowledge and the interest of lesser gods with virility that the marketplace can supply. Not only is the newsboy associated with celebrities, but he also has social relevance as a purveyor of information. He is like a writer – one who is unafraid to comment brashly on society:

Intrusive as a collision, he is
The Zeitgeist's too public interpreter,
A voice multiplex and democratic,
The people's voice or the monopolists' (n.p.)

As a "too public interpreter" he is a symbol of literary celebrity as Layton later envisages it, though here Layton seems to approve of the newsboy's publicity. In the newsboy's "multiplex" voice, one that speaks for both the "people" and the "monopolists," Layton anticipates his many future poems that appreciate contradiction and attempt to avoid being restricted to a monotone. Layton was already thinking about the limitations that stardom – being "too public" and vulnerable to monopoly – might impose on his conception of the poet.

Being too public is a result of what I defined in the first chapter as the metaphor of celebrity: *privacy is publicity*. A star's self-promotional grandstanding can lead to the fusion of private and public personas that leaves the star without a decoy. Layton was concerned that his stardom might catalyse the fusion of selves and, specifically, restrict his freedom of expression. A poet or a private self can survive this fusion, but usually in a diminished condition.

Layton suggests this in another early poem that shows that he was concerned about the public's effect on the private self from the beginning of his career. In "To the Lawyer Handling My Divorce Case" from *Now Is the Place* (1948), Layton begins to realize some of the potential consequences of being too public. In early 1948, Layton divorced his first wife after having a child out of wedlock (Cameron 170). The fact that he was willing to publicize that event in "To the Lawyer Handling My Divorce Case" implies that his personal life, in his opinion, was almost sensational enough for the tabloids,[2] though the poem discloses nothing sordid. Instead, Layton uses the opportunity to consider his private persona's limited ability to protect his private self from the public. I have explained that the private self offers the private persona to the audience as a decoy. When the audience's demands lead the private persona to fuse with the public persona (and the public in general), the public gains power over the celebrity. In "To the Lawyer Handling My Divorce Case," Layton describes a similar fusion of otherwise separate selves in the context of dealing with the public realm represented by the law and the lawyer. Alluding to George Herbert Mead's concepts of "I" and "Me" and his theory of socialization in *Mind, Self and Society* (1934), Layton conceives of himself in two ways: "I" as the subject, the private persona; and "Me" as the object acted upon by the public realm (i.e., the law and the lawyer). When the speaker reflects upon the lawyer peering at him, he says,

> In that instant I have plummeted the infinite distance
> Between I and Me –
> Me is always question-begging, diffident, undersized;
> I am Me
> When my lawyer addresses me. (34)

Compared to the aforementioned letter to Williams in which Layton seems to separate himself from "LAYTON" the commodity, here he suggests that the contemptuous scrutiny of the lawyer fuses "I and Me" – in a mere "instant" eliminating an "infinite distance" between personas – so that both selves become "undersized." Contrary to the expectations of a poet engaged in grandstanding, the speaker in this poem becomes smaller, not bigger. While anticipating – and subtly promoting – his stardom in this poem, Layton acknowledges that celebrity could assimilate his private persona, leaving his private self unprotected and possibly feeling correspondingly uncertain, less confident, and small.

In the late 1940s, perhaps a man could suggest without recrimination that his divorce proceedings were hurting his self-esteem, but as the second wave of feminism gained momentum in the 1960s and 1970s, such proceedings became negotiations of more obvious moral and ethical complexity. Now that "To the Lawyer Handling My Divorce Case" has established that Layton was thinking about his identity, possibly in relation to celebrity and masculinity, I want to explain some of the historical context necessary to any understanding of Layton's stardom. Many of Layton's poems and some of his behaviour in person were allegedly misogynistic, and the historical context that helps to explain the uses of stardom in relation to male identity also helps to explain why he indirectly threatened so many women – and men, I would add – in his poems. History cannot excuse him but it can help to explain him.

Layton's sexism responded partly to a historical crisis of masculinity relevant to celebrity in the aftermath of the Second World War. In *Stiffed: The Betrayal of the American Man* (2000), Susan Faludi explains that men began to feel less control over their lives after the war and that they manifested their frustration with violence against women (9). She argues that men were implicitly promised that "wartime masculinity, with its common mission, common enemy, and clear frontier, would continue in peacetime" (19); however, "World War II ... would prove not the coronation of this sort of masculinity but its last gasp" (20). Although K.A. Cuordileone, in *Manhood and American Political Culture in the Cold War* (2005), admits that describing the condition of masculinity as a "crisis" "might not be a useful historical designation" (15), he states that the various expressions of malaise, doubt, and discontent in society "tended to coalesce around a central theme: the passing of the autonomous male self" (14). Men's control over their lives and their autonomy were felt to be in need of recuperation, and, when men felt that women were interfering with this recuperation, they sometimes reacted with male chauvinism, sexism, or violence. Layton's concern for his freedom was associated with the expression of the sometimes divergent historical desires of men and women.

The second wave of feminism in the 1960s and 1970s was a much-needed challenge to patriarchy, inequality, and women's dependence on men, but it was also one factor – among several – in the post-war crisis of masculinity. In an era when America's war in Vietnam was unpopular and when heroism seemed possible only on screen, men had fewer ways to prove their value as members of society. Filmic celebrity suggested to men that, as images, they could regain their value, but this suggestion resulted in men being newly objectified and thereby feminized by the media. According to Faludi, in "an age of celebrity" (35) men's "public 'femininity'" (39) required them to accept their own objectification, passivity, infantilization, and vanity, which she claims are the same problems "that women have in modern times denounced as trivializing and humiliating qualities imposed on them by a misogynist culture" (39). Layton's response to the condition of post-war masculinity was partly to insult, sexually exploit, or abuse women in his writing, as Joanne Lewis shows in "Irving's Women" (1988), and to some extent in person, as Cameron and later Layton's son David (in *Motion Sickness*, 1999) occasionally report.[3]

To call Layton's work merely "sexist," however, as Lewis does, or to argue that he is beyond definition and beyond reproach, as David Solway does – "it is inadvisable to condemn 'Layton'" (224) – is to ignore how Layton's sexism was motivated in part by a concern for freedom from socially and historically determined ways of thinking and behaving. Although freedom is a problematic concept associated with property and power – in effect, capitalism and all the gross inequity of that system – it is also a goal of selfhood as defined in the individualistic West. In the film *Ladies and Gentlemen ... Mr. Leonard Cohen* (1965), Layton says that poets must "preserve the self in a world that is rapidly steamrollering the selves out of existence and establishing a uniform world." In contrast with what Solway claims and what Layton sometimes affirms,

Trehearne suggests that Layton also feared that his "transformative model of selfhood" ("'Scanned'" 141) would not function in practice because of the influence of his audience. Trehearne asserts that Layton worried about a public that could "render him a fixed fact and deny him further freedom to change" ("'Scanned'" 146). Layton's poems of the 1950s reflect his anxieties about his present society and his stardom, which was emerging into and being formed by that society; those poems gain new relevance when considered alongside the historical development of his own stardom.

When Layton's celebrity was emerging in the mid-1950s, one of his major influences was Friedrich Nietzsche (Cameron 231). Nietzsche's *Thus Spoke Zarathustra* (1883–5) adapts the prophet of the Zoroastrian religion to his own purposes. Although Patricia Keeney Smith suggests that the "creative giant" (189) who appears in Layton's poetry is the "over-man" (*Übermensch*) introduced by Nietzsche's Zarathustra, I would argue, more specifically, that Zarathustra himself is the model for Layton's ideal poet. Significantly, that ideal of the poet developed as Layton became a star poet, and Layton seems to have been thinking about how his ideals would fare in the context of his celebrity. Indeed, these two conceptions of the poet are impossible to separate; Layton constantly wrote of this "creative giant" or ideal poet in relation to audiences, symbols of celebrity (e.g., stars such as the sun), and features of stardom – such as ironic masculinity but especially the religious pretence – that Zarathustra seems to embody.

Layton had read *Thus Spoke Zarathustra* no later than 1958 (likely much earlier[4]), when he quoted from it on the back cover of *A Laughter in the Mind* (1958). Although I have no evidence that Layton consciously decided that Zarathustra would be the model of his star poet, he probably intuitively thought that Zarathustra was an apt pseudo-religious figure, a prophet who ironically claims that "*God is dead!*" (Nietzsche 5, his emphasis). Michael Q. Abraham calls Layton "by turns spontaneous visionary and inflammatory cynic, nihilist-prophet and satirist-clown" (90); these last two roles (prophet and clown) are amply evident in the ironically religious persona that I consider to be Zarathustrian and wherein Trehearne perceives "full-blown ironic egoism, the doubled sense of selfhood's limitlessness and mistakenness" (*Montreal* 213). Zarathustra is an ironic figure – arguably a prophet whose ideas of the *Übermensch* and will to power are theories that he fails to practise exactly. Zarathustra descends from his mountain to become a teacher after ten years of hermitic solitude: "One morning he arose with the dawn, stepped before the sun and spoke thus to it: 'You great star! What would your happiness be if you had not those for whom you shine?'" (Nietzsche 3). Ironically, Zarathustra's rhetorical question for the sun implies that stars need an audience "for whom [they] shine," thereby helping to establish – because he mainly attracts an audience of animals other than people – his religious pretension.

As I suggested in a 2009 article, Layton was attempting to use his pseudo-religious persona to control the metaphor of celebrity – in other words, to prevent various opposites, such as privacy and publicity, from fusing and from thereby threatening his ideals of flux and paradox. These ideals came to Layton partly from the myth of Dionysus, Nietzsche's "favourite deity" (Del Caro and Pippin 124n), and through the character of Zarathustra. Mandel suggests that Layton's ideal of freedom was associated with religion because his ideal "includes everything, which could only mean the manifestation of a god" (*Irving* 33) – a god of metaphor.

As Nietzsche did, Layton chose celestial symbols (Francis, "Layton" 47) to suggest that his star poet can speak for the gods. Zarathustra's association with the sun, a star, is another reason why he might have seemed intuitively correct as a model for Layton's star poet. Chris Rojek argues that "[c]elebrity culture is secular. Because the roots of secular society lie in Christianity, many of the symbols of success and failure in celebrity draw on myths and rites of religious ascent and descent" (74). Regardless of the accuracy of the claim that secularism arose from Christianity, I agree that, obviously, one of the "symbols" of celebrity is the star, which has been cemented into the sidewalks of Hollywood to enshrine celebrity as fame. Many of Layton's poems, such as "Anacreon" (1952), are suffused with sun imagery that also alludes to the Greek god Dionysus. Francis calls Zarathustra a "sunworshipper" and remarks that "hundreds of [Layton's] poems containing sun and flame imagery can be read with deeper insight as the tributes of a Dionysian to his God" ("Layton" 47).[5] Not coincidentally, Layton chose *A Red Carpet for the Sun* (1959) as the title of the book that he might have reasonably assumed would confirm his celebrity. Layton dedicated the book to his mother: in that context, the title also announced that the "son" had earned his "red carpet" treatment as a star.[6]

The poems in the first phase of Layton's career as a celebrity – the mid- to late 1950s – were ambitious, not only in their formal and symbolic complexity but also in their anticipation of higher degrees of celebrity or fame. Using Nietzsche's Zarathustra as a model, Layton imagined the star poet's relationship with his popular audience and concluded – as my upcoming analysis of his major poems suggests – that masculine and pseudo-religious authority would not be enough protection from the public. The star poet's freedoms of expression and self-definition would be compromised, and the achievement of fame – poetic immortality earned with the greatness of his poems – would not be likely. Unable to think of a plausible solution to this problem, especially given that he was already in his forties and maybe not as sexy as his protégé Cohen, Layton became more and more pessimistic about celebrity.

Nevertheless, at the start of this first phase Layton was usually optimistic about his anticipated celebrity and seemed to think that his pseudo-religious persona would help him avoid the typecasting effect of celebrity. Preparing the way for Layton's highly acclaimed *A Red Carpet for the Sun, In the Midst of My Fever* (1954) featured a poem that prominently announced his debt to Nietzsche and foretold his success. "The Birth of Tragedy," named after Nietzsche's book translated with the same title, is a remarkable instance of Layton's grandstanding. By choosing that title, he stands in for Nietzsche,[7] whose name was much more widely known than his. "The Birth of Tragedy" proposes that the ideal poet would be a unifier of "nature's divided things" (n.p.). The poet, "happiest when [he] compose[s] poems" (n.p.), gleefully synthesizes the Dionysus/Apollo binary – on his own terms, not those of the public or any other authority – merging the wild and the rational. According to Mandel, "the poem tells of Dionysius [*sic*] who dreamed the mad dream of perfection and so was slain and became Apollo" (*Irving* 25). The poet says that in himself "nature's divided things" "have their fruition" (n.p.) and that "I am their core. Let them swap, / bandy, like a flame swerve. / I am their mouth; as a mouth I serve" (n.p.). With this poem, Layton introduces himself as a conduit for Nietzsche's "mad dream," as embodied in Dionysus, and predicts the "fruition" of his career.

The cryptic end of the poem would lead me on a tangent if I were to attempt its full explanation, and Mandel offers a helpful reading, so I will merely state that the poem gestures in a way that would later be recognizably Laytonic; it represents his figure of the poet as not only sacrificial but also godly, which means that the poem is potentially significant in Layton's understanding of stardom, even though the poem is not obviously about stardom. In fact, the poet in "The Birth of Tragedy" has no following. Despite Layton's future popularity and his engagement with contemporary politics, in this early phase he separates his figure of the poet from society to elevate and isolate the poet on a higher plane. Although celebrity depends on the pretence – however ironic – of such a plane, Layton had not yet imagined his prophetic poet in the public life of stardom, except in the comparatively mundane "Newsboy." He is a poet without an audience other than the "perfect gods" (n.p.).

Layton made the implicit religiosity of "The Birth of Tragedy" considerably more obvious in "The Cold Green Element," from the 1955 book of the same name, which builds on his understanding of the star as a figure of ridicule, with added emphasis on the effect of social rejection on the self and, ultimately, on freedom of expression. The poem introduces a "dead poet" (n.p.) whose identity soon becomes indistinct from that of the speaker. Immediately after mentioning the "dead poet," the speaker remarks that his own "heart [is] beating in the grass" (n.p.); he will soon be dead, like the dead poet. Celebrity becomes an implicit topic of the poem partly because of the "heart." The image of the heart temporarily living outside the body describes the exposure, to the outside world, of something that should remain internal and private. The source of the threat to the speaker's private self (represented synecdochically by his heart) can be understood only indirectly, through his similarity to the dead poet. Arguably, among what the speaker calls his "murdered selves" (n.p.) is the dead poet, who represents the speaker's private persona: the failed decoy for the public. In the second stanza, the speaker states that "[c]rowds depart daily to see" (n.p.) the dead poet. After staring at the body – sadistically waiting for it to twitch while casually eating their oranges (n.p.) – the crowds "return / with grimaces and incomprehension" (n.p.) to the city. Because he is a public attraction, likely to be forgotten as a novelty, and possibly an identity in crisis because of both his fusion with the speaker and his heart's exposure, the dead poet satisfies some of the criteria of stardom.

Initially, the speaker and the dead poet are separate, so that the speaker can refer to him in the third person: as an undertaker passes him, the speaker nonchalantly says "Hi" and that "a great squall in the Pacific blew a dead poet / out of the water / who now hangs from the city's gates" (n.p.). Later, however, the speaker and the dead poet seem to fuse when the speaker mentions his "murdered selves" "hanging from ancient twigs" (n.p.) like the dead poet hanging in a pseudo-crucifixion on the gates. The ultimate evidence of the fusion is in the final lines, when the speaker says, "I am *again* / a breathless swimmer in that cold green element" (n.p., my emphasis). Also like the dead poet, the speaker drowns in the Pacific Ocean, and not for the first time. The speaker and the dead poet are indeterminate versions of the same self that has reverted to oneness after the death of the celebrity; their sameness means that the fusion of selves is in effect and that celebrity is a sacrifice akin to the one in "The Birth of Tragedy."

The poet's weakness in "The Cold Green Element" helps to counter the later stereotype of Layton as a poet who relied, without reflection, on machismo and a seemingly delusional confidence in his sexuality. "The Cold Green Element" depicts the poet's masculinity and sexuality with a subtle playfulness that complicates its general seriousness:

> I've seen myself lately in the eyes
>   of old women,
> spent streams mourning my manhood,

in whose old pupils the sun became
a bloodsmear on broad catalpa leaves
and, hanging from ancient twigs,
            my murdered selves
sparked the air like the muted collisions

of fruit. ... (n.p.)

Like the dead poet, the speaker is the object of the public gaze; in this case, he is stared at by "the eyes / of old women" (n.p.), who have various powers over him.[8] The ironic humour and self-mockery here are subtle. The syntax implies that "lately" (i.e., since his latest resurrection) the speaker "spent streams" (cried) grieving for the masculine virility that he lost; alternatively, his streams might be seminal fluid that he "spent" (wasted) proving his manhood to an unreceptive audience of old women, not the young ones whom we usually see as the objects of desire in Layton's poems. Either way, the speaker implies that he, too, is old, so old that "the labels / of [his] medicine bottles" (n.p.) seem to have been worn off; his frequent rebirths might have gone on indefinitely without actually renewing his body.

The narrative of this poem ends without recourse to a happier rebirth, even though it does return the speaker to the ocean, an archetypal symbol of the womb (as in other poems by Layton such as "The Swimmer," 1945, and "Thoughts in the Water," 1956). Layton concludes the poem by putting it in the context of the mythic Furies, born of the blood of Uranus, whose son Cronus wounded him for mistreating his wife (Gaea) and children. The Furies had "writhing snakes for hair and eyes that wept tears of blood" (Hamilton 65); they are (or are analogous to) Layton's old women "in whose old pupils the sun became / a bloodsmear." Their job was to pursue sinners into the underworld for their just punishment:

But the Furies clear a path for me to the worm
who sang for an hour in the throat of a robin,
and misled by the cries of young boys
            I am again
a breathless swimmer in that cold green element. (n.p.)

In Greek myth, the Furies usher sinners into the underworld of Hades, but here they "clear a path to the worm." The Furies seem to realize that the worm will punish the speaker in their stead, so if he feels any resentment, it should be directed at the worm. The worm might be a symbol of decay and a phallic symbol (combined: phallic decay). The worm punishes the speaker by aging and emasculating him, so that even "the cries of young boys" can "misle[a]d" him. His sins, whatever they are, give him no power over an audience of "old women" (the Furies) and "young boys," and there is no evidence that he would have better success with middle-aged people of either sex. In the end, Layton implies that the speaker's audience will exhaust his masculine vitality, confuse him, and never welcome him in from "the city's gates." In effect, he fears that his aging will cost him his freedom of expression as a version of the dead poet.

The much less abstract poem "Poetic Fame," from *A Laughter in the Mind*, reiterates some of the concerns of "The Cold Green Element" and helps to support my claim that "The Cold Green Element" has new meaning in the context of celebrity. In "Poetic Fame," Layton is not referring to fame but celebrity, which is often associated with the notoriety that he implies is an aspect of his reputation. Layton sardonically announces that he appreciates "the supporters / who now reach me their hands to put money in, / their collateral being their good opinion of me" (36); he then reveals why he is being sardonic about "their good opinion":

At my approach
the ladies, unsubtle and ugly,
rush their adolescent daughters upstairs;
insert a table between themselves and me
and leer sensuously across the waxed surface.
I do not understand their discordant hints and maneuvers.
Do they expect me to sire tables? (36)

As in "The Cold Green Element," the women he attracts are not young but are obviously older than their "adolescent daughters," and here his reputation suggests that he will not refrain from seducing even "adolescent[s]." Also as in "The Cold Green Element," he is confused by his audience; the mixed signals of "the ladies" lead him to his joke about his reputed desire to fornicate with anyone or anything, including "tables." He therefore concludes the relevant part of the poem by stating that "in this unroyal kingdom a child knows / all poets are dead or they're Englishmen" (36).[9] In other words, he is not even known as a "poe[t]" – only as a lecher, which is, of course, highly reductive. According to "Poetic Fame," he has none of the pleasures of sex that celebrities are supposed to enjoy; his celebrity is also reductive, making him well known but not known well – not honored or understood.

In "Whatever Else Poetry Is Freedom," *A Laughter in the Mind* returns to the problem of celebrity's effect on poetic expression – here represented as musical performance – in relation to the poet's masculinity. As Trehearne argues, the poet expresses a will to be unfixed in the public context of fame; "Whatever Else Poetry Is Freedom" focuses explicitly on the problem of being recognized – and the problem of *not* being recognized. Rather than rely solely on mythological, religious, or Nietzschean models of individuation, the poet attempts to seek individuation and inspiration through the performance of gender (specifically masculinity) but often finds that his performance is not flexible enough to bring him the freedom and individuation that he desires. The poet asserts, "Whatever else poetry is freedom. / Forget the rhetoric, the trick of lying / All poets pick up sooner or later" (7). He likens this lying rhetoric to "the thin voice of grey castratos" (7) and thereby implicates gender in the performance of poetry. Age, again, is an issue, because he also likens the "grey" castrati to the "mist" that "lies inside one like a destiny" (7). Punning on the verb *to lie* recurs throughout the poem to suggest that the poet, the women, and destiny are all deceptive, which generally increases the ambiguity of the poem. Indeed, this pun reinforces the motif of performance, which reminds readers to wonder about the face behind the actor's figurative mask – to question the sincerity of what they read.

The musical performance, which includes a dance, simultaneously raises questions about masculinity and stardom in the context of the poem's titular concern with freedom.

And I who gave my Kate a blackened eye
Did to its vivid changing colours
Make up an incredible musical scale;
And now I balance on wooden stilts and dance
And thereby sing to the loftiest casements.
See how with polish I bow from the waist.
Space for these stilts! More space or I fail! (7)

Machismo permeates this stanza until the last line, the first indication of what the singing poet fears. As someone who "sing[s]," he seems to fear becoming a castrato, a man whose testicles were surgically removed to maintain his boyish voice. Despite Layton's insistence on poetry being freedom, and on poetry enabling the transformation of the self, he implies some limits on what he wants to become. He does not want the ambiguous gender of the castrati. Although ambiguity is nonfixity, his fear of being fixed – in its veterinary connotation – is a fear of losing his masculinity, which (according to the gender stereotype) brings him power to define himself. He expects his sexuality, gender, and identity to be destabilized through performance; he represents this destabilization in the poet's unbalanced posture above the crowd. The poet desperately needs to differentiate himself from the crowd; otherwise, he fears the loss of his balance and his freedom, including the freedom to control his own transformations.

The poet's relation to his audience is based on his transformation of the bodily result of his violent performance of gender – Kate's bruised eye (a brutal cosmetic "[m]ake up") – into a musical performance that raises him on stilts above his audience. His work is "incredible" but he is vulnerable; if the crowd comes too near and interferes with his stilts, he will fall and "fail." The stilts raise the poet above the danger of his audience, which never encroaches as he might have expected. They also imply that the poet is only figuratively on a higher ground, indicating perhaps his sense of righteousness or dominance after having hit Kate, or the implied desire to transcend gender and the violence of its performance. The stilts also imply that the poet's performance is inauthentic clowning, a sublimation of other fears that are never simply explained. He alludes to his ultimate fear when he says, "I smell the odour of mortality. // And Time flames like a paraffin stove / And what it burns are the minutes I live" (8). Falling from his precarious stance on the stilts would mean his death.[10]

Trehearne notes that the audience in the poem is only implied: "This invisible audience, unnamed and unportrayed, is the first indication that 'Whatever Else Poetry Is Freedom' is an articulation of the disturbing relation between the falsely elevated poet and the uncomprehending crowd he addresses" ("Scanned" 145). Indeed, the crowd's absence suggests that the poet is focused so narcissistically on himself that he is his own audience. Is he singing, or speaking, for anyone when he projects "to the loftiest casements"? Layton might be suggesting that his poet sings only to God (as in "The Birth of Tragedy") through those windows, or, if God (like the audience) is absent, then he sings to himself as an alienated, falsely elevated divinity. These possibilities suggest that the poet must be alone and godless to be free, and that the freedom will last only as long as youth, which is the main attraction in an increasingly sexualized culture of stardom. The implications are bleak: spend your youth alone, achieve celebrity but not freedom, and lose it all with age. Layton's highly sexualized, masculine, pseudo-religious persona attempts to resist such an eventuality, especially in the final stanza: "Swivel, / O hero, in the fleshy groves, skin and glycerine, / And sing of lust" (8).[11] Layton surely believed that poetry is freedom, but he was aware of the limitations of both.

These poems from the late 1950s that implicitly or explicitly express Layton's concerns about celebrity represent the star poet as an ironically religious, masculine but emasculated figure. Zarathustra was his model – Dionysian, prophetic, clownish, and associated through the image of the sun with celestial, celebrity symbolism. Layton's Nietzschean poems defined freedom as a paradox that poetry could demonstrate, but he anticipated that celebrity would reduce his multiplicity to the singular – fuse his private and public personas – thereby narrowing the range of his options for self-definition and expression. Although the star poet is a paradox, too – unable to achieve promotion to fame while also preserving flux – and to some extent derives from that paradox a pseudo-religious authority, the audience eventually emasculates him; the public's control over the celebrity's sexuality is greater than the celebrity's power as a pseudo-religious figure. Layton thereby suggests that having a popular audience inevitably means losing control – despite the power that masculinity and the religious pretence are expected to bring; furthermore, losing an audience is a sign of age, of being a has-been, and of having little hope of achieving fame – poetic immortality – after death.

The scepticism and apprehension of these early poems contrast starkly with Layton's eager optimism, which he expressed in letters to friends, as his celebrity increased at the end of the 1950s (leading eventually to many more poems that concern themselves explicitly with stars and stardom). Making the transition to the second phase in his career with *A Red Carpet for the Sun*, Layton enjoyed three particularly significant experiences of public acclaim in 1957, 1958, and 1959. The first was a 1957 reading at Queen's University. According to Layton in a letter to Pacey, "The students' response – well, it was glory, glory all the way. ... Unblushingly I confess this was a proud moment for me; for this was the acid test, and by all the rules of the game, I had passed it" (qtd. in Cameron 281). The second was, in 1958, a "taste of glory riding on the coattails of Leonard Cohen, the younger *CIV/n* poet" (qtd. in Cameron 282): Layton wrote that he "descended on Leonard Cohen's nest in Birdland, where he gives poetry readings to the accompaniment of a jazz orchestra" (qtd. in Cameron 282); Layton admitted that Cohen was the "staple goods" (qtd. in Cameron 282) and did not seem jealous. Layton was probably thrilled to realize that he would not be alone as a celebrity among poets of that era, and he felt himself at the centre of a "groundswell" (Cameron 281) in Canadian poetry.

The third experience was especially important to Layton: the book launch for *A Red Carpet for the Sun* in September 1959. According to Layton, "[e]veryone in TV or Radio, in the Newspaper or Bookselling game was present when I made my great entry ... I was flanked by Aviva [his third wife] on one side, and by Leonard Cohen on the other, and I needed both of these to run interference for me as the mob bore down" (qtd. in Cameron 289). Jaffe makes an instructive claim to help explain the significance of this account of the launch of *A Red Carpet for the Sun*: "despite relentlessly advancing the cult of the singular artist ... modernism's existence is repeatedly marked by the need for the unpaid work of others, others who were frequently women" (96). By "flank[ing]" himself with Cohen and Aviva, Layton not only grants them the power to protect him but also feminizes them as lesser accomplices to his singular celebrity (figured here as a quarterback or running back – a metaphor of masculine sports also seen in poems such as "Poetry as the Fine Art of Pugilism," 1973). In these three moments in the development of Layton's celebrity, however, Layton is secondary to Cohen in at least one of them. These examples suggest that Layton himself thought that his celebrity was brightened by the presence of Cohen, who was, after all, two decades younger. Layton was proud of being connected to Cohen, and Cohen, in exchange, benefited from his association with Layton at the maturity of his poetic power. Although Cohen was in attendance, Layton remained the centre of attention – and would for around four more years.

Francis argues that the publication of *A Red Carpet for the Sun* was a significant event "not only for Layton's career and for McClelland and Stewart, but also for Canadian poetry in general. Jack McClelland audaciously printed 5,000 copies of *Red Carpet of the Sun*. Within a few weeks more than 2,000 copies had been sold in both paperback and cloth editions, and 5,000 copies were sold within the year" (Francis, "Adjusting" 81). For that book, he won the Governor General's Award and reportedly spent hours bowing in preparation for the ceremony (Cameron 296–7). He was gleeful because of the prize, no doubt, but also ironically amused to be celebrated by the public that he so often insulted. After thirteen years of constant toil, Layton had proven himself, and by 1964 *A Red Carpet for the Sun* had sold 7,500 copies (Cameron 369). Probably no other Canadian poet had ever before enjoyed such success, not until Purdy and Cohen achieved higher sales for their respective *Selected Poems* in the mid- and late 1960s. Neither Layton nor his critics refer to him as such a sensation after any other event in his career. He continued to gain attention on television and radio, but the excitement of his celebrity peaked with *A Red Carpet for the Sun* and its aftermath.

Layton was still the star of Canadian poetry in 1963, when he published *Balls for a One-armed Juggler*, which contained "A Tall Man Executes a Jig." He had written the poem in 1961 (Cameron 329) but chose, uncharacteristically, not to publish it immediately. Although Layton explains "A Tall Man Executes a Jig" as a poem about the poet's transformation of pain, suffering, and evil into art (*Tall Man*), it also shares themes of poetic self-referentiality, of sexuality, of resurrection, of animosity toward the crowd (represented in this case as gnats), and of Zarathustrian religiosity with earlier poems such as "The Birth of Tragedy," "The Cold Green Element," and "Whatever Else Poetry Is Freedom." It is distinct from these poems, however, because it shows that the poet – instead of trying to avoid being held captive by the crowd – *envies* the people in the crowd for *their* lack of freedom. The crowd then withdraws its gift of sexual love because his masculinity is not procreative. The audience that he accepts in their stead (a snake) represents his poetic sublimation of sexual desire left unfulfilled by the audience that initially accepted him as a celebrity. Like the highly abstract poems from the 1950s that have already been considered in this chapter, "A Tall Man Executes a Jig" is not obviously about stardom; however, it is obviously about audiences and grandstanding, and it stands out during a time when Layton was writing much more often than previously about celebrities themselves (such as movie stars, politicians, and other literary celebrities).

"A Tall Man Executes a Jig" reprises the Nietzschean themes related to celebrity in Layton's earlier poems. The tall man is Layton's most Zarathustrian character: as in *Thus Spoke Zarathustra*, the tall man is in a landscape where the "ruddied peaks ... pierced the sun" (112) and he cannot attract a human audience. Zarathustra initially attracted animals that substituted for disciples instead of "the proper human beings" (Nietzsche 265). Both the tall man and Zarathustra are unhappy because of their relationships with their audiences; their art, their teaching becomes their recourse: "Do I strive for *happiness?*" asks Zarathustra (Nietzsche 266); "I strive for my *work!*" Similarly, in "The Birth of Tragedy," Layton's poet says that he is "happiest when I compose poems." Furthermore, Zarathustra claims that God is dead and tries to replace him as a prophet; again similarly, the tall man witnesses "the sun [sink] down, / A dying god" (112) and eventually succeeds in an ultimate creative act that supplants God's jigging, which is analogous to the writing of poems and to performances such as dance. The tall man is a figure of the poet; as Smith observes, "[the tall man's] story turns out to be about man as poet, and ultimately, of course, about Layton himself" (195).[12]

The poem's gnats are a symbol through which Layton adjusts his view of freedom and celebrity. The gnats, tiny but nevertheless more visible than the audience in "Whatever Else Poetry Is Freedom," represent the public that the poet both desires and fears. When the tall man sees a swarm of gnats approach, he realizes that they will "assault" (111) him. Unlike the tall man, the gnats have no concept of freedom, but experience only varying degrees of captivity as if they were on a chain gang: "Jig jig, jig, jig. Like minuscule black links / Of a chain played with by some playful / Unapparent hand" (111). The "hand" is that of God, who enslaves the gnats on a "chain" that he dangles from heaven. The tall man watches the gnats "drop upon his sleeveless arm" and begin to sting him until he becomes a "maddened speck" (111) among them. (Cohen seems to have adapted this scene with Martin Stark's mosquito bites in his 1963 novel *The Favourite Game.*) Their assaults threaten to make him gnat-like: chained by them, to them, and to a higher power – and indistinguishable from his audience. Although the threat to his freedom makes him mad (crazed), he is also, temporarily, happy:

> Still the assaults of the small flies made him
> Glad at last, until he saw purest joy
> In their frantic jiggings under a hair,
> So changed from those in the unrestraining air. (111)

He is "glad" because he is so tall and the bugs puny; however, when his arm hairs trap the flies, he interprets their "frantic jiggings" as "purest joy," a joy greater than the masochistic gladness that he feels when they assault his exposed skin. Their joy ends his. A potential figure of celebrity, he fears that the crowd's parasitic verve might restrict his freedom and absorb his individuality, but he envies the crowd that can be happy without being free.

The tall man's general unhappiness brings him a temporary feeling of great status: "He stood up and felt himself enormous" (112). Motivated by unhappiness, in the third stanza he feels a creative power akin to Donatello's mastery of stone. Although he temporarily "feels his forehead touch the emptied sky" that the "dying god" has now vacated, the gnat-audience's jig continues in godless chaos, in "[m]otion without meaning, disquietude / Without sense or purpose" (112). He has been unable to bring meaning to the multitude that worships him so sadistically. Possibly because the gnats were impressed with the tall man's presence, they return (after being scattered by the wind) with "a bee, who, seeing / But a tall man, left him for a marigold" (112). Bees seek flowers for their sustaining pollen, which also contains the male gametes that fertilize other flowers when the bee moves from plant to plant. The bee, therefore, potentially symbolizes a woman who finds neither sustenance nor sexual potency in the tall man. She has an individuality that the gnats do not; perhaps for that reason, she "see[s] / But [or only] a tall man." In other words, the bee is not compelled by what the tall man feels to be his "enormous" stature or status; she sees the tall man as the performer that he is. In contrast with the bee, the gnats seem to represent an audience composed of parasitic men, not women. The tall man might have "held / A loved and lovely woman in his arms" (112), but that relationship was in the past. Extending his suggestions in earlier poems about the star poet's impotence, Layton suggests that the tall man's masculinity – represented here as a tolerance and even enjoyment of physical pain – turns away his potential audience of comparably independent women.

Dejected, the tall man "drop[s] his head and let[s] fall the halo / Of mountains" (113); in his humility, he seems to attract the snake, his third and most genuine audience. The snake appears as "temptation coiled before his feet: / A violated grass-snake that lug[s] / Its intestine like a small red valise" (113). Although he was prepared to stop thinking of himself as a Zarathustrian surrogate for a divine, "halo[ed]," creative power (i.e., a star poet), the tall man rekindles the godly creativity that he had sought from "the wheeling fire of the sun" (112) when he sees the mortally wounded serpent. As a "temptation," the snake might represent Satan, but in its "violated" condition, it also represents all the animals mutilated by people in Layton's many cruelty-to-animals poems. Rather than be tempted to either sadism or mercy, the tall man "wept because pity was useless" (113). He warns the snake, "Your jig's up; the flies come like kites" (113). He initially does nothing but wait for the second return of the gnats, which herald the end of the snake's life and "jig." His declarative authority over the jig, and the prophetic announcement about the coming "flies" – with their connotation of Beelzebub – restores the impression of religious significance that he had abandoned earlier.

When the snake dies, the tall man acts as the executor of the snake's last will. We can infer the terms of that will based on what we know of the tall man and of the other audiences in the poem. The tall man might know the snake's will because their minds are melded in a "fellowship of death" (114). Indeed, when the snake dies, the speaker reveals that the tall man's "mind" has a "flicking tongue"; thus, the snake is a symbol of his imagination, which revives, becoming a dragon, a flying snake that might spout the "green flame of life" and the "thin wreaths of cloud" that "coiled above his head, transforming all" (114). By reanimating the snake and reviving the dying sky (a symbol of the mind and of God), the tall man asserts the creativity of the imagination over that of the body. Furthermore, he seems to channel the snake-audience's desire for *freedom* – because the snake was possibly heading for the tall man to escape its killer, which is associated with the enslaved gnats that herald its death.

By insinuating Layton's preoccupation with freedom in the context of *execution*, which also means the infliction of death, the poem implies that Layton is marking the end of a major phase of his life in art, his jig. The tall man – a symbol of Layton that, like the clown on stilts in "Whatever Else Poetry Is Freedom," puts him in the shoes of a bigger man in an act of grandstanding (literally standing tall) – does not literally die, but his life does transform. The tall man's union with a disturbingly mutilated phallic symbol (the snake) suggests that he has been emasculated by an audience that rejected him. The transformation might demonstrate the power of resurrection known to us as Dionysian vitality, Christian redemption, and Nietzschean flux, but it also poignantly implies that Layton lost hope of achieving freedom through stardom. The tall man, like Layton, seems to anticipate the fading of his celebrity and the resignation of being his own audience in solitude. We saw similar symbolism in

"The Cold Green Element" and "Whatever Else Poetry Is Freedom," but there is much here that we did *not* see in those earlier poems: first, the poet's temporary envy of the audience's pain and lack of freedom; second, the preference for an audience of one rather than an audience of many; and third, the bittersweet but remarkably positive closing image. The end of "A Tall Man Executes a Jig" suggests that the tall man overcomes his masochism and begins to value himself without the attentions of an audience; thus, he crowns himself with the snake after having "doffed his aureole of gnats" (112) along with his halo. The poet affirms his self-esteem in a gesture of freedom that also seems like a grand finale, a flourish. Layton was compelled to reassure himself that even after losing or rejecting his audience, he could jig a poem of hard-won joy.

Few of Layton's later poems continued to imply that the star poet has religious significance, but they continued to suggest that masculinity was essential for self-promotion. Although some of Layton's most important poems from the 1950s and the beginning of the 1960s can be interpreted as comments on celebrity, he produced fewer long and complex poems after that time – nothing to compare with "A Tall Man Executes a Jig" as a grand gesture of concern that gains relevance in the context of celebrity. He was, however, representing stardom much more explicitly, beginning more and more to use his poetry in a self-reflexive strategy of his own promotion. In the second phase in his career, the obviousness of his poetry about celebrity and the relative lack of poems such as "A Tall Man Executes a Jig" were signs not only of the peaking excitement of his celebrity but also of the stress of maintaining his status when his celebrity was likely to fade.

Perhaps because he sensed his celebrity had reached its peak in Canada, Layton redoubled his efforts and cast his eye to the bigger markets – and some of the bigger celebrities – of America and Europe. In the same year that he was writing "A Tall Man Executes a Jig," he published *The Swinging Flesh* (1961) and imagined himself in contrast with widely recognized foreigners. His use of his own name in many of these poems (and that of his wife in some cases) shows that he is involving his private persona, but the self-promotion in these poems means that his public persona is also in use, and their simultaneous, fused presence is the metaphor of celebrity at work. So soon after the major milestone of Layton's literary celebrity, no one should be surprised to notice this fusion in *The Swinging Flesh*. Disregarding "Prizes" and its outrageous claim that the poet would have won not another "prize" but "[i]mmortal fame" if he had "praised" (169) a woman's vagina, I will focus on two other poems in the book that involve foreign women who are represented as, or are assumed to be, more widely recognized than Layton himself. The first is "The

Day Aviva Came to Paris," which was written for his wife, an Australian; and the second is "Why I Don't Make Love to the First Lady," which was written for Jacqueline Kennedy, later Onassis, whose husband was then president of the United States.[13] In these poems, Layton exaggerates the scope of his celebrity by association with women from other countries – much as he later does with Norman Mailer but with predictable differences in his treatment of him because of his sex (i.e., violent confrontation rather than implied seduction).

In "The Day Aviva Came to Paris," Layton describes "the Frenchmen" who set down books by "their famous writers" (150) to gaze at Aviva's nude body. He offers Aviva compliments (seeming not to realize that they are sexist), but he mainly seems interested in indirectly congratulating himself for having a beautiful wife who is as well known in France as he imagines he is. He imagines "the Frenchmen" cheering, "'Vive l'Australienne! / Vive Layton who brought her among us!'" (151). Although he temporarily worries that the Frenchmen will "bury [him and Aviva, alive,] in the Panthéon" (151), the poem ends as Aviva is "raised up / into [his] hairy arms by the raving emotional crowds" (152). Layton was not to my knowledge well known in France, though he was, many years after he wrote this poem, recognized in other countries outside of North America.[14] The importance of this poem is its ironic fantasy of his worldwide stardom, which he continues to understand in problematically masculine ways.

The irony of that fantasy is not apparent in the compliments to Aviva as much as it is in his representations of the French. Whereas "the Frenchmen" say that they are in awe of Aviva's "blaze of pubic hair" (150) and her "adorable ass" (151), Layton calls her "an undraped Jewish Venus" (151) – a description less coarse but no less objectifying because "undraped" can refer to models posing for sculptors and painters. He focuses on his wife's attractiveness and what that means to him; "[t]he day you came naked to Paris," Layton writes, "[t]he tourists returned home without their guidebooks, / The hunger in their cameras finally appeased" (150). She is the object not only of the touristic gaze but also of that of an audience of "millions of Frenchmen" (151). The Frenchmen fare not much better than Aviva in Layton's representation of them as foolishly humble – having "learned ... to think of themselves / As not excessively subtle or witty" (150) despite the example of Voltaire, whom he mentions – but also excitable: their "applaudissements and bravos / Bombinating along the Boulevard Saint-Germain" (152). Layton indirectly disparages both Aviva and the Frenchmen. Like most of Layton's sensational or controversial poems, "The Day Aviva Came to Paris" is curiously flawed and only partly ironic; as a strategy of promoting himself abroad, it is so unlikely to succeed that it seems parodic. Although the poem seems to promote Layton by association with Aviva, it also demeans or mocks everyone in the poem – Layton included, but Layton less obviously.

In "The Day Aviva Came to Paris," Layton is mocking himself and his own celebrity by exposing the ridiculousness of the notion that he would be recognized anywhere else but in Canada – a ridiculousness evident in the hyperbolic representations of the effusive appreciation that the Frenchmen show for his wife and him. His awareness of his relatively inferior celebrity suggests that, despite evidence of the fusion of selves in this poem, he retained a critical faculty for assessing his literary stardom even at its actual historical peak. "The Day Aviva Came to Paris" reveals not only Layton's cynical opinion about the potential of his celebrity but also his willingness to subject himself, and his wife, to comic and demeaning appraisals.

He is almost as insulting toward Kennedy as he is to Aviva in the first lines of "Why I Don't Make Love to the First Lady": "Of course I could have her! // In a flash, with a snap of my fingers" (173). The speaker admits that he is "arrogant" and "degenerate," but he also states that he has "a sense of honour" that prevents him from competing for women with men, such as "President Kennedy," who do "not write verse" (173). As in "Poetry as the Fine Art of Pugilism" but less obviously, Layton implies that poetry is a way of proving one's manhood. While the president loses sleep because of a tense "international situation" (174) that involves actual wars and threats of escalation, Layton imagines that his status as a writer of "verse" gives him a power that is greater than the president's ability to make war: power over women. Making love, then, is the higher power. As usual, however, Layton undermines his own manhood. Although his pretext for not "running off" with "[m]y lovely, unlucky Jacqueline" is "honour," he plans to "wait until / the international situation has cleared. / After that it's every poet for himself" (174). The free-for-all implied in this last line is a playful suggestion of what Layton really seems to want: the freedom to pursue even the most unrealistic of goals, such as having the "First Lady" as the object of his attention. Of course, he would also be wise not to aggravate America's commander-in-chief during the escalation of the Cold War. Audaciously, Layton sent a copy of the poem to the president and his wife (Cameron 315), which indicates a remarkable lack of judgment but also – more important – a mischievously funny, unrealistically ambitious tactic of self-promotion to audiences beyond Canada.

His tone soon returned to its previous seriousness in *Balls for a One-armed Juggler* (1963), which contains a remarkably high concentration of poems that refer to other non-Canadian celebrities. As I quoted in the first chapter, Layton was "[a]s a celebrity ... a purely typical Canadian product, a blow-up of our national inferiority complex" (Dudek, "Layton" 92), which is rarely more evident than in these poems. Many of Layton's past and future references were to Cohen, but the surprising number in *Balls for a One-armed Juggler* – not much more than a year before Cohen began to surpass Layton's celebrity – is suggestive. *Balls for a One-armed Juggler* contains poems about Marilyn Monroe ("Elegy for Marilyn Monroe"), Ernest Hemingway ("Silence," another elegy[15]), Alexander Trocchi ("For Alexander Trocchi, Novelist," who was also a notorious drug user), and Mailer. "The Dazed Steer," dedicated "for Norman Mailer," is also explained in my aforementioned article because Cohen later responded to that poem; it has a somewhat different role here. Cohen excepted, not one of the mentioned celebrities is Canadian; Trocchi was Scottish, but along with the others his celebrity was established in the United States. Arguably, with *Balls for a One-armed Juggler* in 1963, Layton began to consider his own celebrity more seriously than he had only a couple of years earlier with *The Swinging Flesh* in 1961 – with less self-deprecation and more desperation. Compared to "The Day Aviva Came to Paris" and "Why I Don't Make Love to the First Lady," Layton's poems for Monroe, Hemingway, Trocchi, and Mailer are sober, even grave. His solemnity was probably the result of thinking that celebrity was a factor in the deaths of Monroe and Hemingway, and that Cohen needed to be cautioned about seeking inspiration through drug use as Trocchi did. Layton's concern for himself as a celebrity, too, was now emerging with less abstraction than it did in poems such as "The Cold Green Element" from the 1950s.

"The Dazed Steer," therefore, boldly puts Layton into a contest with another celebrity: Mailer. "The Dazed Steer" describes a presumably fictional encounter between the speaker (i.e., Layton) and Mailer: "He greeted me by saying: / 'What if I hit you in the belly?' // We squared off" (84). The ensuing staring contest ends when Mailer "turn[s] his head / like a dazed steer" (84). The confrontation is unexpected, almost random, though Mailer and Layton are very similar, both being antiestablishmentarian Jewish celebrities with high ambitions for their writing. In "The Dazed Steer," Layton invokes Mailer to show what company he keeps, even if they had never met, and he proposes a celebrity face-off. Despite the implication of "Poetry as the Fine Art of Pugilism," never in Layton's poems does he, as speaker, actually engage in a fist-fight with anyone – though he mentions, retrospectively, "[giving his] Kate a blackened eye" in "Whatever Else Poetry Is Freedom." Instead, he shows remarkable sympathy for Mailer by suggesting he knows "that someone or something / had dealt him a blow / from which he'd never recover" (84). The "blow" might have been Layton's indomitable gaze, but it might also have been something else – perhaps Jewish history but perhaps also an effect of stardom – that had compelled Mailer to seek in Layton an outlet for his frustration.

Although Cohen later chides Layton for his macho bluster in this poem in "Dear Mailer" from *The Energy of Slaves* (1972), "The Dazed Steer" subtly implies that Layton might have also anticipated or even experienced a blow like the one he says Mailer received. They stare at each other as if they were mirror images, almost alike enough to come to a "draw" (84). Because "The Dazed Steer" is in the context of other poems (as I will explain) that seem to recognize the negative consequences of celebrity, its conclusion suggests that Mailer's problem might be reflected upon Layton. The unspecified blow to Mailer is intelligible to Layton because he experienced a similar blow: the experience of rapidly rising celebrity and its consequences.

The problem occurs, as Layton articulates in "The Predator," when one's "fame's against / him" (50) and one's reputation precedes him. Although "The Predator" makes no other direct reference to "fame" or celebrity, it describes a "little fox / [that] was lying in a pool of blood, / having gnawed his way out to freedom" (50). In this chapter, my argument has been that Layton's concern for "freedom" is often a response to the typecasting effect of celebrity. Here, the fox died because of its self-amputating attempt to escape a trap, but the fox's fame is such that "one suspects him of anything" (50), even faking his own death: "His evident / self-enjoyment is against him also: / no creature so wild and gleeful can ever be done for" (50). The speaker's appreciation for these Nietzschean qualities of freedom, joyfulness, and determination is obvious, but rebirth and transformation no longer seem to be as effective as they were in "The Cold Green Element" and "A Tall Man Executes a Jig." Layton asserts, "But this fox was ["done for"]; / there's no place in the world any more / for free and gallant predators like him" (51). For animals such as the fox, "their freedom is their death" (51). When the speaker claims that "[m]an sets even / more terrible traps for his own kind" (51), he might be suggesting that there is no "freedom," not even in "death," from "fame" turned "against" the fox – or against Layton.

It seems inevitable that Layton's well-known poems about animals and insects victimized by cruel humans would be a conceit that he would eventually associate with celebrity; his representation of Mailer as a "dazed steer" is only the most obvious example. In "The Cage," also from *Balls for a One-armed Juggler*, the speaker is trapped as if he were an animal such as the fox in "The Predator": "me / Blinded and raging in this huge cage" (14). The imprisoned speaker in "The Cage," however, concentrates more on his audience than on himself. His audience tends to be from the working class – "janitors, whores," a "blacksmith," "stonemasons," and "ironmongers" – with the exception of the "bank presidents" (14); notably, there are no presidents of countries or their spouses: no Kennedys. This is the general public. "The Cage" does not mention celebrity directly, but Layton implies that some highly visible men are sacrificed by the public to sublimate its violent, animalistic urges.

The only violence that the public does is to the imprisoned speaker, who is not only caged but also wounded in such a way that his masculinity is compromised. When the blacksmith offers, to the other members of the audience, "to blind" (14) the speaker, he is offering to destroy the speaker's phallic power of the gaze.[16] The effect of imprisonment and injury on the speaker is to elicit various emotions of shame, fear, and powerlessness: "I turn away to hide my terror / Lest my unmanliness displease them" (14). His "unmanliness" recalls the emasculated speakers from earlier poems by Layton, such as "The Cold Green Element." If there is any equivalence between the "[b]linded and raging" speaker and Layton, he is clearly neither happy about the effect of scrutiny on masculinity nor happy about the social usefulness of scrutinized men; if they serve a religious function, it is sacrificial, not prophetic – except in the sense that Layton seemed to be intuitively correct about the fate of so many celebrities (the list is long) after the tragic early deaths of Monroe and Hemingway.

The paradoxical combination of Layton's fear of stardom's consequences and his frustration at not achieving even greater stardom was evident in 1964's *The Laughing Rooster*, which revealed Layton at the extremes of his outrageousness, anger, and misogyny. Robin Skelton's review of *The Laughing Rooster* was negative but perceptive, arguing that Layton's poems depend on "an egocentricity which assumes that the poet's personality is more important than the poems, that any expression of personal idiosyncracy has poetic potential, and that self-dramatization is an adequate substitute for structural control" (63).[17] In other words, Layton was attempting to rely on his celebrity instead of his poems for his success. Specifically, he was attempting to generate controversy by indulging his abusive public persona. In "An Imperfect Devotion" (1993), Gary Geddes mentions an occasion when Layton insulted Margaret Atwood, who had been invited to read from her work at York University sometime between 1969, when Layton began teaching there, and 1976, when Atwood described the incident (Cameron 372, 496n). Geddes explains: "The gifted but insecure poet, trying to gain control of a public situation where he feels at a slight disadvantage, resorts to verbal pugilism" (20). The "slight disadvantage" is an understatement; Atwood was a rising star in Canadian literature and posed an additional threat to Layton because of her feminism. Furthermore, Layton's literary celebrity had peaked,[18] and his strategy of relying on his star power or shock value was no longer effective. A more determined than innovative self-promoter, Layton in the mid-1960s resorted to strategies that had worked in the past – and continued to write bad poems.

Some reviewers would continue to think of Layton as "probably the least dispensable Canadian poet now living" (Ross 22), but by 1964, Canadian poetry had developed beyond Layton's influence (Cameron 364, 371), and Cohen was eclipsing his celebrity. The clearest sign was that the National Film Board documentary, which had begun as a project about Layton, Cohen, Earle Birney, and Phyllis Gotlieb in 1964, became in 1965 simply *Ladies and Gentlemen ... Mr. Leonard Cohen*. Rather than squabble over the film's emphasis, Layton tried to find the cause of his fading celebrity and, in a letter to Pacey, "explained the puzzling centrality of Leonard Cohen in the filmed tour of 1964 as the result of Layton's too-frequent appearances before the public" (Cameron 371). His overexposure was one reason that his celebrity waned; the next big thing was Cohen, and Atwood and feminism were beginning to show that Layton and his "*chutzpah*, vituperation [and] exuberance" were unfashionable (Cameron 371–2).

By the mid-1960s, Layton was overexposed and felt threatened by the effects of celebrity and his own compulsion to promote it. Layton himself had contrasted what Trehearne calls his "transformative model of selfhood" with his fear of being captured or captivated by his own public self. In 1965, Layton said, "The last thing I want to see happen to me is to be taken captive by my own image. I want freedom and blessed independence – even from myself. Perhaps mostly from myself" (qtd. in Cameron 373). Despite hinting that he was the cause of his own "captiv[ity]," he did not stop promoting himself. Cameron devotes two chapters in *Irving Layton: A Portrait* to showing that Layton redoubled his effort to maintain recognition while his reputation was waning. In 1961, his charisma and opportunistic controversiality were still affording him "media coverage ... no other poet could compete with" (Cameron 367–8), but for most of the 1960s *Fighting Words* was off the air in Canada (Allan). Layton gained attention on air again in the 1970s, but his style "seemed too grand, too forced, too confident of right and wrong to express the more muted anxieties of the next generation" (Cameron 368). Layton continued to enjoy strong book sales until the early 1970s (Cameron 425) and generated controversies with letters to the editor in the *Globe and Mail* throughout the 1970s, but Marian Engel wrote, in 1973, that "[t]he man who took the underpants off Canadian poetry [now] sings an unfashionable tune" (31).

In the third phase of Layton's career as a celebrity, he wrote with considerably less angst about his status, which preoccupied him less than when he was younger. The tone of his later poetry is more reflective and generous (especially to women), and the voice is quieter and more directed outward – toward social problems that he no longer thought that poetry should solve. His representations of himself are sometimes playful, as in "Shakespeare," which appeared in *Nail Polish* (1971). Most of the poem is a comic exaggeration of the frustration that poets feel because of Shakespeare's "forever unapproachable star" (19), a degree of celebrity that Michael D. Bristol has called, to describe Shakespeare, the "big-time" (10). In my argument, the "big-time" is the equivalent to fame or poetic immortality.[19] The poem begins,

My young son asks me:
"who's the greatest poet?"
Without any fuss I say, Shakespeare.
"Is he greater than you?"
I ho-ho around that one
and finally give him a hard "yes." (18)

His son then asks if he would ever be greater than Shakespeare, and the speaker firmly says no. He also says, but not to his son, that he is

hoping my fair-minded admission
won't immediately blot out
the my-father-can-lick-anyone image
in his happy ignorant mind
and take the shine away
that's presently all around my head. (18)

The halo resulting from the "image" of the father who can beat other men is a sign of religious pretension and problematic masculinity that Layton wears more lightly here than in the past (as when he removed "the halo / Of mountains" in "A Tall Man Executes a Jig"). "Shakespeare" is not seriously pretentious. The poem ends with a good-humoured joke about still having a chance to be greater than Shakespeare – mainly because Layton's "six-year-old son" (20) has a promising imagination that might enable him to extend the patriarchal lineage of celebrity that, as I explained in my aforementioned article, Layton and his symbolic son Cohen had drawn between each other – but Layton's tone remains mellow despite the subtle competitive zest. Layton was capable of adjusting his attitude to celebrity after it had sufficiently waned.

Layton's emphasis on Shakespeare's "greatness" (20) is a sign that, by 1971, Layton had regained some of his focus and began to recover his original ambition: fame. He admits that "there's nothing to be done / about that bastard's unsurpassable / greatness" (20) but concludes by saying that he and his son have "got our bid in, Old Bard" (21). Some evidence suggests that he was, indeed, increasingly recognized in some media, as the tables in the appendix show. He was perhaps becoming a more general star as his literary celebrity lost currency and became fame. In the years between 1978 and 1989, for example, Layton was mentioned at least five times per year in the *CPI*, and, notably, many of those mentions were honorific; they were tributes to his past achievements rather than inquiries into his current affairs – another sign of fame. His major poems of the 1950s can be considered accomplishments, even instances of "greatness," but they did not earn him fame until he stopped promoting his stardom so fiercely that it cast doubt on them by association. He became somewhat famous as the era of celebrity in Canadian poetry, which he helped to define, was ending. If he had concentrated less on his celebrity – and had written more poems such as "A Tall Man Executes a Jig" and fewer poems such as "Prizes" – he probably would have achieved a higher degree of fame, though almost certainly not that of Shakespeare.

Layton's experience with celebrity might have convinced him that he would always be Canada's most widely recognized poet, but he was already forty-seven when *A Red Carpet for the Sun* arrived at the end of the 1950s, and in the next decade the burgeoning culture of youth, feminism, and civil rights became less hospitable to Layton's pedantic tirades, misogyny, and megalomania. Later comments on his work (even the positive ones) blamed not only shifting cultural values for Layton's gradual displacement but also his stubborn style. Arguably, the restrictiveness of his celebrity outlasted his actual celebrity and led Purdy to write, in a 1979 review, that "Layton has been imitating himself for years, in a perfect parody of his own style, and has written nearly all of his poems before, some many times" (qtd. in Cameron 422). Similarly, in 1983, Cohen commented – with admiration, it seems – that Layton "will never grow, his work or himself. His sense of the urgency of the poetic identity is unparalleled" (qtd. in Cameron 359). In spite of Layton's theories about the poet's freedom, other poets were already noticing that Layton's work seemed fixed and repetitive by the late 1960s, and he was never relieved of this stigma in his lifetime. He laboured to have his poetry and its various satirical messages recognized not simply because he was a star but also to prove that his stardom's typecasting effect would not ruin his poetry. Although in that respect he often failed, he crafted several poems, especially in the 1950s, that proved him imaginative, perceptive, and critical in his anticipation of celebrity.

By appearing on television and increasingly in other popular media in the 1950s, Layton helped to make celebrity possible for Canadian poets after the Second World War and helped to define the terms of reference for the public personas of later star poets. His problematic masculinity and religious pretension were later re-enacted and then rejected by Cohen, Michael Ondaatje, and Gwendolyn MacEwen, who also wrote poems about their stardom – and, sometimes indirectly, about how it differed from that of Layton. Unlike Cohen and Ondaatje, Layton maintained his literary celebrity for several years despite his lack of success in writing in other forms. He admitted, "I'm simply not one of [the poets who seem easily to switch from form to form]" (qtd. in Cameron 400). He accepted, to some extent, his typecasting; he committed himself to his public persona until the end of the 1960s and did not moderate it much until the 1970s. He wanted fame but understood his celebrity to be a threat to his freedoms of expression and self-definition. For someone of such devotion to Dionysian and Nietzschean values of vitality and flux, the typecasting effect, which seems to have been internalized enough to affect his identity, was an artistic and even existential problem.

4 *Fighting Words*: Layton on Radio and Television

No Canadian poet has a reputation for both self-aggrandizement and outrageous provocation comparable to that of Irving Layton, and he earned that reputation partly on radio and television. Many of his important appearances in the national broadcast media happened in the half decade from 1955 to 1960, when his self-described "BOOM IN LAYTON" (*Wild* 63) was ongoing. During the era of celebrity in Canadian poetry, he was featured on widely heard radio programs such as *Anthology, Ideas, As It Happens, Assignment, This Is Robert Fulford,* and *Morningside*; and on television on *Tabloid, 90 Minutes Live, Telescope, Take 30,* and others – but it was *Fighting Words* on both radio and television that was especially promotional for Layton. *Fighting Words* was one of the Canadian Broadcasting Corporation's most popular shows (Nash 242), and he was often one of its guests. Its format was debate: a moderator offered controversial statements to be discussed by four panellists, often "personalities." Authors who debated with Layton on the show included Canadians such as Miriam Waddington, Morley Callaghan, Earle Birney, and Hugh Garner, but even Ayn Rand appeared on one occasion; they argued about topics such as pornography, dirty jokes, violence against women, American foreign policy, censorship, and, of course, high and low cultures, mass media, and celebrity. Some aspects of Layton's persona in addition to his reputation as a contrarian emerged from these debates, but his involvement also helped him appeal through controversy to both popular audiences and the intelligentsia, thereby widening the scope of his celebrity and improving his bid for fame.

Much of Layton's success in the national media of the 1950s can be attributed to his combination of speaking well and acting a little bad. He realized that he would be more likely to draw attention to his poetry if he spoke with authority on major issues in the arts and culture during the emergence of integrated mass media in the mid-twentieth century. He also must have known that CBC TV and CBC Radio, despite their establishmentarian ethos at a time of increasing nationalism in much of Canadian culture, were also significant opportunities to reach a growing popular audience – one that did not always want traditional commentary on the issues. In the context of *Fighting Words*, he was a little more tactful on radio than on television. For his popular audience, he acted the roles of instigator, rebel, devil's advocate – what Sam Solecki calls the *enfant terrible* ("Introduction" xv). For his public of academics and the literary establishment, he was considerably more measured and diplomatic, especially when the other guests on the same CBC programs might have upstaged him with narrower or more extreme views. These publics also existed in unison, of course, and so his behaviour on air was sometimes inconsistent, even perplexing. But one constant of his appearances was his willingness to argue, to emphasize disagreement rather than agreement, and – as perhaps the only Canadian poet to be a "regular" on both television and radio – he thereby helped to make room in public space for poets as critics.

He did not recite his poetry on *Fighting Words*, however. Acting as a critic, could he advertise himself as a poet? Layton probably thought so. He would never have admitted to playing the role of critic rather than poet; he would call them the same role. Douglas Grant, who later appeared with Layton on *Fighting Words*, spoke about the roles of poet and critic in an address on private and public poetry at the 1955 Canadian Writers' conference at Queen's University. Grant argued that the poet is "radical" and private (in an age of lyricism) compared to the "conservative" public, and that the critic is "a person of divided allegiance" (34). Grant concluded that "[t]he good critic attempts to maintain the precarious balance, and in so doing fulfils his purpose: which is, first, to illustrate the issues in dispute between the writer and the public, and, second, to prevent their instinctive divergence from becoming extreme" (35). Like Grant's "good critic," Layton's ideal poet would be able to reconcile those occasionally opposite positions. This partly accounts for the variations in his claims on *Fighting Words* about the public and publicity, which are almost always bad in his writing but sometimes good on air.

Although some of Layton's earliest comments in the broadcast media show him to be cautious about television (e.g., an appearance on CBC Radio's *Citizens' Forum* on 12 December 1956, in which he argued that the social problem of conformity is a result of "mass pressures"), within a couple of years he was more willing to endorse it, possibly because he was recognizing it as a vehicle of his own promotion. Among other gestures, he appealed to the public by stating that television was becoming important to democracy. On radio's *Fighting Words* on 28 January 1958, Layton engaged with Callaghan and two professors from the University of Toronto on the topic of politics on television.

They were debating American foreign policy and the conversation led to questions about Dwight D. Eisenhower's and John Diefenbaker's recent uses of the media for political ends. Layton claimed that television

> gives the opponents of a political straw man a chance to get up and knock him down. I think television too by opening more channels of communication, by enabling much more controversy to take place before the public, in some way can undo the damage of this kind of made-up personality and made-up campaign and issues.

This partial defence of television is somewhat contrary to his implied criticism of mass media in his discussion about conformity on the aforementioned *Citizens' Forum*. It is also contrary to the typically negative representation of the public in his poems, where the public damages his own "made-up personality" and not vice versa. Here he gives the public credit, as he rarely did in his poetry, for its discernment. The implication is that the public will become aware of political issues through controversy, and that controversy – ideally "much more" of it – is good for democracy. Because his public persona was beginning to rely on controversy as publicity, he saw the personal and social reasons for endorsing television.

Perhaps Layton was speaking as a critic rather than a poet, which would help to explain the inconsistencies in his views, but consistency itself was also of interest to him in this 1958 radio debate. One of the professors from Toronto, John Irving, disagreed with Layton's hypothesis about the potential of television to fall under despotic control with a cogent argument about wealthy businessmen controlling the media (at least the privately owned media), and Layton conceded the point. Nevertheless, given the last word in the debate, Layton concluded: "I think [television] gives the American public or the Canadian public – any public for that matter – the chance to test the personality against the words, and this is something that is I think most important to the democratic process." Layton might have been assuming that the public can distinguish between a "personality" or persona and the "words," but both are potentially inauthentic, and (as the previous chapter demonstrated) he eventually worried about not preserving the difference between the authentic and inauthentic man. Consistency was the trait that Layton was looking for in politicians in their statements and attitudes to the public. Ironically, his own statements were inconsistent, but he almost always had a positive attitude toward controversy, and controversy demands that one be willing to play the devil's advocate. He would be a bad politician by his own measure of consistency – unless he were controversial. Lacking confidence in public figures, he sometimes tried to be optimistic about the public in general. Although he would often depict the public as a menace in his writing, perhaps he felt obliged on air to recognize how the public and the media's publicity could be good.

Layton's opinion remained critical of public personalities and stardom in another debate on radio later in the same year, but he began to extend his criticism to the public that had been so discerning only months earlier. On 11 November 1958, Nathan Cohen, the host of *Fighting Words*, offered the following hypothesis to a panel that included Layton and Rand: "If you become a public figure, you can no longer be sincere as a writer."[1] Layton agreed:

> I would go along with that, Nathan. I think the important thing for a writer is really anguish and solitude. I think he's sincere when he's alone with his thoughts. I think he loses something of that when he becomes a public figure and then sort of disintegrate [*sic*] in the general miasmal sophistries and illusions of the teeming millions. He's got to keep himself pure. And the only way he can do that, the only way he can preserve his integrity, is by avoiding becoming a celebrity or a public figure. It seems to do something to the integrity of a writer when he becomes a person pronouncing on current fashions, current opinions, and the current madnesses and manias and obsessions affecting the world today.

The "BOOM IN LAYTON" had ostensibly started in 1955, so Layton must have realized that he was beginning to become the same "celebrity or ... public figure" that he was criticizing. There is more than a little hypocrisy in his foregoing statement, even though he had not yet won the Governor General's Award for *A Red Carpet for the Sun* (1959). Here we can see how Layton's view of the public as a critic was beginning to align with the view that he had already articulated as a poet. He now referred not to the public's keen, upstanding minds but to its "teeming millions" who deceive and are deceived. In referring to "disintegrat[ion]," he was arguably also alluding to the identity crisis that is associated in his poetry with becoming a star, becoming too public. Stars and their fans, and the public more generally, all get his criticism.

His disdain for the "millions" suggests that he understood himself on occasion as a man set apart from an imagined low culture of uneducated masses. Cohen's next statement for debate – that "[t]he people pay for television and the dulling of perception between true and false" – garnered general approval from Layton, who chose to respond as a teacher. He remarked that he was astonished to realize that many of his students could not comprehend a few simple lines of poetry; he suggested that they have difficulty distinguishing good from bad and have no taste. Rand agreed, and Layton politely thanked her (a notable instance of two elitist writers agreeing from otherwise opposite ends of socio-economic ideology). By calling attention to his job in the classroom, he associated himself with other teachers.

So, he was a populist but also wanted to associate himself with knowledgeable people *and* the elites among them – the intelligentsia. In an earlier televised debate on *Fighting Words* on 6 December 1956, he spoke out against Callaghan, whose statement about a lack of "intellectual life" in Montreal was in question. Layton implied that Callaghan's opinion was problematically restricted to the anglophone population and claimed that Montreal's communities of French and Jewish intellectuals were vibrant and cosmopolitan. As he sometimes did, he got the last word with a pointed rebuttal: "May I further add, Morley, that because your field does not lie in poetry, and the chief glory and majesty of the Montreal intellectual life lies in the poetry, you are in no position to judge." Simultaneous vigorous responses met this statement, but the host rang the bell (an actual bell!) because the allotted time had elapsed. Layton was raising another question for debate: the implicit competition between poetry and prose fiction in Canada. He was managing to advertise himself to poets, academics, and other potential intellectuals in Montreal, maintaining a sense of their exclusivity, and his own, in Canada's cultural centre at that time.

On a similar topic four years later, after his winning of the Governor General's Award, Layton aligned himself once again with the intelligentsia but seemed even more elitist in contrast with one of the other panellists on *Fighting Words*. On 31 January 1960, Layton appeared on television with three others, including Waddington – another leftist Anglo-Jewish poet but one who was "an important counterweight to Layton's work and his public persona" (Ravvin 127). On *Fighting Words*, her opinions were respectful of less educated people, in contrast with Layton's left-leaning elitism. The question to be argued was whether Canadian intellectuals ever "crawl out of their ivory towers except to go on CBC panel shows." Layton claimed that "the Canadian intellectual is in a very small minority" and then cited a statistic about the "great majority of Canadians" who are not educated well enough to care about issues or understand them. Intellectuals (i.e., professors) are "a small class of people," he said. "Canadians by and large do not give two hoots about education." Instead, "tobacco, alcohol, and hockey games" are interesting to them. Waddington responded by saying, "Mr. Layton – I'm very suspicious of what Mr. Layton has said. He's marshalled here a lot of facts, but you know facts and the truth are two different things, Mr. Layton – " "Not when I put them together," Layton said. The half-joking arrogance of such a remark might have been amusing to viewers who shared his opinions, but probably not to Waddington and others who were more sympathetic to people excluded from the upper class or other privileged groups. Layton did not have the money to be included in the upper class, but his education at McGill University and his work as teacher and professor were relatively prestigious (i.e., cultural capital), and here he seemed to have forgotten his earlier street-tough persona and the scholarship on Marxism in his master's thesis.

Nevertheless, although he implied in this debate that he was a member of the elite, he also seemed to have a tactic for appealing to alienated others. He argued that most Canadian intellectuals were not, as he was, engaging with enough controversy. Waddington argued that "pseudo-intellectuals" enjoyed "quite a showing" on CBC TV. Layton responded immediately with a rhetorical question about whether there are any intellectuals in Canada (or at least on CBC) who ever "do anything" and are taken seriously. Layton then asked his other panellists if they could name any public intellectuals who were willing to advance controversial arguments and actually argue about them rather than merely acknowledging differences of opinion. Another panellist, the aforementioned Grant, then said with circumspection that "Mr. Layton is precisely one of the intellectuals that is being referred to." Layton, rather pleased to be referred to as such (even though it was his own implicit referral), nevertheless claimed, "I don't want the *ad hominem* argument to reflect me at all." Using a Marxist keyword, he continued by saying that Canadian intellectuals are "alienated" and "isolated" compared to their emboldened counterpoints in Britain and the United States. "What really happens, what really happens [he said, beginning to repeat himself as other voices attempted to direct the conversation] – and this is very interesting because it gets me hot under the collar – you'll find there is no controversy among Canadian intellectuals. They only note that an argument has been set against them ..." But Waddington disagreed with his premise. "There's no virtue in controversy *per se*. I think that's a very half baked way of looking at things," she said as Layton attempted to interrupt by voicing disagreement. She concluded,

> I think Mr. Layton you have a marvellously persuasive eloquence, but it is a half truth when you start to pan the Canadian intellectuals and compare them unfavourably with the English ones and the others ... Maybe we should define *intellectual*. Maybe that's what we're wrong about. I think the true ones don't often get on the [CBC] panels.[2]

Although Waddington was right in implying that *intellectual* is a term with class connotations, with the benefit of hindsight we can also see that Layton was potentially appealing to more than one class of alienated people. By complaining about people's being taught to "stay inconspicuous," he implied that alienation could be overcome through publicity. He thereby joined intellectuals to the proletariat instead of the relatively powerful intelligentsia, and he indirectly supported the Habermasian idea that the public and even the mass media can be critical despite their perpetuation of hegemony. Layton's attempt to generate controversy in his debate with Waddington can be interpreted as an attempt to renew his faith in the public through publicity, and to help them both, as poets (and as Jewish writers), to gain political influence through discourse in new media. His manner was less divisive than it seemed.

It seemed controversial, however. What good were his controversies? And were they a public good? Waddington was sceptical of a "virtue in controversy" itself, but the issue was really the lack of public debate about social problems germane to art and literature. For Layton, poetry and the new media enabled poets and critics to influence society. The wide scope of his television and radio broadcasts suggests that, whether his effect was good or bad, it was public. In the plural, his controversies varied from good to bad, supportable to indefensible. In general, his controversy was good, because it attracted attention to poetry and criticism that, in a partially free society, have a social benefit when they motivate discourse in the mass media. Although Grant in 1955 did not think that poetry could have a social benefit except "in quietness" (37) and privacy, poets such as Layton and Waddington were translating some of the implications of their poetry into critical, public statements. They were not broadcasting their poetry itself on *Fighting Words*, which suggests that the show's producers and perhaps radio and television themselves allow the role of critic to be more radical than that of the poet on air; regardless, Layton believed that the roles are inseparable, and he probably also hoped that the mass media could do good by reaching a variety of cultures in unison and without always separating them into publics.

This generality is admittedly a problem, and Layton's enthusiasm for controversy sometimes overcame his anxiety about the public and his caution about the mass media's role in the development of an educated, democratic, free society.[3] The question of freedom was current at the time; Isaiah Berlin's 1958 lecture on "Two Concepts of Liberty" suggested that an uncritical desire for freedom in overly general terms could be manipulated (through propaganda, for example) to the detriment of freedom. For example, later in the same year as Layton's debate with Waddington, a panel on television's *Fighting Words* was convened on the topic of censorship – which is sometimes construed as an issue of the freedom to speak versus the freedom from public offence. Layton used that opportunity to discuss intellectualism again, and to bring together high and low cultures on the basis of the value of freedom – a major concern of his poetry. On 19 June 1960, the panellists on *Fighting Words* – Layton, Birney, Garner, and the reporter Frank Tumpane – were asked to consider the formation of the censorship committee in Ontario and the decision to repeal the long-standing ban in Ontario of D.H. Lawrence's *Lady Chatterley's Lover* (1928). Layton argued that

> Intellectuals will defend the right of people to read anything that they want to. And I think with very good reason. Intellectuals are aware of the evils of censorship. They realize that generally speaking it isn't the smut that's censored, it's always a very good book, say *Lady Chatterley's Lover* or James Joyce's *Ulysses* – these are the books that the censor-morons, to use the phrase that D.H. Lawrence used for them, generally go after. And for this reason, intellectuals defend the right of everybody to read whatever they want. If it's smut, then let them read smut.

Garner then claimed: "I would like to go on record as being a so-called intellectual who *does* read smut. I rather like pornography, and I think that 99% of the people on this television network likes pornography ... Let's some of us at least argue for it for a change." Layton seemed to enjoy the terminological ambiguity and responded, "I agree wholeheartedly with Mr. Garner." Attempting to clarify, Garner then added, "I personally do not read girly magazines ... But I do like good pornography." He did not explain this distinction, but Tumpane responded by observing that Garner was implicitly differentiating between "smut" and "pornographic books with a serious literary intent." Although Layton was more moderate than Garner and some of the others at other times in their conversation, here Layton was willing to allow people to read "whatever they want," even if it is smut. His conviction in the importance of individual freedom, as a generality, allowed him to appeal to "everybody."

Layton's public was not, of course, universal, partly because his own public persona alienated various audiences – including many women *and* many men in literary circles and academia who disliked his occasional crassness and his attempts to lure them into debate. His poetry even suggests that he wanted an adversarial relationship with the same public to which he wanted to appeal. In "Poetry as the Fine Art of Pugilism" from *Lovers and Lesser Men* (1973), a poem that might have been inspired partly by his earlier appearances on *Fighting Words*, Layton alludes to his many poems that insult other poets. He calls some of his attacks "squib[s]" (69), a term that refers both to short, satirical "lampoon[s]" (*OED*) and to potentially disappointing plays in sports, such as a short hit in baseball or a short kick in American football (*OED*). The allusion to sports played before grandstands and to hitting (and, amusingly, kicking) in the contexts of boxing and poetry is a sign of Layton's grandstanding and maybe an attempt at humour. Despite the poem's mean tone and its anti-intellectualism, it is germane to his earlier attempts at reconciling high and low cultures. In the poem, he aligns himself and his "social station" (69) with boxers, who are associated with the lower classes, and yet he suggests that his fighting words in poetry become a "Fine Art," as if both boxing and poetry were upper-class concerns (and indeed they are, but not as they are typically represented). Few boxers or "fine artists" would agree with his simile and later metaphors, and the speaker himself is perhaps too bitter to believe it, but – using figurative language in an attempt to bridge a cultural divide – he vigorously proposes it anyway, regardless of its potentially critical reception.

Although Layton offended many readers, other members of his public often responded favourably to his irrepressible personas, which helped his book sales to remain strong (in comparison to other sales of poetry) into the early 1970s. The eventual overexposure that I described in the previous chapter was partly the result of Layton's controversial topics losing their novelty as he grew older and the idealism of the 1960s faded. His public might have felt eventually that he was more boring than offensive, though he remained newsworthy in some contexts because he was increasingly outspoken on the topic of religious politics associated with Jews. His popularity lessened to a literary degree, and he became a canonical Canadian poet: widely (though superficially) read, even famous, but not likely to instigate new public debates.

The mass media of radio and television were definitive, through Layton, in the era of celebrity in Canadian poetry. They were subjects of debate and also the contexts in which those debates occurred. Issues of conformity, democracy, sincerity, elitism, alienation, and celebrity derived in part from the noticeable influence of the mass media, and Layton was one of the few Canadian poets to appear in those media to confront those issues. By performing as a contrarian and controversialist, he both approved and disapproved of the public and the mass media, but he helped to promote himself to a range of audiences – from elite to popular. For Layton, publicity could ease social stratification and yet could threaten stars. His own stardom was evident in his many appearances on television and radio, and his statements in those media indicate not only a related wariness but also an excitement. Only Margaret Atwood and Leonard Cohen exceeded Layton's success in the era of celebrity in Canadian poetry, and for very different reasons: Atwood exploited and helped to define the second wave of feminism and the growing educational market for Canadian literature, especially prose fiction; and Cohen exploited a culture of youth that identified with popular song as a poetic alternative to the literature of the establishment. Layton's *Fighting Words* gave them a model of involvement in the mass media for them to accept or reject; as a result, they surely understood how controversy in the media could promote them.

5 Recognition, Anonymity, and Leonard Cohen's Stranger Music

In 1993, Leonard Cohen published a career-spanning selection of poetry and song called *Stranger Music*. This book brought together poems and song lyrics that were mutually promotional. It was thereby Laytonic in attempting to further integrate the high and low cultures associated with those arts. Although the title *Stranger Music* seems to acknowledge the defamiliarization produced by the juxtaposition of texts that had previously appeared in very different formats, the book also intends to familiarize Cohen's fans with other aspects of his writing. The title has various other implications: that his poems are music; that his music is stranger than other music; that it is music for, or about, strangers. The latter is the focus of this short chapter on a few of Cohen's songs from the 1960s and 1970s that express ambivalence about recognition and anonymity through his various public personas.

Such ambivalence develops to an eventual resolution in the metaphor of celebrity that I explained in the first chapter. The personas ultimately come together – to the detriment, at least symbolically, of the private self – thereby enacting the identity crisis that can result from stardom. Although Cohen represents the public negatively, he is not often so critical as Irving Layton, Michael Ondaatje, and Gwendolyn MacEwen are in representing the public as hags, killers, and demons (among other figures). The comparatively ambiguous figure of the stranger is one of Cohen's symbols of the public. In *Publics and Counterpublics* (2002), Michael Warner observes that "[a] public is always in excess of its known social basis. It must be more than a list of one's friends. It must include strangers" (74). "The appeal to strangers in the circulating forms of public address thus helps us to distinguish public discourse from forms that address particular persons in their singularity" (Warner 85). By including strangers in his public, Cohen acknowledges that his audience is large enough to contain people that he does not know or cannot recognize. By assimilating the public into the figure of Cohen the celebrity, he identifies with strangers but also gives them his identity, thereby encouraging members of the public to identify with him as fans – while he is the one to surrender anonymity and privacy to publicity.

Although this chapter focuses on Cohen's musical lyrics, one technical aspect of his musical recordings is worth considering as it relates to his celebrity. With few exceptions until Phil Spector's production and co-authorship of Cohen's *Death of a Ladies' Man* (1977), Cohen's songs had been recorded to give the impression that the singer is close to the listener. The high degree of articulation on the vocal tracks suggests that Cohen was very near the microphone in the studio. His closeness is further emphasized by his whispery delivery, by the frequent lack of reverb effects on his voice, and by the minimal instrumentation. In an early review that indirectly acknowledges how these recording techniques promoted Cohen's celebrity, the music journalist Robert Christgau stated that Cohen's voice "has been called monotonous but it is also the most miraculous vehicle for intimacy that the new pop has yet produced" (qtd. in Devlin 56). By referring to Cohen's voice as "miraculous," Christgau endorsed the pretence of religious significance associated with stardom, and by acknowledging the resulting "intimacy," he corroborated part of my argument about the metaphor of celebrity in the first chapter. Cohen's voice, as we usually hear it, implies that we must know him well to be so close to him, and for some fans the sense of identification could be a "mystical sense of union" (Crocker 62).

One of Cohen's earliest musical and public personas implies that anonymity is a personal sacrifice and a consequence of religious devotion. His debut album, *Songs of Leonard Cohen* (1967), established the themes of anonymity and recognition with "The Stranger Song," which was also the song he performed for his musical debut on national television in 1966 on Adrienne Clarkson's *Take 30* (Devlin 20). In the song, Cohen identifies with a difficult, spiritually searching dealer in "the Holy Game of Poker." "I know that kind of man," he sings. "It's hard to hold the hand of anyone / who's reaching for the sky just to surrender." The dealer's gesture of capitulation and faith has the potential to isolate him from others – and to stop them from knowing him as the singer claims he does – but in the next verse his attitude to the heavens persists: "Like any dealer he was watching for the card that is so high / and wild he'll never need to deal another. / He was just some Joseph looking for a manger." Although the dealer is referred to as "some Joseph," the name is symbolic, and it preserves his literal anonymity while implying that he is saintly, as Joseph is in the Gospels.

The dealer's mysterious identity and his speaking in the song raise the question of Cohen's identification with him. The extent of a writer's identification with his or her characters or personas can never be determined, especially when they are various, but "The Stranger Song" implies that the writer, singer, persona, and character share an identity. Partially echoing the claim in one of the poems from *The Spice-box of Earth* (1961) that "[o]nly strangers travel" (35), Cohen sings: "And taking from his wallet an old schedule of trains, he'll say, / I told you when I came I was a stranger." He then refers to "another stranger" who is also a dealer, "his golden arm dispatching cards," and the figures multiply; there are the two dealers, the singer, and the addressee ("you"). Their coexistence as one figure or their mutual identification becomes a possibility when one of the dealers or the singer says to the addressee, "It's you, my love, you who are the stranger." The chill provoked by this line is the result of the uncanny suggestion that we, the listeners, are not familiar enough with ourselves to realize that we are strangers. It is the spectre of identity crisis and the effect of ventriloquism. The origins of the voices in the song are sometimes momentarily uncertain: the first-person "I" reappears in the seventh verse ("I've been waiting ..."), but Cohen immediately disowns the voice by singing that "he talks like this." Only the addressee's voice is set apart with quotation marks when the song appears as a prose poem in *Stranger Music*, suggesting that the other figures are at least partially interchangeable. Cohen also sings that "it comes to you he never was a stranger," thereby contradicting earlier statements about the dealer's anonymity and inviting the listener to assign the stranger's identity to the most widely recognized person involved in the song: Cohen himself. His public persona becomes ironically and impossibly anonymous, in addition to religious, in "The Stranger Song."

In this song, the dealer hopes to give the "high" and "wild" card to some other player who could win and end the game, and this willingness to be one or more than one loser reappears on Cohen's next album. On *Songs of Love and Hate* (1971), "Famous Blue Raincoat" reveals two personas in competition with each other, and some version of Cohen is the loser of the game. Again, Cohen's identity is not clearly distinguished from his personas, but the song depends on his being recognized and, to a lesser extent, on his reputation as a ladies' man. His self-referentiality is evident not only in his signature at the end of the song – "Sincerely, L. Cohen" – but also in the raincoat itself, which Cohen bought in London in 1959 and which was stolen in 1968 (Nadel 73). In the symposium on the song in *Intricate Preparations* (2000), Bill van Dyk observes that the speaker "is living on Clinton Street, in New York, as Cohen was at the time he wrote the song, but he is addressing someone who owns a 'famous blue raincoat,' which is also obviously Cohen ... So the physical facts suggest that both men are Cohen" (103) or (to acknowledge their status as representations) his personas. In the liner notes for the reissue of *Songs of Love and Hate*, Anthony DeCurtis writes that the raincoat has become "a symbol of mystery, identity and creativity" (14), and Cohen himself also becomes figurative and fictional in the song – though he implies that this is not to his advantage.

Cohen is the actual writer of the song, but his signature and the multiplicity of his personas imply that he is not its ultimate authority. Participating with Van Dyk and others in the symposium, Judith Fitzgerald claims that the "L. Cohen" signature "smacks of an almost self-flagellating zeal" (Scobie, *Intricate* 106), a masochistic gesture that accords with other gestures of self-destruction and self-questioning that I consider in the next chapter. Van Dyk also wonders if Cohen is "addressing a duality within himself" (Scobie, *Intricate* 103), as in these lines:

And what can I tell you, my brother, my killer?
What can I possibly say?
I guess that I miss you. I guess I forgive you.
I'm glad that you stood in my way.

Van Dyk concludes by stating that the narrator "is his own brother, his own killer; he stands in his own way" (Scobie, *Intricate* 104). In his contribution to the symposium, Stephen Scobie quotes from his *Signature Event Cantext* (1989) to argue that when writers sign their own names in their texts, they abandon "the property-rights of their (as)signed station in order to invade the text, to appear in poems in their own name ... The effect is always equivocal: to detach the name from its position of power ... and to set it free in the text ... is to risk losing control altogether of the logocentric presence of the author, and of his author-ity" (qtd. in Scobie, *Intricate* 114).

I would extend these arguments by noting that "L. Cohen" and not "Leonard Cohen" is identified as the man who has been or might be killed in "Famous Blue Raincoat." Celebrities tend to be referred to with both of their names (except in academic contexts), so Cohen's public persona, "Leonard Cohen," is probably the "killer" who has torn his "famous blue raincoat." He has killed Cohen's private persona, the "L. Cohen" who sings about a private life with "Jane" that the public persona has disrupted. Although personas multiply most obviously in contexts of performance, celebrity can destroy the multiplicity that they offer; the public persona eventually takes over – even symbolically kills – the private persona.

Whenever the various personas are noticeable in Cohen's songs, they are figures in conflict with each other. In "Field Commander Cohen," from *New Skin for the Old Ceremony* (1974), Cohen refers to himself in the third person as if he were a military agent – "our most important spy / wounded in the line of duty." Spies rely on their fake identities to achieve their goals, and, after the war, Cohen exposes his spying persona, who has

> come back to nothing special,
> such as waiting rooms and ticket lines
> and silver bullet suicides
> and messianic ocean tides
> and racial roller-coaster rides
> and other forms of boredom advertised as poetry.

Rarely was Cohen so explicit about suggesting that he wanted a life more exciting than that of a poet, which is seemingly the second life of his "Field Commander." Cohen then addresses the Field Commander and encourages him to return to "stand guard" in his role as a spy, though, as I suggested in the introduction to this book, returning to privacy from publicity is a difficult challenge. The Field Commander remains a public figure who is a singer like the actual Cohen, who describes himself as a spy-like (or fan-like) eavesdropper:

> then I overheard your prayer that you be this and nothing more
> than just some grateful faithful woman's favourite singing millionaire
> the patron saint of envy and the grocer of despair
> working for the Yankee dollar.

Without knowing whether Cohen was a millionaire by 1974, we cannot insist on a strong similarity between the two singers (the Field Commander and the actual Cohen). Nevertheless, what fan of Cohen could fail to see his likeness in his description of the retired spy's popularity, religiosity, attitude of "despair," and blatant cynicism about the commercial interests in his music? Cohen's public personas in this song – poet and singer – are trading places, even fusing, and their engagement with each other involves the potential conflict of any criticism, such as the dismissals of boring poetry and obsequiously commercial music.

When a third role, the "lover," is named in "Field Commander Cohen," the question is whether the singer is already the actor in that role. "Lover, come and lie with me, if my lover is who you are," Cohen sings in a voice that is not obviously differentiated from possible others, raising questions about both the speaker's and the lover's identities. The speaker's suspicion implies that he is the Field Commander, who as a spy would have been pragmatically distrustful. Whoever he is, he describes the lover as the "sweetest ... child" and then encourages him or her to allow "the other selves" to be comparatively agitated and violent, so that "love is pierced" and "hung / and every kind of freedom done." The "un" rhyme in these lines suggests that Cohen is preoccupied with negation, which in turn suggests that the phrase "freedom done" does not mean *accomplished* but *completely finished*. Given the song's various ironies of criticism and identity, it is probably not an optimistic tale of a war winning freedom. As in war, in "Field Commander Cohen" we cannot always be certain who is acting the good parts or the bad parts. We can be certain only that Cohen is identifying with figures of differing degrees of recognition and anonymity, possibly in an effort to describe his experience with celebrity.

In the aforementioned songs, the lovers mentioned are sometimes anonymous and sometimes not (e.g., "Jane"). In "Chelsea Hotel #2," also from *New Skin for the Old Ceremony*, Cohen maintains the privacy and anonymity of the lover – only to disclose her identity in live performance. In this song, he invokes Janis Joplin (Nadel 144–5) by singing, "I remember you well in the Chelsea Hotel / you were famous, your heart was a legend." He later regretted the indiscretion of identifying Joplin at concerts (Nadel 145; Devlin 63), possibly because he believed her to have disliked such recognition, and possibly because of the first stanza, though the oral sex that it reveals was not so transgressive in the culture of the 1960s and afterward.

The line about fellatio is potentially sexist because it reduces the power of a woman's voice, her "talking so brave and so sweet," to a subservient act that gives pleasure to a man, and his timing was rather insensitive because Joplin had died only four years earlier, in 1970, of an accidental overdose of heroin (Gaar par. 2). The potential for this song to function as a tribute to Joplin is partly squandered by the line about fellatio and by the dismissive, anticlimactic ending: "that's all, I don't even think of you that often." Elsewhere in the song, however, Cohen adjusts his disrespectful attitude with his wistful and yet regretful admiration of Joplin's struggle to cope with celebrity. Perhaps those sentiments are why the "limousines wait" respectfully for the celebrities to finish their intercourse in private.

In fact, Cohen seems to admire Joplin's resistance to publicity. In the chorus, he sings, "But you got away, didn't you, babe, / you just turned your back on the crowd."[1] In his view, her desire to be unrecognized might be a good reason to honour her by generally forgetting her – by not thinking of her "that often." Cohen was probably also thinking of her death as the reason that she "got away," and he might have wondered if the only way to "tur[n] your back on the crowd" is to die, as Joplin did in 1970. The singer does not explain whether he admired her for escaping celebrity through death (not necessarily suicide) or for knowing what she wanted; the singer also says, "I never once heard you say [presumably to the crowd]: / 'I need you, I don't need you, / I need you, I don't need you.'" In other words, according to Cohen, Joplin did not express ambivalence about the crowd, whereas he did – as in this song. In "Chelsea Hotel #2," the singer admires Joplin because she escaped from the slavery of her celebrity one way or the other. He resents his comparative ambivalence about his own.

Although his music in the late 1960s and early 1970s is the most representative, the themes of recognition, anonymity, and privacy can be traced beyond 1974 in Cohen's albums, particularly to "Fingerprints" and "Paper Thin Hotel" from his 1977 album *Death of a Ladies' Man*. "Paper Thin Hotel" is relatively unimportant in terms of the identity of Cohen's persona, but the lyrics to "Fingerprints" reveal that he was thinking about leaving no traces of himself that would allow him to be identified. This theme appears also in the song "True Love Leaves No Traces," adapted from his 1961 poem "As the Mist Leaves No Scar." The lyrics to "Fingerprints" are also adapted – from the poem "Give me back my fingerprints" in Cohen's *Parasites of Heaven* (1966). In the song, the rollicking country-and-western accompaniment that Spector wrote for the lyrics increases the levity of a poem that was already unusually – and misleadingly – light-hearted. The singer explains that he has rubbed off his fingerprints by touching his lover too often. As a result, he sings, "I don't know who I am." In the poem, the speaker's lover takes his fingerprints hostage so that he will love her mind instead of her body – an idea he insensitively "[doesn't] pretend to understand" (73). He later seems to regret his focus on her body and his own. In the song, the dichotomy of mind and body is not as apparent, but the singer retains a sense of regret or disgust – insinuating, in a reversal of sexual stereotypes, that his lover corrupted his purity by knowing him carnally and privately:

> Sure I'd like to marry you
> But I can't face the dawn
> With any girl who knew me
> When my fingerprints were on

He refuses to marry someone who knew him when he had a personal identity. Only anonymous interactions, including anonymous sex, are acceptable to him now. If any agent of the law were to track him through his fingerprints because of his sexual transgressions, he would be protected. He has come to accept the necessity of his own leave-taking or disappearance.

The aforementioned themes in "The Stranger Song," "Famous Blue Raincoat," "Field Commander Cohen," and "Fingerprints" are indications of Cohen's anxiety about stardom's effects on his identity in the late 1960s and 1970s. Perhaps not coincidentally, in the year following *New Skin for the Old Ceremony*, one of Cohen's mentors was also thinking about these issues. Louis Dudek remarks in his *Epigrams* (1975) that "[f]ame is mainly the privilege of being pestered by strangers" (qtd. in Stromberg-Stein 1). Although Cohen was evidently willing to blend in among strangers in these songs, his poetry treats stardom harshly because of its effects on his identity – such as its creation of tension between his personas, which can become indistinguishable. Becoming a stranger and joining the public is, in fact, a way to simulate the identity crisis of the metaphor of celebrity, and this tactic suggests that Cohen was sometimes performing a role that would be dangerous to his selfhood if he were using the stranger as a figure of privacy instead of another public persona. In his poetry, the question of the threat to his privacy is developed with further complexity.

6 "I like that line because it's got my name in it": Masochistic Stardom in Cohen's Poetry

Leonard Cohen sang in "Bird on the Wire" (1969), "I have tried in my way to be free." Cohen's concern for freedom was motivated not only by his mentor Irving Layton's poetic manifestos but also by his close observation of Layton's mid-career. In the late 1950s and early 1960s, Cohen watched Layton experience a degree of celebrity never before achieved in Canadian poetry, and yet his own celebrity soon reached heights that were far beyond Layton's grasp. In chapter 3, I argued that Layton understood that celebrity constrained his freedoms of expression and self-definition despite his insistent individualism. Cohen realized that Layton's ideal of freedom was a fantasy and then accepted, more willingly than Layton, that his identity would be redefined by his stardom. Cohen's "way" of being "free" was ironic; it involved renouncing Layton's individualistic style of freedom and accepting the consequences of being too public. What I interpret as Cohen's metaphor of celebrity as slavery – especially as implied in *The Energy of Slaves* (1972) – was his way of describing, and then exploiting, a star's initially voluntary loss of control over his or her identity.

Cohen's experience of celebrity was also implicitly masochistic, given that he associated celebrity with slavery. Masochism is commonly understood to involve performances of slavery. Many of Cohen's poems and some of his songs imply that celebrity's oppressiveness can be psychologically internalized and thereby affect identity and selfhood. Cohen's metaphor of celebrity as slavery needs to be explained in the context of *the* metaphor of celebrity. In the first chapter, I explained how celebrities create personas that not only attract attention but also initially draw it away from their private selves; however, they then experience the metaphor of celebrity – *privacy is publicity* – a consequence of their self-promotion that occurs when the fusion of the private and public personas leaves the private self without a decoy for the audience. The result has been explained as "identity confusion" (Rojek 11) and the public's "invasive reconfiguration" (Latham 110) of the private self. As Cohen implies, when the public persona threatens to dominate the private self, the character of celebrity becomes sadomasochistic.[1]

Cohen's painfully negative representations of stardom helped to dramatize and criticize what I call the era of celebrity in Canadian poetry, whose peak was largely defined by his career. As I argued in chapters 2 and 3, the era of celebrity in Canadian poetry began around 1955, when Layton emerged as the first poet to be widely recognized in post-war media such as television. Layton's celebrity peaked in the late 1950s when he published his award-winning *A Red Carpet for the Sun* (1959); in 1965, the film *Ladies and Gentlemen ... Mr. Leonard Cohen* began to introduce Cohen to a national audience and signalled that Layton was already becoming *passé*. A year after Cohen started his career as a popular musician in New York City, the phenomenal success of his *Selected Poems: 1956–1968* (1968) won him the status of the star poet of highest degree in Canada. As his celebrity intensified, his representations of his various selves – private and public – became increasingly negative. His sadomasochistic poems help to explain the oft-noted confusion between his personas and his private self.[2] One of my later suggestions in this chapter is that Cohen then symbolically killed his public persona (or committed its suicide) in *Death of a Lady's Man* (1978) and rejected his stardom;[3] that symbolic death at the end of the 1970s coincided with the end of "star-making" (Messenger 944) in Canadian poetry, leaving Layton and Cohen as that era's definitive figures.

As in Layton's case, Cohen's early ideas about freedom – which his metaphor of celebrity as slavery later critiqued – developed as he anticipated and began to achieve celebrity. His interest in slavery was an extension and inversion of Layton's interest in freedom.[4] In *Leonard Cohen* (1978), Stephen Scobie notices that the concern with freedom begins to appear in Cohen's *The Spice-box of Earth* (1961), especially in "A Kite Is a Victim" and "You Have the Lovers." Referring to "A Kite Is a Victim," Scobie observes that "[s]omehow the beauty of the poem tends to gloss over the unpleasantness" (*Leonard* 26) of its titular focus on a victim. Even that early in Cohen's career, however, his ideas about freedom were explained in terms of masters and slaves who often switch positions; even earlier, in *Let Us Compare Mythologies* (1956), he was beginning to think of how his public persona would dominate his private persona. Linda Hutcheon has argued that these "inversions" of masters and slaves "recur in all Cohen's work" ([Poetry] 42); the difference between his two earliest books and *The Energy of Slaves* is that the mood of the former still seemed romantic. Around the time of *Flowers for Hitler* (1964), especially in "Style" and its thematically related poems in *Parasites of Heaven* (1966),

Cohen rejected Layton's ideal of freedom. *The Energy of Slaves* made that rejection extremely obvious, partly because it is the first of Cohen's books to deal with celebrity directly (though his earlier poems become newly relevant in the context of his developing celebrity); it suggested that artistic "energy" could be gained from the figurative slavery resulting from stardom. His last book during the era of celebrity in Canadian poetry, *Death of a Lady's Man*, was a new beginning as much as an ending; it questioned – even renounced – the features of the public personas of literary celebrities, especially poets, that Layton had hoped would help to ensure his freedom: masculinity (of the problematic kind) and a pretence of religious significance.

Layton attempted to ensure his freedoms of expression and self-definition in part by exploiting these two features of the stardom of poets. Most celebrities, consciously or not, accept that their personas will play roles that scholars have now understood to be pseudo-religious (Frow 201, 204; Turner 6–7). Furthermore, poets who were celebrities have been criticized for perpetuating masculinity's exclusive, aggressive, and sexist tendencies (Glass 18; Jaffe 165). In the first chapter, I defined such exaggerated performances of masculinity and religiosity as *grandstanding*: standing in for someone grander – a bigger man or even a god. Cohen indulges in such performances but eventually seems to choose less problematic ways of imagining himself. By the late 1970s and *Death of a Lady's Man*, Cohen was attempting to rebuild his ego with genuine religion – Buddhism[5] and, later, the Judaism of his heritage – and a less sadomasochistic conception of masculinity than that of his earlier books.

Whereas Layton's ideal of freedom was especially individualistic, Cohen's was relatively communal – or, more accurately, multiple; his emphasis is on brothers and brotherhood in "Style" and in *Parasites of Heaven* (which makes various claims about freedom that seem relevant in the context of "Style"). Beyond his emphasis on multiplicity, Cohen's ideal of freedom is not easy to define; it is being "like a bird on the wire" and "like a drunk in a midnight choir." In *Parasites of Heaven*, Cohen writes: "So long I've tried to give a name to freedom, today my freedom lost its name ... Every act has its own style of freedom, whatever that means" (23). His "whatever" is important. The lack of easily interpretable claims by Cohen about freedom suggests that he would not or could not define it; this lack also implicitly explains his later focus on slavery, for which he could and would suggest a definition: celebrity.[6]

In "Cohen's Life as a Slave" (1978), Eli Mandel provides an alternate definition, but it, too, associates this figurative slavery with celebrity. Mandel suggests that Cohen, faced with the "conflicting demands" of "audience" and of "art" (212), "turn[ed] from high to low culture in response to the demands of audience" ("Cohen's Life" 218). Reading Cohen's poem "Alexander Trocchi,

Public Junkie, Priez Pour Nous" from *Flowers for Hitler*, Mandel states that in Cohen's work "slavery is defined simply as art and addiction. Art is opposed to work; it is habit, need, no longer the romanticized purity, focus, and concentration of the Trocchi poem, but the routine dreariness of meaningless necessary repetition" ("Cohen's Life" 221).

Mandel's remark is perceptive but oversimplifies Cohen's implied definition of slavery. It is not "simply ... art and addiction." Indeed, its "meaningless necessary repetition" also describes the tautological aspect of celebrity's excessively replicated images (and imprimaturs), which I explained in the first chapter as one of the threats that celebrity poses to authors as purveyors of meaning. In response not only to this threat but also to what Mandel calls a "history of horror" that is implicitly the Holocaust, Cohen seems to indulge in "sado-masochism" and extends his own trauma into "a public nightmare," mounting a "bitter attack on both audience and art" ("Cohen's Life" 213). With literature in jeopardy, Mandel suggests that Cohen's "anti-literary" (215) persona in the early 1970s is an acknowledgment of poetry's status: "*The Energy of Slaves* remains valuable because it elucidates with the precision we used to call poetry the failure of contemporary poetry" ("Cohen's Life" 224). Determined to work within the limits of what poetry could still do, Cohen sought inspiration in the so-called "low culture" and found it by imagining himself both as an "attack[er]" and as a slave (even a sacrifice) to a popular audience.

Cohen's thinking about slavery developed from his oft-noted interest in martyrdom, which was an early sign of his religious pretence. The interest in martyrs revealed in his poems, novels, and songs leads Michael Ondaatje to claim that Cohen is "the scapegoat of success" who "shift[s] from scapegoat to martyr" (*Leonard* 59). Cohen was devoted to his own "pop-sainthood" (Ondaatje, *Leonard* 59). His "sainthood" was related to his being a "pop" star, and martyrdom was implicated in that success. Cohen anticipated the aforementioned "invasi[on]" by the public and understood it to be the price of his celebrity – a sacrifice, more accurately, to his audience. Scobie might not accept this; he argues in his *Leonard Cohen* that the martyrs and saints in Cohen's poetry are "not [selves] sacrificed to some higher cause; the sacrifice of the self *is* the higher cause" (10, his emphasis).[7] Celebrity, however, is rarely so selfless; it is inescapably relational, and every star depends on an audience. Especially in *Parasites of Heaven*, Cohen implied that his ambivalent relationship with his audience had been psychologically internalized. His martyrdom, however pretentious it might be, can be interpreted as the result of the public persona demanding the submission and sacrifice of the private persona. Because of this sacrifice or martyrdom, the masochism of his private persona is implicitly religious.

There are and have been numerous theories of masochism in psychoanalysis (Finke 2), yet those that tend to be used in literary studies come from Sigmund Freud, Jacques Lacan, and Gilles Deleuze, despite more recent developments in the practice of psychoanalysis (Balázs 166). My intention in this chapter, however, is not to contribute directly to psychoanalytic literary studies but to studies of Cohen's poetry and stardom. Of the three recognized types of masochism, my focus is not on the "erotogenic" variety, whose commonly accepted definition is misleading,[8] but on the masochism that Freud called "feminine" (Finke 6) and Deleuze "passive" (Deleuze 110). The Freudian usage means the "sexual perversion in which a man adopts what is assumed to be the naturally passive position of a woman" (Finke 6; see also Silverman 10, 189). I call this *feminine masochism* to maintain the emphasis of Cohen's critique of the masculinity that star poets assert along with their pretended religious significance.[9]

The different types of masochism are not mutually exclusive; feminine masochism is similar to the third type, what Freud called "moral masochism," which refers to the social ramifications of the relationship between the punitive superego and the guilty ego (Finke 6). The superego is likely to be sadistic, and the ego masochistic, because the superego dominates the ego (Deleuze *passim*). Deleuze argues that sadism and masochism cannot fuse in an individual as sadomasochism, which is a faulty category (13); in his analogy, "a genuine sadist could never tolerate a masochistic victim ... Neither would the masochist tolerate a truly sadistic torturer" (41), mainly because the masochist would need to teach and tell the sadist what to do, and the sadist, wanting to control all the pain, would refuse. Cohen might disagree; he actually mentions sadism as a tendency of what seems to be his public persona in some of his poems, and yet they often also describe masochistic feelings and fantasies of the private persona. Notably, these personas are sometimes almost indistinguishable.

When my argument about the celebrity's fusion of selves is considered in the psychoanalytic terms that Cohen proposes, a new possibility emerges: that, contrary to Deleuze's reasoning, a star can have both sadistic and masochistic tendencies. In *Masochism and the Self* (1989), Roy F. Baumeister argues that masochists "define their roles as slavery" and that "[s]lavery nullifies identity. The masochist's wish to be a slave is a desire for the removal of the social self" (85).[10] Partly because sadism might also be involved in "building up" (Baumeister 195, 197) the sadist's sense of self, Cohen's celebrity can be understood as a sadomasochistic "reconfiguration" of the self – both the private self's deconstruction and the related construction of the public persona.

Cohen's metaphor of celebrity as slavery, which becomes evident at last in *The Energy of Slaves*, implies that he took masochistic pleasure and gained artistic "energy" from his celebrity despite its ramifications for his freedom and his identity. Although Francesco Alberoni once called celebrities "The Powerless Elite" (1972), celebrity itself is powerful, and for Cohen the challenge of surviving its invasion of his privacy and its effect on his identity was as inspirational as dangerous. His performance of masochism was tactical. In "Masochism and Identity" (2000), Robert Tobin argues that some masochists pretend to be subordinate to subvert the identities imposed on them by institutions that are otherwise assumed to do good for them (33, 37). On the topic of subversive performances in *Gender Trouble* (1990), Judith Butler argues that gender is obviously a contrivance because it must be performed repeatedly to induce the belief that it is natural (140–1); it can therefore be subverted through parody (138–9). It follows that masochistic practices can parodically subvert hierarchies – such as master and slave or man and woman – that help to determine identity. By creating what Tobin calls "only the appearance of subordination" (40), "the slave can demonstrate a masochistic power" (49). In the late 1960s and early 1970s, Cohen allowed celebrity to make him appear inherently sick – a masochist – so that he could criticize celebrity. Regardless of its actual effect on his mental health, his celebrity appeared to dominate him – an appearance that elicited the sympathy of his fans.[11]

Cohen's tactical representations of "feminine" or "passive" masochism are especially relevant in the post-war contexts that reveal what might be called a crisis of masculinity. In chapter 3, I addressed three issues related to the historical manifestation of that crisis after the Second World War: men's shaken confidence in their autonomy and control over their lives (Cuordileone 14; Faludi 9); their objectification and feminization in "an age of celebrity" (Faludi 35); and their strategic bonding, which enabled them to promote themselves and each other as writers (Jaffe 165) and to counter assumptions about the femininity of writing poetry (Davidson, *Guys* 48). Feminine masochism's supposed perversion is that it involves men who perform roles that are contrary to what is stereotypically expected of their gender. After 1945, men could not easily fulfil the expectations of their gender; rather than change their behaviour, though, they often performed their masculinity more stubbornly. Loren Glass states that "[h]istorians of sexuality tend to agree that the postwar era ... is characterized by the increasing fragility of patriarchal authority, which generates the sorts of strident masculine response we see in writers like [Norman] Mailer" (182). The representations of sadism in Cohen's poetry are indeed strident at times, but their masculinity is also often ironic. The title of his somewhat later album *Various Positions* (1984), which Ira Nadel interprets as a motto for Cohen's entire life by adopting the same title for his biography of Cohen, suggests that Cohen wanted to occupy both masculine and feminine positions – to play "various" roles: sadist, masochist, and others.

Early in his career, Cohen was thinking about the splitting of his self into various personas in anticipation of his own celebrity. When Cohen published *Let Us Compare Mythologies* in 1956, Layton had recently announced a "BOOM IN LAYTON" (*Wild* 63, his emphasis) because of the success of *In the Midst of My Fever* (1954). With Layton as a precedent, literary celebrity of a higher degree than before the war was now possible for Canadian poets. In "Poem," Cohen implies that he understands the separation of himself into the private self and both the private and public personas, a separation that is typical of celebrities before the fusion of selves that I described in more detail in the first chapter. Here is "Poem," brief but in full:

> I heard of a man
> who says words so beautifully
> that if he only speaks their name
> women give themselves to him.
>
> If I am dumb beside your body
> while silence blossoms like tumours on our lips
> it is because I hear a man climb stairs
> and clear his throat outside our door. (64)

Although "Elegy" was the first poem in his first book, "Poem" announces (ambivalently) Cohen's presence on the scene. The context is indoors, in the ostensibly private life of the poet, but the public realm – as Cohen's anticipated celebrity – is about to intrude.

Most critics (such as Nadel and Michael Q. Abraham) think that the poem describes a rivalry between two men for one woman, but the poem also suggests that Cohen understands himself as a split subject ("I" and "a man"), one who is "dumb" but also poised to appear as a star poet or singer by joining the other in the bedroom. "Poem" is therefore an early example of Cohen's grandstanding: a metaphoric self-promotion that involves standing in for someone grander.[12] Here, the poet is beginning to think of how to stand in for the celebrity or singer; he is almost certainly thinking of how he might also "clear his throat" and use his voice to seduce women. "Poem" anticipates Cohen's actual success as a singer while foreshadowing his difficult experience with stardom that becomes explicit in *The Energy of Slaves* and *Death of a Lady's Man*: the public persona, skilled at the seduction of women with words, arrives at the bedroom door of the private persona and causes him pain; it is the subtle introduction of the central theme of sexual guilt and masochism in Cohen's poetry and songs such as "Famous Blue Raincoat" (1971), which can be interpreted, like "Poem," not as a love triangle but as two sides of the same self vying for another's love. The multiple selves and their potential fusion – their joining each other in the room – indicate that Cohen, even at the age of twenty-two, was anticipating celebrity and accurately predicting its consequences.

In contrast with Layton's prolificacy, Cohen was not quick to publish a second book; it would be five years until *The Spice-box of Earth* appeared in 1961. Abraham accounts for the gap between books by explaining that "Cohen was unwilling to engage himself any further in the adolescent angst which characterized his first book. Such displays of suffering, no matter how well-intentioned, had become so popular that they had lost all meaning" (108). There remain, however, numerous "displays of suffering" in Cohen's later poems. Although he did downplay his "adolescent angst" after *Let Us Compare Mythologies*, he also established masochistic and sadistic personas. These personas appeared before he actually was a star – which suggests that he was imagining how to dramatize celebrity that he could reasonably assume would be his, thanks to his relationship with Layton. In the five years after *Let Us Compare Mythologies*, Cohen probably wondered how to renew the "meaning" of "suffering" in the "popular" context, how to validate the experience of celebrity that he had seen Layton deal with in the late 1950s, and – by doing so – how to promote himself.[13]

Cohen would begin to experience unsurpassed popularity – and then celebrity – as a Canadian poet not long after the publication of *The Spice-box of Earth*. He introduced that book with "A Kite Is a Victim," which expresses his thoughts about freedom and slavery – and his prototypical sadomasochism – at an important transition in his own career. Abraham explains that, "[i]n contrast to the uncertainty so prevalent in *Let Us Compare Mythologies*, the kite is a clear metaphor for the tension between limitation and freedom" (109). "A Kite Is a Victim" includes several elements that might have been borrowed from Layton, but the most prominent is the theme of restricted freedom related to the implication that the speaker is both a teacher (a "master") and a clown (a "fool"): "You love it because it pulls / gentle enough to call you master, / strong enough to call you fool," and "you can always haul it down / to tame it in your drawer" (1). The kite, as Cohen later makes clear, represents "the last poem you've written" and is "a contract of glory / that must be made with the sun" (1). Emphasizing the intermittent tug of the kite in the poet's hand through the half-rhyme of "pull" and "call," Cohen suggests that his "calling" of poetry – with its vocational, religious connotation – is not free of restrictions; slavery is implied, and the contrast between the "master" and the poet reveals the masochistic dynamic of domination and submission.

In *Leonard Cohen*, Scobie makes a similar argument: because the kite is also "a victim you are sure of" (1), the poem has "sadistic implications" (26).

Because "the personalities are interchangeable" (Scobie, *Leonard* 27), the poet strong enough to "haul ... down" and "tame" the kite becomes the one who is weak "under the travelling cordless moon" (1). In the end of the poem, he is submissive, praying that he will be "worthy and lyric and pure" (1), but these are the same qualities that Cohen begins to rebel against in his next book, *Flowers for Hitler*, by concentrating on worthlessness, victimization, and depravity in the aftermath of the Holocaust and the destructiveness of the Second World War.

Cohen's fascination with evil and pain was obvious, however, even in *The Spice-box of Earth* (and earlier, as in "Lovers" and "Letter" from *Let Us Compare Mythologies*). The sadomasochistic tendencies did not mean that he was always writing about physical or symbolic pain; humiliation was also prominent. In "The Cuckold's Song," the representation of his own humiliation promotes Cohen because it is funny and self-reflexive. The poem's speaker is a poet who writes about having been cuckolded and says, "I wonder if I give a damn at all" (47). This potential apathy is characteristic of sadism, not masochism, according to Deleuze (117, 124), but Deleuze also argues that irony is sadistic (125) and humour is masochistic (126) without accounting for ironic humour such as that in "The Cuckold's Song." The masochism that coexists with this sadism appears not only in the lengthy descriptions of how the speaker was cuckolded but also in his indirect self-promotion: "I repeat: the important thing was to cuckold Leonard Cohen. / I like that line because it's got my name in it" (47).[14] Cohen's use of his own name does not guarantee that any actual cuckolding occurred, but it reveals that he was willing to establish a private persona that would invite speculation about his private life. Cohen was not yet a celebrity, but his use of his own name is self-promotional, despite – or because of – the self-deprecation. He was therefore speaking through both his public and his private personas – an instance of grandstanding that anticipates, as in "Poem," the fusion of selves. Being cuckolded gives the speaker an opportunity to write a poem that will be provocative enough to promote "Leonard Cohen," and yet by appearing sadomasochistic, he can indirectly criticize stardom.

In *Flowers for Hitler*, however, Cohen also wrote explicitly about celebrity – and with considerable appreciation for it. Now Cohen was writing about celebrities other than Layton, as Layton was also doing. In fact, they sometimes wrote about the same other celebrities. One was Mailer and another was Alexander Trocchi,[15] a Scottish novelist and painter who moved to the United States in 1956 and became a notorious heroin addict and promoter of drug use. In 1961, Trocchi was charged with giving drugs to a minor and, if convicted, might have faced the death penalty. He later escaped to Montreal and met Cohen there (Scott 88, 92). Cohen wrote "Alexander Trocchi, Public Junkie,

Priez Pour Nous" to commemorate that meeting and generally to acknowledge Trocchi's public status as a celebrity – and junkie.

Trocchi appears in that poem as a saint to whom Montrealers such as Cohen might pray for prayers in return. By representing Trocchi as a religious figure, Cohen acknowledges and affirms the religious pretence of celebrity. He also suggests that Trocchi is a martyr; Cohen admires him for his "purity" (45) but also describes the effect of Trocchi's heroin addiction on his body and mind. In an aforementioned quotation, Mandel argued that art and addiction are "slavery" in this poem. I agree; Cohen implies that he wants and even masochistically needs – and needs to share – that slavery. Otherwise, his career might become like that of other poets, who "work bankers' hours / retire to wives and fame-reports" (45). To avoid the tedium of knowing "fame" only through "reports," Cohen looks to Trocchi for inspiration and in thanks. Cohen refers to himself in the poem's newspaper headlines as "Famous Local Love Scribe" (47) because he has been "[i]mplicated" (47) in Trocchi's escape from the United States and Canada; the poem is a thank you to Trocchi for having made Cohen notorious, "a fanatic" (47) – with the religious connotation of that term – who has to answer questions from the police but is now part of a brotherhood (with its religious connotation, too) of stars.

The popularity that Cohen achieved with *The Spice-box of Earth* became celebrity with the publication of *Flowers for Hitler* in 1964 and the NFB documentary of the promotional tour that followed. Cohen attracted attention away from other poets who might have experienced stardom because of the film – notably, Layton. The documentary had been conceived to include Layton, Earle Birney, and Phyllis Gotlieb – who were all much older than Cohen – but it finally purported to introduce only Cohen to a national audience as *Ladies and Gentlemen ... Mr. Leonard Cohen*. Cohen wryly said that "[f]or some technical reason only the parts of the film that dealt with me seemed to have been good" (qtd. in Harris 28). The "technical reason" was Cohen's wider appeal in the context of the media's new focus on the burgeoning youth culture, a culture that contributed to "[t]he great boom of young poets [that] began in 1964" (Dudek, "Poetry" 117). The filming of *Ladies and Gentlemen ... Mr. Leonard Cohen* and this "boom" are significantly coincidental milestones of that year.

Although Cohen had already anticipated celebrity, *Ladies and Gentlemen ... Mr. Leonard Cohen* was the first instance of his national celebrity. The filmmakers helped to promote him not only by focusing on him but also by presuming to reveal his private life. In *Understanding Celebrity* (2004), Graeme Turner explains: "We can map the precise moment a public figure becomes a celebrity. It occurs [when] media interest in [one's] activities is transferred from reporting on [one's] public role ... to investigating the details of [one's] private [life]" (8). Most of the film concentrates on what we are supposed to assume is Cohen's private life: he walks around Montreal, shops for food, sleeps in a hotel room, plays guitar with his friends, bathes, talks with his mother, and writes poems; we also see pictures of his lover Marianne living in Greece. Nowhere is his private persona more evident than in these scenes. Their supposedly private details are aspects of his performance in the film, which seems to erase the distinction between his private affairs and his life in public. Cohen seemed prepared to exploit this lack of distinction and his heightened exposure in the popular media.

In the aforementioned scenes in the film, Cohen's public persona is not evident; he is not obviously performing until, in the bath, he writes "*caveat emptor*" on the marble wall. Viewing himself later in a screening room (and aware by then that he had become the star of the film), he explains to one of the directors that he "had to for a moment act as a double agent for both the filmmakers and the public; I had to warn the public ... that this is not entirely devoid of the con." Notably, he writes "*caveat emptor*" and not "*caveat lector*," warning the *buyer* in the commercial realm of celebrity and not the *reader* in the supposedly separate realm of the book. As a "double agent," he not only speaks on the public's behalf and dispels the illusion of public access to his private life but also endears himself to the public. In most of the film, Cohen appears comfortable with the closeness – even the fusion – of his private and public personas; it helps the public to feel connected to him as the star of the film, and this intimacy promotes him.

In the same year that *Ladies and Gentlemen* was being filmed, Cohen produced a book that was for him "a revolution of style" (Ondaatje, *Leonard* 39), which also reflected on his thinking about masters and slaves. In my article on Cohen's poetic dialogues with Layton, I showed that Cohen used the crucial poem "Style" in *Flowers for Hitler* to describe his "slavery" (27) – an ironic enslavement to a "style of freedom" (his words, but from *Parasites of Heaven*) that he had learned from Layton and Layton's generation, for whom "freedom" seemed to require an arms race and the potential for nuclear apocalypse during the missile crisis involving the United States, Cuba, and the Soviet Union in 1962. In rejecting that style – but in performing masochistically to express its influence on his poems of this era – Cohen came of age as a poet and continued to imagine ways of using his voice to speak to larger audiences.

Radio is prominent in "Style" not only as a technology of forgetting but also as a technology of stardom. In "Style," the "early morning greedy radio eats / the governments one by one the languages / the poppy fields one by one" (28) without pausing – a chain reaction that imitates a nuclear explosion. The radio records the disappearance or the mutation of culture as it is "eat[en]" by war. Given Layton's and John F. Kennedy's invisible presence as celebrities in the poem's historical subtext (Layton being arguably visualized only in the symbol – and a somewhat comic one, furthermore – of "the giant rooster" in line 40), it is significant that the poem mentions radio and not television. Cohen's focus is not on image but on sound. When the speaker says that he does not "believe the radio stations / of Russia and America," he adds, "but I like the music" (27). Although the radio is "greedy," its greed threatens "governments," "languages," and "poppy fields," not "music." The lyrics ("the language") of Cohen's later music are at least as important as its purely musical elements, but here Cohen's "anti-poetic" (Ondaatje, *Leonard* 43) voice is speaking against words – speaking as if words could be survived by music, or poetic celebrity could be survived by musical celebrity, which would diminish the emphasis on language. He was envisioning his mastery of a different discourse, even if his future career in music would soon lead him to feel much more seriously enslaved.

The motif of a brotherhood in crisis that Cohen introduces in "Style" – with the bomb that "makes toward me brothers" (28) – and extends in *Parasites of Heaven* is another sign of his rejection of Layton's style of freedom, which was for Cohen too individualistic. Cohen's desire for inclusion was ironic, given that he really was living in isolation on a Greek "Argolic island" (27). The individualism of Layton and "America" seemingly left Cohen disoriented, lonely, and – perhaps worst of all – afraid that he might also forget "the style [he] laboured on" (28), which might have been Layton's but might yet have become his own. Thus, "I" appears sixteen times in the first half of "Style," and only five times in the last half – a diminishment of lyrical subjectivity. The movement toward the relative collectivity of the "brothers" is ambivalent. Cohen wrote a poem in his journal in 1967 that read, "I want to live alone / in fellowship with men" (qtd. in Nadel 146). Partly because of this ambivalence, the movement toward fellowship or brotherhood reveals a personal crisis – a crisis of freedom described here as slavery.

The ambivalence in Cohen's view of style in relation to freedom reappears in the prose poem "Here we are at the window" from *Parasites of Heaven* two years later: "So long I've tried to give a name to freedom, today my freedom lost its name, like a student's room travelling into the morning with the lights on. Every act has its own style of freedom, whatever that means" (23). Surely alluding to Layton's famous invocation in "Whatever Else Poetry Is Freedom" (1958), Cohen's "whatever" is familiar to us now as a mantra of apathetic youth. He had stopped believing in freedom as Layton had defined it. In *Parasites of Heaven*, Cohen writes that "[f]reedom lost its name to the style with which things happen" (23), implying not only that Layton's style could make nothing "happen" but also, perhaps even thankfully, that freedom had become anonymous (having "lost its name") in response to Layton's self-referential individualism (which is not to suggest that Cohen stopped referring to himself in his poems or songs thereafter). Cohen might have wanted to be free and anonymous instead of free and known as an individual.

Scobie argues that "[t]his is the terrible force of Cohen's destruction of individuality: that he endorses [that destruction]" (*Leonard* 9); Cohen offsets the loss of individuality by resolving to join, on equal terms, the rebellious community of student-prisoners: "Brothers, each at your window, we are the style of so much passion, we are the order of style, we are pure style called to delight a fold of the sky" (23). This cryptic declaration implies that the speaker is trying to convince his "[b]rothers" that they have a "call[ing]": to rebel and, if necessary, to sacrifice themselves to "a fold of the sky" – that is, to heaven. Although Layton's public persona was rebellious, it was not usually so communal. As I wrote in my article on their poetic dialogues, Cohen began to realize that Layton's influential style and preoccupations were too idealistic: freedom could be theorized, but it was a fantasy. Conceding the impossibility of achieving freedom (at least in Layton's pseudo-religious way), Cohen would later find inspiration in figurative slavery and imagined community in *The Energy of Slaves*.

The faith that Cohen seemed to put in brotherhood in *Parasites of Heaven* did not mean, however, that he wanted only one alternative to Layton's style of freedom. Rather, he suggests elsewhere in *Flowers for Hitler* that he simply wanted many alternatives (and perhaps Layton could be included among them, on equal terms). "Why I Happen To Be Free" begins with the least ambiguous of its suggestions about the speaker's freedom:

> They all conspire to make me free
> I tried to join their arguments
> but there were so few sides
> and I needed several (59)

Perhaps, therefore, Cohen later imagined the brotherhood in *Parasites of Heaven* as a way of multiplying the "sides" that he could "join." Here, he implies that his freedom is associated with having "several," not "few," sides – "various positions" again.

Cohen appraised and eventually rejected Layton's style of freedom, choosing a less individualistic and more communal approach to both freedom and celebrity (a necessity for anyone thinking about being a musician and playing in bands), but he refused to define freedom in "Style" or in *Parasites of Heaven*. This decision might have been a strategy that partly ensured that his freedom would not be co-opted or redefined by others. What he implied about slavery in "Style" eventually became more obviously related to stardom after the start of his career in music, when his representations of masochism became much harsher.

The year 1966 was a watershed for Cohen. It was the year Cohen decided to become a singer (Nadel 141), the year he began living occasionally at the Chelsea Hotel in New York City, the year he wrote "Suzanne" for Judy Collins to record, and the year he said that popular music would be the future of poetry (Nadel 150) and that "the time is over when poets should sit on marble stairs with black capes" (qtd. in Nadel 156). He also published *Parasites of Heaven*. Although he dedicated the book to Layton, Cohen was no longer following Layton and other modernists by making obscure references to literary history, religion, or mythology in his poems. Popular culture was his new reference point. Cohen revised Layton's Dionysian and Messianic personas with "pop-sainthood" based in youth culture. With *Parasites of Heaven,* Cohen also began to wonder about his celebrity's consequences – possibly based on experience he now had, rather than anticipation based, in part, on what he knew of Layton's experience.

In "Nancy lies in London grass," Cohen uses his own name again (as in "The Cuckold's Song") and implies that, with *Parasites of Heaven* and his higher degree of celebrity, his identity was changing. The speaker implies that difference when he says, "Leonard hasn't been the same / since he wandered from his name" (33). Although Cohen's reference to only his first name suggests that the other "name" is probably "Leonard Cohen" the public persona, his reference to himself in the third person suggests that the speaker is different from both his private persona ("Leonard") and his public persona ("Leonard Cohen"). The speaker might be a third party, someone entirely unconnected to the real Cohen; however, another possibility is that "Leonard Cohen" might be speaking incognito (the equivalent of wearing sunglasses and a false moustache) so that he does not draw attention to his celebrity. (The previous chapter and the next poem I consider both remark on this issue.) Regardless, the situation becomes somewhat less ambiguous when Cohen's themes related to celebrity appear after he includes "Leonard" in a list of other names: "Nancy," "George," "Michael," and "Robert" – who are presumably his "friends" (33).

They are martyrs, crucified, and "Leonard" seems to be among them. Although not all martyrs are celebrities in Cohen's poetry, his own celebrity is associated with martyrdom. These martyrs in particular are not masochists, because their bodies were "torn on crosses / that their visions meant to leap"

(33); they wanted to avoid pain. Nor are they sadists, though "they hate / the company they keep" (33) as they suffer; they are not inflicting pain on each other, and they are not noticeably enjoying each other's pain. Nevertheless, the poem brings together most of the themes familiar to his readers and fans: religiosity and pain – even masculinity, because male names outnumber female names four to one. Cohen's celebrity was not really an issue of his biography yet, given that it was just becoming national in scope (Bouchard R3), but his references to his own name demonstrate that he was still working on his identity. Deliberately or not, he was representing himself with increasing ambiguity and with a greater sense of consequence (e.g., crucifixion).

The confusion about the speaker in "Nancy lies in London grass" is also evident in *Parasites of Heaven*'s "He was beautiful when he sat alone," which is more direct in suggesting that sadism and masochism could both characterize celebrities. In this prose poem, the speaker claims outright: "I'll tell you why I like to sit alone, because I'm a sadist, that's why we like to sit alone, because we're the sadists who like to sit alone" (66). He also uses the third-person singular to include another man, who is uncannily similar to the speaker: "He was beautiful when he sat alone, he was like me ... he was holding the mug in the hardest possible way so that his fingers were all twisted" (66). The painfully "twisted" fingers imply that "he" is a masochist and, because he is "like" the speaker, the speaker might also be a masochist; however, the speaker also calls himself "a sadist." Furthermore, the intended hearer of his monologue is "Miss Blood" (66), whose name suggests that the speaker is sadistically interested in hurting her – drawing "[b]lood."[16] His tendencies are both sadistic and masochistic, which is relevant because both Cohen's private and public personas are seemingly there.

The identity crisis associated with celebrity is evident in the confusion and fusion, as "we," of Cohen's private and public personas. The speaker of "He was beautiful when he sat alone" reveals that the other man is writing a song but has only the last line: "*Don't call yourself a secret unless you mean to keep it*" (67, his emphasis). The songwriter (later called a "singer") is remonstrating with either himself or the speaker (or the audience of his music) for complaining about privacy (the "secret") without actually protecting it.[17] The question of whether the songwriter really is a songwriter is never answered; in fact, it is only complicated when the speaker says, "He thought he knew, or he actually did know too much about singing to be a singer, and if there actually is such a condition, is anybody in it, and are sadists born there?" (67). He then responds to his own question and hints at his own identity: "It is not a question mark, it is not an exclamation mark, it is a full stop by the man who wrote Parasites of Heaven" (67). The speaker assumes that everyone knows his name: "Leonard Cohen," the public persona. The fusion of the personas is evident because the speaker is not merely "like" the potential singer; he is implicitly the writer of "Parasites of Heaven" who decided, in that same year, to become "Leonard Cohen" the singer. Cohen is writing about the moment when the private and public personas fuse, which, for him, is also the moment when the poet becomes the singer. This identity crisis is worse than usual, perhaps, because Cohen was partly rejecting the poetry of his apprenticeship – "the style [he] laboured on."

Parasites of Heaven is also concerned with the popular culture that supports celebrity in music and film more than in poetry. The poem "A cross didn't fall on me" revises the nostalgia but disaffection of "Style" with the bored, ironic attitude of youth.

A cross didn't fall on me
when I went for hot-dogs
and the all-night Greek
slave in the Silver Gameland
didn't think I was his brother
Love me because nothing happens (14)

The poem dismantles or negates both religion and myth. It insinuates that Christianity is fading by suggesting that crosses are tumbling down as if the sky were falling. It also exploits an enjambment to transform what I expected to be a reference to Greek myth into a reference to the popular culture of video arcades and movies. The "Greek slave" did not recognize him as a "brother," so their shared slavery might be only a pretence of Cohen's newly embittered view of celebrity; perhaps the Greek man thought that this star poet was slumming, which some critics alleged of Cohen (Filip 74). Even so, "nothing happens," regardless of the speaker's status. Leading to "[l]ove" by dwelling on negation – for example, "didn't," "nothing," "not" (14) – the speaker also dismantles romance. Instead of having intrinsic or traditional value, love is what one feels or does to alleviate boredom, like going to the movies, which provide the template for hopelessly unrealistic relationships:

Do you have any idea how
many movies I had to watch
before I knew surely
that I would love you
when the lights woke up (14)

Here Cohen implies that popular culture involves a brotherhood of bored "slave[s]" who are conditioned by "many movies" to seek "love." Although this dull, figurative slavery might be different from relatively innovative performances of masochism, no one should have trouble seeing Cohen's perspective on a culture of youth whose boredom and disappointment are masochistically reinforced by their own meaningless hedonism and distraction.

When the poem ends, Cohen reveals his growing understanding of celebrity as violence done to the private self. The speaker notes that the plentiful "stars," which are common symbols of celebrity, try to "keep" privacy, but he cynically counters, "Have you ever noticed how private / a wet tree is / a curtain of razor blades" (15). In other words, the stars have only the privacy provided by a curtain of razor blades. With so many blades, they have so many opportunities to kill themselves – a conceit Cohen later makes explicit with the small razor blade icon at the start of every poem in *The Energy of Slaves*. Beyond masochism, suicide is the ultimate solution, if it can be called that, to the lack of privacy suffered by celebrities.

Both in his poetry and interviews, Cohen associates these suicidal tendencies in celebrities with memory loss and historical change. In "A cross didn't fall on me," the speaker wants to "grow / wings and lose [his] mind" – in other words, become an angel and end his human consciousness through suicide, but he cannot even remember why: "I confess that I've / forgotten what for / Why wings and a lost mind" (15). (There are also signs that he is not entirely hopeless – on the same page, he intends "to find / a passage or forge a passport" and learn "a new language" – but he does not seem convinced by these possibilities.) Cohen might not have been serious about killing himself, but following his two-month recovery after his binge-writing of *Beautiful Losers* (1966) on amphetamines, he said: "I would like to say that it made me saintly" (qtd. in Ruddy 18) – that is, like a martyr, though his statement hardly reveals any conviction of his really being a martyr. Nevertheless, he claimed that the binge left him with partial memory loss and a dwindling sense of personal freedom. Seemingly in a state of disillusionment, he said, "There will be no more history anyway. ... We won't have the old historical sense. People will live in a state of amnesia" (qtd. in Ruddy 18). Cohen was beginning to suggest that the concerns demonstrably related to stardom in his poems were not only speculative but also personal.

The peak of Cohen's celebrity (in the context of the era of celebrity in Canadian poetry, being that he had later comebacks) was soon upon him. Around the time of the release of his *Selected Poems*, Cohen arrived at a level of poetic celebrity that has probably never been matched since. The peak of his celebrity, of course, was not owing strictly to his poems, but also to his music, in which he made an American debut in 1967 at the Newport Folk Festival and on CBS's *Camera Three* (Hutcheon [Poetry] 21–2).[18] By 1978 his books had been translated into eleven languages; he had sold over two million books and over nine million albums (Amiel, "Leonard" 56). These figures show that his albums in general were more popular than his books – though his albums would consistently reach a minimum of "gold" status (depending on the country) only after 1984's *Various Positions*.[19] Of his books, *Selected Poems* was notable for selling 700,000 copies in its first ten years in the United States alone (Amiel, "Leonard" 56); it sold 200,000 in the first three months (Ondaatje, *Leonard* 5). As my comparisons between the sales figures of different poets in chapter 2 show, Cohen's celebrity was of a vastly higher degree than any of them, with the eventual exception of Ondaatje and especially Margaret Atwood.

While the film *Ladies and Gentlemen ... Mr. Leonard Cohen* was the first instance of his celebrity,[20] the popular magazines *Saturday Night* and *Maclean's* did not begin to publish stories about Cohen's private life and personality until 1968, when he had just begun seriously to exploit celebrity's imprimatur – its transferability, as a "textual signature" (Jaffe 3) or "stylistic stamp" (Jaffe 20), between forms and genres. Although I argued in chapter 2 that literary celebrity in Canada is meaningfully contextual, celebrity in general can focus on the celebrity's image and thereby enable cross marketing and spin-offs regardless of the commodity's form, making "literary and dramatic form ... irrelevant" (Boorstin 158). Undoubtedly, the success of his first album boosted the success of his *Selected Poems*, but Cohen argued in 1969 that his poems and his songs were the same thing: "Some were songs first and some were poems first and some were situations. All of my writing has guitars behind it, even the novels" (qtd. in Nadel 175). He was cross marketing himself – with retroactive effects on the popularity of his two novels, especially *Beautiful Losers*. Theoretically, the imprimatur applies its authority arbitrarily because the license and what is licensed are not necessarily connected (e.g., a retired boxer can sell electric griddles). It is transferable between people as shared or inherited authority and between forms and genres as a spin-off. Cohen could have used his imprimatur to sell Armani suits but sold books – books that tended to criticize the same tactics he used to become successful.

He thereby alienated some of his readers and some other poets (Nadel 175), who tried to brand him differently: as a sell-out, or as someone who had never been authentic – neither as a figure of popular culture because of his roots in Montreal's wealthy Westmount neighborhood, nor, I would add, as a figurative slave. According to Aaron Jaffe in *Modernism and the Culture of Celebrity*

(2005), however, the imprimatur functions not only to regulate the market but also to enable elite artists to retain high cultural value despite popular success (26). Jaffe implies that the authority of the imprimatur sufficiently complicates critical evaluations and substitutes for traditional criteria of merit (31–3). Thus, Cohen's high cultural value might have been beset by allegations of inauthenticity motivated by his popular success, but his facility for adapting into different forms, genres, and roles was a sign of talent that no one could reasonably deny.

Recorded so soon after his celebrity became international, "Bird on the Wire," from his second album, *Songs from a Room* (1969), associates Cohen's multiple roles with his freedom – as he did earlier in the aforementioned "Why I Happen To Be Free" from *Flowers for Hitler*. Cohen sings about himself in six different roles: "a bird," "a drunk," "the worm," "a knight," "a baby," and "a beast." The bird and the drunk are explicitly related to his freedom: "Like a bird on the wire / Like a drunk in a midnight choir / I have tried in my way to be free." The sadomasochism related to Cohen's celebrity is evident in his representation of himself as a "worm on a hook" and when he sings, "Like a baby stillborn / Like a beast with his horn / I have torn everyone who reached out for me." The pain that he has inflicted on his audience makes him feel guilty; the singer then "swear[s]" that he will use "this song" to atone for what he has "done wrong," but the end of the song is sceptical of his atonement: a "beggar" tells him "not [to] ask for so much" while a "pretty woman" "crie[s]" to him, "Hey, why not ask for more?"

What he really seems to ask for is the freedom to have so many roles. In a rare acknowledgment by a star poet in Canada that the audience is not a homogeneous threat, Cohen suggests that his comparatively appealing audience, the "pretty woman," encourages him to ask for "more" atonement. But she is recommending greed, which will only exacerbate his feeling of guilt. In response to her recommendation, the song ends as it began: "Like a bird on the wire / Like a drunk in a midnight choir / I have tried in my way to be free." The repetition of diverse similes is protection from the metaphor of celebrity; Cohen seems to want neither one audience nor one role for himself that the audience could command. His multiplicity is freedom.

In the years between 1968 and 1972, Cohen's celebrity had lifted Canadian poetry to the height of its popular status; simultaneously, however, Cohen went on "hiatus" as a poet, recorded two albums, went on tour, "committed himself to Zen" (Nadel 175), and ostensibly suffered through a depression. His concert before "ten thousand fans" (Nadel 177) at the Royal Albert Hall in London was reviewed as a display of "captivating self abasement leaving deep impressions of a sad and tortured wasteland" (qtd. in Nadel 177). He reflected later upon the recording of *Songs of Love and Hate* (1970) and said, "absolutely everything was beginning to fall apart around me: my spirit, my intentions, my will. So I went into a deep and long depression" (qtd. in Nadel 180). He told a journalist, "now I'm thirty-six and greedy. I'm willing to be this ... My greatest need is to be interesting to myself" (qtd. in Nadel 180). He also said that suffering "has led me to wherever I am. Suffering has made me rebel against my own weakness" (qtd. in Nadel 180) – presumably his egotism. The private persona in these interviews – if that is what it is – offers some of Cohen's reasons for representing celebrity as a status that only masochists could appreciate. His next book, *The Energy of Slaves*, was the most obvious of his responses, in art, to his status as a celebrity. Despite his previous assertion of the equivalence of his poems and his songs, in *The Energy of Slaves* he was beginning to wonder how poetry would fare in the context of celebrity.

The book repeatedly suggests that a new historical age has begun, one which debases poets and poetry by supplanting love poems with grotesque antipoems. In "The poems don't love us anymore," the speaker says that he sees poems "half-rotten half-born ... / lying down in their jelly / to make love with the tooth of a saw" (117). The poems, he suggests, are aborted fetuses that were discarded by their unloving parents (authors), fetuses that "don't want to love us [and] / ... don't want to be poems" (117). Apparently disgusted with "all the flabby liars / of the Aquarian Age" (115) in "How we loved you," Cohen suggests that the Aquarian Age culture of peace and love had been (or is) naïve. Thus, in "You tore your shirt," the speaker stares at someone's injured breast or exposed heart, and says,

I put my hand
on what I saw
I drew it back
It was a claw (89)

The speaker's basic diction, primitive rhythm, and limited awareness of himself are animalistic; they seem associated with the sadistic impulse to cause injury by "claw[ing]" at someone else. The poem concludes by suggesting that the speaker is a dangerous animal and symbolic slave kept in a cage by whomever he had wounded: "You throw me food / and change my dirt" (89). Status loss – from free person to slave or to animal – is another aspect of some performances of masochism (Baumeister 158–9), such as this poem. *The Energy of Slaves* reveals Cohen's fascination with pain and his opinion of the end of poetry as he once knew it.

The Energy of Slaves therefore returns more seriously to the topic of suicide that *Parasites of Heaven* implied with "A cross didn't fall on me." In "This is a threat" (reproduced here in full) Cohen clearly links self-hatred or self-pity with celebrity:

This is a threat
Do you know what a threat is
I have no private life
You will commit suicide
or become like me (62)

The speaker's relationship with "You" is similar to the relationship between the speaker of "Nancy lies in London grass" and the other man – the private persona – whom the speaker says is "like me." Here, "[y]ou" might become, he says, "like me." Nevertheless, the "threat" is not that the speaker will sadistically hurt the reader; nor is it the prediction of the speaker's suicide, because that suicide already happened – perhaps accidentally – when he sacrificed his "private life." Instead, the threat is a classic catch-22: kill yourself or become "like" the speaker whose private persona has killed himself. Hypothetically, these are cases of accidental suicide (not sadistic murder at the hands – or claws – of the public persona or the public) because the private persona and even the private self are usually complicit in some of the decisions that make the fusion of selves possible for celebrities. For people like Layton and Cohen who anticipated some of the negative results of stardom, some loss of their privacy was a known risk, and of course the threat of this poem is also the poem itself, because it is a vehicle of publicity. In general, the threat is a warning to would-be celebrities – fans, including the readers – about the mockery of fulsomeness that suffices for the private life of a star.

Even more explicitly, "His suicide was simply not a puzzle" suggests that stardom is a cause of suicide. The plural speaker of the poem addresses "Leonard" and sadistically commands him to "[s]ing for" (94) the suicide case. The cause of death is obvious to "those of us / who photographed him" (94) but is cryptic to the reader. In brief, the suicide case appears to have shot himself in the head while lacing a girl's "huge new boot / with a boa constrictor," and the paparazzi (the poem's narrators) are spying on the scene from above "on the rim / of a bullet hole looking down" (94). The girl, her boot, and the snake are hard to explain except as a dominatrix and her fetishes, which put emphasis on the suicide case's masochism, and he seems to have been a star, someone "photographed." Furthermore, he seems to be someone similar enough to

"Leonard" that "Leonard" could "wear his raincoat" (94). The raincoat is more evidence that the private persona has died as a result of celebrity, because it might be the one in "Famous Blue Raincoat." "Leonard" refers not to Cohen himself but to the private persona, who might live on to elegize the suicide case but is also uncomfortably like him.

Although Cohen himself was rumoured to be suicidal around this time, Nadel states that in 1974 he admitted, "I'm too old to commit suicide. It would be unbecoming" (qtd. in Nadel 194). Tragically, however, a fan whom Cohen had met during his 1972 tour had killed herself while he was finalizing *The Energy of Slaves*. "Cohen was mentioned in her suicide note" (Nadel 194), and she had reported in an earlier letter to him that "your soul entered mine then and some union took place that almost killed me with its INTENSITY" (qtd. in Nadel 193, her emphasis). In the first chapter, I suggested that the metaphor of celebrity – *privacy is publicity* – could also apply to fans, for whom the celebrity is the public that invades or is welcomed into their private lives. The diction of this fan – "some *union* took place" (my emphasis) – supports my argument about the metaphor of celebrity, which is potentially implicated in this death.

Despite such seriousness, no one should ignore the possibility that Cohen's especially disturbing representations of celebrity in *The Energy of Slaves* are the result of the bitter realization that his stardom in poetry had reached its highest degree and would begin to fade (a realization, I argued in chapter 3, that prompted Layton to attempt various desperate strategies to maintain his own literary celebrity). Another possibility is that these representations were intended to promote Cohen by eliciting the sympathy of his audience, and in some especially shocking examples, his representations of stardom might be intended solely for self-promotion through controversy. The epitome is almost certainly the darkly comic, problematic short poem "the 15-year old girls." Its speaker refers to the girls that he was attracted to when he was the same age, and then he claims, "I have them now" (97). He concludes:

> it is very pleasant
> it is never too late
> I advise you all
> to become rich and famous (97)

The insinuations of paedophilia and transgressive hedonism are outrageous but also emphasize the unusual mixture of sardonic and deadpan comedy in the poem. The poem does not really encourage men to seek sexual pleasure from "15-year old girls"; its implied advice is to avoid riches, fame, and the humiliation of seeking girls instead of women. Nevertheless, when Cohen's relationship with Suzanne Elrod deteriorated later in the 1970s, he reportedly did have a fling with a fifteen-year-old (Nadel 210). Without seeking to confirm or deny those reports, I interpret the irony of this poem in the context of the book's other poems about loneliness that criticize celebrity and that depend on the reader's prior awareness of Cohen's celebrity. Because the metaphor here in *The Energy of Slaves* is that celebrities are slaves, "the 15-year old girls" is concerned with the speaker's lack of genuine power and his feelings of being emasculated and trapped because he is "rich and famous."

Remarkably, "the 15-year old girls" might be the only poem by Cohen that explicitly refers to pleasure in the context of celebrity. It is therefore one of the only poems that could help to explain the paradox of erotogenic masochism. Unfortunately, that paradox cannot be resolved here – first, because Cohen is not providing a case study; second, because Cohen does not give voice to the girls and their experience of pleasure, pain, or any combination of both. Even if they were real and he did give them voice, their words would be suspect because he wrote the poem. The gross, patriarchal abuse of sexual power (Cohen was thirty-eight when this poem was published) implied in "the 15-year old girls" might be sadistic, but we, as readers, are privy only to representations – certainly ironic and possibly false – of being rich and famous.[21]

An example that helps to explain the problematic masculinity and sadomasochistic complexity of "the 15-year old girls" is "Dear Mailer," which was a delayed response (by nine years) to Layton's "The Dazed Steer" (1963). It is a crucial poem in the poetic dialogues of Layton and Cohen. In "Dear Mailer," Cohen addresses Mailer, another celebrity who happened to be Jewish and antiestablishmentarian. Cohen's commentary on that masculinity needs to be considered in relation to Layton's earlier representation of his imaginary defeat of Mailer. Here, defending Layton – regardless of whether that is needed – on the assumption that Mailer is "The Dazed Steer," Cohen writes in *The Energy of Slaves*:

> Dear Mailer
> don't ever fuck with me
> or come up to me
> and punch my gut (103)

– which was the threat in "The Dazed Steer." Describing his public persona as "armed and mad" (103), Cohen also describes a harsh retaliation against Mailer: "I will k – l you / and your entire family" (103). The implication is that Cohen – the "Leonard Cohen" who has fused with "L. Cohen" from that other well-known letter, "Famous Blue Raincoat" – is stronger or at least more aggressive than his mentor Layton. The epistolary form, however, suggests that Cohen has the protection of distance – and is too late to help, anyway, in 1972. Cohen's overreaction is less a shock than a parody of Layton's machismo; with deadpan comedy it supports the assertion that "a virile masculinity bordering on caricature became central to the public image of celebrity authors" (Glass 18) in America (a claim I would extend to Canada, though mainly in relation to poets, as I explained in chapter 2). Cohen acknowledges that Mailer might "humiliat[e]" (103) him – a subtle masochism that partly subverts the more obvious, potentially sadistic impulses of the poem. "The masochist is insolent in his obsequiousness, rebellious in his submission; in short, he is a humorist" (Deleuze 89), as Cohen seems to be in "Dear Mailer." Here, the elision of the word *kill* implies that violence is holy or unspeakable, but it also suggests – along with the epistolary form – that Cohen does not have the "gut[s]" to kill someone.

Interpreted together, "Dear Mailer" and "the 15-year old girls" suggest that Cohen's private persona is seeking humiliation (another sign of masochism) because he cannot compete with other men, either in physical contests or in sexual conquests of women, though his public persona asserts otherwise. The problematic sense of humour in these poems reveals itself in what Thomas P. Balázs calls "masochistic play" (13). According to Balázs, "masochistic play relies primarily upon the manipulation of symbolic pain" (186). According to Baumeister, masochists tend to "seek pain without injury. In a sense masochists *fictionalize* pain ... They want *safe* pain" (14, his emphasis). Cohen's "Dear Mailer" is an obvious example of a scenario of "safe pain" or "symbolic pain," and "the 15-year old girls" possibly refers to symbolic pleasure. Cohen's sense of "play" is also a reminder that he might be falsely representing himself as a slave of celebrity and that he thereby takes some control over his personas and what they mean to others. In both "Dear Mailer" and "the 15-year old girls," the speaker is implicitly a loser; his "masochistic play" suggests that Cohen is attempting to parody and thereby subvert stereotypes of male stars and men in general.

Much of Cohen's self-deprecation was related to his musical career and his impression of its effect on his freedom. In 1973, the year before *New Skin for the Old Ceremony* was released, Cohen announced that he intended "to quit the music business" (Pirrie 66). In an issue of the magazine *New Musical Express*, Alastair Pirrie stated that "[a]mong his friends, [Cohen] would often claim that he hated the business of selling his songs to people, and he hated the society that made this necessary" (66). Cohen reportedly said to Pirrie, "I'm no longer a free man; I'm an exploited man. Once, long ago, my songs were not sold;

they found their way to people anyway. Then people saw that profit could be made from them; then the profit interested me also" (qtd. in Pirrie 66). His complaint was that his celebrity not only "exploited" him but also tempted him to be greedy. Cohen was making statements about his figurative slavery not only in his poems.

The Energy of Slaves is the appropriate conclusion to this chapter on masochistic stardom, but Cohen's next book, *Death of a Lady's Man,* needs at least a partial explanation now (and perhaps more in the future) partly because it was Cohen's final comment on his status during the era of celebrity in Canadian poetry. It made relevant changes to his masculine persona and to his religious pretence – without abandoning themes of sadomasochism but with new hope for his relationship with the public. It was, as I suggested earlier, his attempt to figuratively kill or commit the suicide of his public persona – and to find something genuine beyond stardom.

Although he had somewhat abandoned the religious pretence of his earlier books by shifting his reference point to secular, popular culture in *Parasites of Heaven* and *The Energy of Slaves,* Cohen returned to it in *Death of a Lady's Man,* which he envisioned as another version of the *I Ching* (Hutcheon [Fiction] 51). For many years, Cohen had been increasingly interested in the counsel of his master Roshi, whose Buddhist teachings and whose Zen "emphasis on suffering" (Nadel 201) seem to have influenced Cohen's ideas about celebrity in his later career, and seem to have been compatible with Cohen's interest in masochism.[22] Scobie's aforementioned argument – that "[t]he self is not sacrificed to some higher cause; the sacrifice of the self *is* the higher cause" – is more valid in the context of Buddhism than it was in *The Energy of Slaves,* when Cohen understood that he had to sacrifice himself to popular culture, if for no other reason (besides self-promotion) than to expose celebrity's power. Cohen's Buddhist training helped him to deconstruct not his private self (as far as any member of his public can know) as much as his tenacious public persona – and to rebuild his ego with genuine religion and a healthier, less sadomasochistic conception of masculinity.

Although Cohen fails to kill his public persona in "The Price of This Book," he hopes that an appeal to his readership could help him to prevent the fusion of his public and private selves: "I am ashamed to ask for your money. Not that you have not paid more for less. You have. You do. But I need it to keep my different lives apart. Otherwise I will be crushed when they join, and I will end my life in art, which a terror will not let me do" (168). Nowhere in Cohen's poetry is his concern about the metaphor of celebrity expressed so directly, and his being willingly "ashamed" is another representation of masochism. The "terror" is partly the potential that the fusion of selves occasioned by celebrity would "crush" his literary longevity. Hutcheon argues instead that Cohen's public and private selves had long been "inseparable" ([Fiction] 51) and that "only through the cooperation of the reader [can the writer make] himself and his text both live and live on" ([Fiction] 55), but the author remains ambivalent about the fusion. Tragically, the "price" of attempting to unite with his audience while fantasizing about keeping separate selves might have been the failure of Cohen's actual marriage (Nadel 203).

Another tragedy and another shame in *Death of a Lady's Man* seem to inspire a fantasy of the end of stardom. The context of "How To Speak Poetry" is explicitly a mediatized world in which the celebrity's lifestyle starkly contrasts with that of other people: "We have seen newsreels of humans in the extremities of pain and dislocation. Everyone knows you are eating well and are even being paid to stand up there [on stage]. ... This should make you very quiet" (196–7). The underlying guilt or humility should change the star's way of life: "Do not pretend that you are a beloved singer with a vast loyal audience ... The bombs, flame-throwers, and all the shit have destroyed more than just the trees and villages. They have also destroyed the stage. ... There are no more footlights. You are among the people" (197). Thus, the poet is not a "beloved" musical star or even an immortal poet, but a simple and present speaker unmediated by the stage or the television. The hypothetical relationship is postcelebrity.

The disappearance of the public persona, however, has no decisive effect on either exposing the speaker's privacy or ensuring that it is guarded. The speaker tells himself (among possible others): "Respect the privacy of the material. These pieces were written in silence. ... Let the audience feel your love of privacy even though there is no privacy" (197). He is implying that he has a sense of self (which underlies his "love of privacy") even if his public persona, or the public itself, is so involved in his life that "there is no privacy." Although stars undoubtedly feel this paradox more intensely than most people do, most of us have at least the remains of a sense of self, though we might be open to the possibility that everything we think of as private is, in fact, somehow shared or somehow determined for us by the public and its agents. Quite possibly, such a state of being – total exposure – would be shameless, even emotionally inconsequential, and performances of masochism would lose their function and appeal.

Although *Death of a Lady's Man* begins sadomasochistically – with Cohen's masculine persona humiliated and "torture[d]" (12) when the speaker dismisses his potentially sadistic thoughts of "mastering" a woman, thereby initiating "the obscene silence of my career as a lady's man" (11) – it ends by seeming to use religion, instead, to appease or sublimate his frustrations. The "silence of [his] career" seems to imply a devotion to Buddhism rather than celebrity. Having replaced martyrdom and pop-sainthood with Buddhism, and having abandoned the pretence that he is "a lady's man," he divides and refuses the two main pretences of celebrity for poets and thereby conquers his celebrity. Quite possibly, by doing so, he is also able to salvage the better aspects of masculinity and religion. With the pressures on Cohen's private life seemingly eased, his fictional editor is able to end the book optimistically: *"I see in the insignificance of these pages a shadow of the coming modesty. His death belongs to the future. I am well read. I am well served. I am satisfied and I give in. Long live the marriage of men and women. Long live the one heart"* (212, his emphasis). The "modesty" and the "one[ness]" are signs that the self has become whole again – as the private self, not as the fused personas. Healthier marriages, real or not, might now be possible; indeed, before the fictional editor's final comments, Cohen describes a version of himself as being stiff with age or injury but still determined to live well: "Leonard / He can still be seen / hobbling with his love" (212).

Death of a Lady's Man was, symbolically, the closing bookend to the era of celebrity in Canadian poetry. Leading to that milestone, Cohen also defined the highest degree of celebrity available to poets of that era, an achievement that was possible because he was also a popular musician with an international following in Europe and the United States. Not everyone who started as a poet and became a literary celebrity in Canada was successful in his way. Although his celebrity seems to have been a serious detriment to his private life, the problem with his style of freedom was that it was initially defined for him by an earlier star – Layton – and was unrealistically individualistic. By reimagining Layton's freedom as a fantasy and his own freedom as the assuming of "various positions," Cohen developed the metaphor of celebrity as slavery. He found creative "energy" or inspiration in that slavery; as masochists do, he submitted himself to humiliation and pain inflicted upon him by a seemingly greater power: celebrity, which might even be understood as a sadomasochistic state of being.

By performing as a victim of celebrity – a sadomasochist, with the emphasis on *masochist* – Cohen was able to be critical of it even while he exploited its effect on his identity for the purpose of his self-promotion and the writing of poems. In particular, he was critical of the masculinity associated with star poets and, in general, of the religious pretence of celebrity. The eventual symbolic suicide or natural death of his public persona in 1978 coincided with his living as a Buddhist rather than as a self-described martyr. It was the end of a ten-year process of recovering his ego, redefining his private life, and reimagining his poetry without celebrity as either an aspect of his identity or a significant inspiration. Cohen later said, in a 1993 interview, "There's ten years of my life I don't remember and I don't want to remember" (qtd. in Sullivan 179). If those ten years are the decade between the peak of his literary celebrity in 1968 and the symbolic death of his celebrity in 1978, he did much worth remembering.

7 Celebrity, Sexuality, and the Uncanny in Michael Ondaatje's *The Collected Works of Billy the Kid*

Balancing the integrity of his privacy with an interest in the public – and the public's interest in him – has been a concern of Michael Ondaatje almost since the beginning of his career. The relationship between privacy, which he seems to crave (Jewinski 10), and publicity, which he seems to disdain (Marchand par. 5), is not only germane to his life but also to the representation of celebrity in his work. Ondaatje published his first book around ten years into the era of celebrity in Canadian poetry. As I explained in the previous chapters, this era began with Irving Layton's appearances on television in the mid- 1950s and ended not long after the announcement of the symbolic death of the era's most popular celebrity, Leonard Cohen, in *Death of a Lady's Man* (1978). Ondaatje's poetic texts during this period focused intensely on the subject of public recognition. He extended Layton's and Cohen's critiques of celebrity by writing, in much more literal detail, about the experience of losing freedom to stardom. This chapter and the next show how he imagines the effect of celebrity on the sexual and racial identities of historical figures who sometimes became legends; ultimately, he suggests that celebrities are disciplined by the public when their sexual orientations or racial identities do not reflect social norms.

Although this chapter focuses on *The Collected Works of Billy the Kid* (1970) and a specific argument about the book's unexpected representations of Billy as a star, it first needs to explain in some detail how Ondaatje's thinking about celebrity related to that of his precursors – especially Cohen – in the era of celebrity in Canadian poetry. Perhaps the most evident development in Ondaatje's critique of celebrity is that he tended to write about other celebrities, not explicitly himself, whereas Layton and Cohen sometimes named themselves (and each other) in their poems. What I called "grandstanding" in the first chapter is not the same for Ondaatje as it is for Layton and Cohen, whose self-aggrandizement was focused explicitly on themselves. Ondaatje wrote about himself as if he were Billy the Kid, for example, but his standing in for someone else not only implicated him in self-promotion but also removed him to a more critical distance. Paradoxically, Ondaatje's descriptions of the effects of celebrity are more intimate than those of his precursors. Perhaps Ondaatje did not imagine his immersion in the lives of other celebrities as totally as Gwendolyn MacEwen did in that of Lawrence of Arabia, but he risked the emotional involvement that method actors have with their characters. He imagines himself both as another (e.g., Billy the Kid) and as an Other – someone for whom celebrity might entail the exposure of his difference from his society, as the following chapter will also argue in relation to *Rat Jelly* (1973) and *Secular Love* (1984).

From early in his career, Ondaatje was making statements in his poetry about the effects of celebrity, but he was also making statements, as a poet in academia, about the public's interest in the private lives of celebrities. After graduating with his master's degree from Queen's University, he taught at the University of Western Ontario, where he seemed to hope that his creative writing would help him to get a tenured job even though he did not have a PhD. According to Ondaatje's unofficial biographer Ed Jewinski, "[b]y 1970, Ondaatje's reputation [for poetry] was well established, and he was often invited to read [his poems] at universities" (59). Jewinski states that during the question period at one such reading, Ondaatje argued that "readers should pay attention to the poem, not the poet" (59). Ondaatje mainly followed his own advice in the writing of *Leonard Cohen* (1970), his only academic book, and felt that "nothing is more irritating than to have your work translated by your life" (3). Seeming to understand, even before he became a celebrity, that his reputation would generate interest in his private life, in academic contexts he warned scholars and general readers not to pry.[1]

Unfortunately, resisting one's celebrity tends to intensify it (Moran 54), and associating oneself with celebrities sometimes leads to becoming one. Even when seeming to be critical of celebrity in *Leonard Cohen,* Ondaatje was making his own more likely. Ondaatje's readings at universities were different, in number and degree of publicity, from what he calls the "circus" (35) of Cohen's 1964 reading tour, but to some extent he was doing what he said Cohen was doing: "following a public rather than a private rhetoric" (35). Furthermore, by writing his monograph around the peak of Cohen's celebrity at the end of the 1960s, Ondaatje was probably seeking not only academic credentials that would lead to a tenured job but also attention – though he might have preferred to see such attention directed not at himself but at his poetry.

To do unto Cohen as he ostensibly would have done unto himself, Ondaatje uses the introduction to *Leonard Cohen* to reject the cult of personality that supports celebrity: "I have intentionally avoided Cohen the recent public personality," he writes, "and ignored detailed biography" to try to "be objective about his novels and poetry" (3). Unsure of whether fans of Canadian poetry were sincere in their appreciation, Ondaatje quotes Lawrence Breavman from Cohen's *The Favourite Game* (1963): "in this country writers are interviewed on T.V. for one reason only: to give the rest of the nation a good laugh" (qtd. in *Leonard* 3). He argues that literature should be defensible without recourse to the questionable status of the author. When he later considers Cohen's *Parasites of Heaven* (1966), he criticizes it because "[t]he poems are only valid when they go hand in hand with the author, [and] they cannot survive by themselves" (56). Ondaatje seems to prefer the earlier poetry, especially *The Spice-box of Earth* (1961), which made Cohen very popular but which appeared before his reading tour and the film *Ladies and Gentlemen ... Mr. Leonard Cohen* (1965) that documented it. One impression of Ondaatje's study is that Cohen's poetry worsened as his popularity became stardom.

In *Leonard Cohen*, Ondaatje seems averse to celebrity – at least to Cohen's celebrity – but when he comments on some of Cohen's highly self-reflexive poems, he also seems impressed that his subject could "cleverly" exploit "the prostitution of personality that comes with success" (4). Eventually, he even argues that "Cohen himself" emerges from his poems as the "mental and social cripple" (14), "the wounded man yearning for the glorious death which will mean sainthood" (13). Ondaatje defines Cohen's saints as "perverted" (37), as "beautiful losers" (53), and as representations of the author – "Saint Leonard" (60) – in the role of "the sacrificial guinea pig" (36). His sainthood becomes "pop-sainthood" (4, 59) in the context of his celebrity, which is also evident because it seems to affect "Cohen himself" and not only a persona. Because pop-sainthood is related to "glorious death," it partly falls into the heroic category of celebrity (Marshall 7) and gets implicit approval. The emphasis on "wound[s]" and "sacrific[e]" reinforces the negative stereotype of celebrity that Lorraine York has noticed in Canadian literature (York, *Literary* 42), but, because this martyrdom is part of what Ondaatje admires in Cohen, *Leonard Cohen* contains a subtle though ambivalent endorsement of celebrity.

No such endorsement can be found in *The Collected Works of Billy the Kid*, where an almost completely negative opinion of celebrity is juxtaposed against the ambivalence of *Leonard Cohen*, which was published in the same year. The contrast between the two texts is partly the result, I would argue, of metaphor's tendency to encourage totalizing fantasies (sometimes worst-case scenarios), and Ondaatje's standing in for Billy the Kid and other stars is an enactment of metaphor with a high degree of commitment to such fantasies. The metaphor of celebrity, as I explained it in previous chapters, invokes religion (as seen in Cohen's persona of the saint) and masculinity (as in so much of Cohen's poetry) as aspects of the public's power, and Ondaatje's representations of Billy help to subvert that power – though Billy as a character is almost completely destroyed by the public. One of the attempted subversions is that his sexuality might not conform to traditional social norms; another is that Billy's religiosity is not aligned with Cohen's pop-saintly precedent. Instead, it is relatively secular; it arguably evokes paranormal events rather than traditional religion. The paranormality helps to elicit uncanny feelings and even an outright fear that help *The Collected Works of Billy the Kid* to act as a dramatic condemnation of celebrity and its ramifications for various freedoms.

The Collected Works of Billy the Kid is not obviously a ghost story, but it is obviously about death and implicitly about sexuality. Smaro Kamboureli has observed that "[Billy] is already dead when he utters his first monologue" ("Outlawed" 120); Dennis Denisoff has extended the work of other critics who have noted Billy's ambiguous sexual orientation (52–3), and he convincingly demonstrates that "[i]mages of homosocial desire ... proliferate" (65) in various scenes throughout the book.[2] Billy's sexuality and death, however, are connected in ways that have not yet been addressed in the criticism. Billy is dead, and some evidence suggests that at least part of his story is narrated when he is a ghost – whose strange perspectives, *déjà vu*, and invisibility (which is memorably suggested by the blank photograph that introduces him) enable him to acknowledge "homosocial desire" that is otherwise repressed. His *déjà vu* is to some extent both the return of the repressed and *his* return, as a ghost, to the narrative of his life and his celebrity. Not only is he shown to us, or made a show of, in various media of publicity in the book, but he is also literally pursued by a figure of the public: his friend turned nemesis, the sheriff Pat Garrett, who is introduced to us as a "[p]ublic figure" (28). Billy's ghostliness helps him to escape into privacy and partially subvert his celebrity, which otherwise enforces the sexual values of the public in much the same way that Garrett does.

Celebrity, sexuality, and the uncanny have a relationship in *The Collected Works of Billy the Kid* that is never self-evident: they revolve around an unspoken aspect of Billy's private life. Garrett sometimes drags Billy into the public to demonstrate his authority, but he arguably kills Billy to keep a secret about the extent of homosocial desire among men in the Wild West. Marlene Goldman and Joanne Saul suggest that "ghosts signal the return of a secret, something repressed" (646); Goldman and Saul then inquire about the "types of secrets" that are "encrypted" (646) in Canadian works of art. Many of those "types" are political, and certainly those that are "repressed" are likely to be sexual. There are, of course, many reasons why sexuality is political; Billy's sexuality is political because he can influence social norms as a star. His secret is implicitly threatened with exposure by the media, but his death prevents the secret from becoming public. Although his murder is sensational enough to increase the degree of his celebrity and transform him into a legend, it also benefits him (a small consolation) with the ghostly invisibility that enables him to insinuate his secret throughout his book.

Billy is not openly critical of his celebrity, but it is arguable that he tends to resist celebrity because it naturalizes the heterosexual masculinity expected of cowboys, lawmen, and outlaws. Manhood, defined implicitly in terms of some heterosexual men's view of women as sexual objects, is "*the* ideal" (Tompkins 18, her emphasis) of the Western genre.[3] Although Ondaatje's Billy might be said to perform as that kind of man by having sex with women, including "Miss Angela [a.k.a. Angie] Dickinson" (64) – whose name alludes to Angie Dickinson, a star of movies such as the Western film *Rio Bravo* (1959) – he also appears to be afraid of women's sexuality, as in a sex scene where he is "paralysed" (16) by Angie's vaginal secretions and demonstrates "extreme physical passivity" (Owens 125). Billy does not entirely conform to the Western ideal of masculinity. His threat to the public as a celebrity who could popularize outlaws (and, if he were outed, might also popularize other sexualities) eventually concerns the sheriff Garrett, who presumably knows his secret and thus kills him to uphold the law – including the unwritten law of heterosexuality. In *Publics and Counterpublics* (2002), Michael Warner argues that "being in public is a privilege that requires filtering or repressing something that is seen as private" (23). He argues further that "to challenge the norms of straight culture in public is to disturb deep and unwritten rules about the kinds of behavior and eroticism that are appropriate to the public" (Warner 24–5). For Billy to be an outlaw of ambiguous sexual orientation in the Wild West, he has to be invisible – possibly a ghost – not only to avoid reconfiguration by oppression but also because the public generally refuses to expose its members to anything but normative or heterosexual expressions of desire.[4]

His ghostliness (of which I will offer necessarily indirect evidence) is uncanny, and the uncanny and celebrity both rely, though with different effects, on familiarity. Sigmund Freud defines the uncanny as a type of "the frightening" (124) that "can be traced back every time to something that was once familiar and then repressed" (154). Like the uncanny, celebrity depends on what is "the most familiar" (Boorstin 61) – on an image, a name, or a slogan so temporarily recognizable that it is known for its well-knownness (Boorstin 57). In the case of stardom, familiarity is the result of presence in the mass media, which tends to reproduce mainstream social norms. Celebrity can happen on the small scale of the local hero, and on that scale, celebrities can express a subculture's "own notions of freedom, fantasy, and needs" (Marshall 56). On a larger scale, celebrity is usually involved in a "dominant culture ... working toward an ideological positioning of ... subordinate cultures within consumer capitalism" (Marshall 56). As a live man, Billy the Kid cannot safely speak for a culture unconcerned by ambiguous sexuality, partly because Pat Garrett's "dominant culture" refuses to allow Billy to become so familiar that he could integrate into the general public without being feared as an unknown. As a ghost who haunts the text he supposedly authored, Billy defamiliarizes his story and hints to his readers about sexuality in the Wild West, but – even if he wanted to – he cannot come back to life and reveal anything directly to the public, and Garrett therefore triumphs in general. Through the mass media, celebrity usually expresses the public's familiar, normative, exclusive values, whereas the uncanny expresses what the public wanted to keep out of sight.

Celebrity, sexuality, and the uncanny therefore seem to be involved with each other in *The Collected Works of Billy the Kid*. As concepts involving secrecy and visibility, they are important to any understanding of Billy's desire to hide or be seen – to be private or public. In an article about Ondaatje's own celebrity and its effect on his novel *In the Skin of a Lion* (1987), Kamboureli argues that the narrator of that novel appropriates the figurative invisibility of the immigrants in his society. Unnoticed, the narrator occupies "a spectatorial position" from which he "constructs their image" (Kamboureli, "Culture" 50). In referring to this gaze, Kamboureli refers to "a politics that constantly shifts from being that of the spectral to being that of the spectacle" ("Culture" 50); she is partly suggesting that Ondaatje exploits the immigrants of *In the Skin of a Lion* by representing them from a comparatively privileged perspective. Although Kamboureli is not writing about spectrality in the context of the paranormal, her remark can apply to *The Collected Works of Billy the Kid*. "Spectral" and "spectatorial," Billy is a ghost whose invisibility allows him to watch the same people who watched him while he was alive. Ultimately, celebrity, sexuality, and the uncanny are concepts that help us to realize the extent both of Ondaatje's willingness to imagine experiences of alterity and his empathy for people who live and die without fully accommodating oppressive social norms.[5]

Ondaatje's interest in the mitigation of celebrity's consequences is related to his interest in celebrity's alternatives. It is arguable that he thinks of celebrity as a transition into a related form of recognition, such as legend, which might preserve someone's recognition after celebrity has passed. Although he sometimes uses the term *fame*, Ondaatje is not writing about that when he writes about people such as Billy. In *The Collected Works of Billy the Kid*, the only terms used to describe how Billy is recognized are "legendary" and "legend" (82, 97). A legend is an "unauthentic" story "popularly regarded as historical" (*OED*); it is rarely based on enough information to be treated as history by historians. Ondaatje has said that he is drawn to "unfinished stories" (qtd. in Witten 10). He is drawn, in fact, to characters who became legends after many of the details of their lives were lost to time. Ondaatje often writes about stardom – about burnouts, comebacks, and sudden fade-outs – yet that is not the status that he would seem to want for his characters. Whereas celebrity seems to promise access to every detail of the lives of the stars that audiences covet, legend refuses such access; it prefers a certain obscurity.

Billy's legend is based on the historical fragments of his celebrity and the missing pieces of his biography. *The Collected Works of Billy the Kid* contains many kinds of texts, which all contribute to the impression of a collection of found documents that can only partially represent Billy's history despite the inclusion of supposedly autobiographical poems. Interviews with people who knew him and photographs of them, an excerpt and illustration from the "comic book legend" (as described in the book's credits) of *Billy the Kid and the Princess*, an "EXCLUSIVE JAIL INTERVIEW" promising that "THE KID TELLS ALL" (81) – these texts are more a part of the popular media than they are staid historical documents; indeed, as Dennis Cooley convincingly argues, even Billy's way of seeing is photographic (217) and cinematic (223).[6] Ondaatje's book has the gossipy flair of movies and tabloids (even stardom in general), but it also conveys a sense of having failed to provide a total picture of Billy; this incompleteness is conducive to legend – and a legend, like a ghost, is never fully there.

Perhaps Billy's legend saves him from celebrity – as one of the blurbs on the back cover of the 1970 edition suggests in claiming that, in writing the book, Ondaatje saves Billy from "superficial pop immortality." Ondaatje gives him "immortality" of the supernatural kind to complement his status as an icon of "pop" culture. In the first poem of the book, a list of "the killed" (n.p.) refers to Billy's death even though he is speaking the poem. Claiming to have killed twenty people, Billy also names those who have been killed or maimed by his enemies:

> Charlie, Tom O'Folliard
> Angela D's split arm,
>   and Pat Garrett
> sliced off my head.
> Blood a necklace on me all my life. (n.p.)

The extreme indentation on the line that names "Pat Garrett" helps to make the next line startling by forcing the reader's eyes to "slice" left. Readers who already know the legend might also be startled to see Garrett – Billy's nemesis – on a list of those killed by Billy's enemies. Furthermore, these lines reveal that Billy is either already dead or might be able to predict how he will die. If he is not dead and can predict the future, then he is a prophet; if he is an accurate prophet, then he will soon be dead anyway – and evidence suggests that he is *not* accurate, because Garrett kills him by gunfire and not decapitation. Adding to these uncertainties is the later suggestion that Garrett "killed the wrong man" (103), but Billy's immortality is not likely the result of having escaped or faked his death. If he is dead but conscious and able to compose poems, then we might assume that he has the immortality of a ghost.

Asked in his "EXCLUSIVE JAIL INTERVIEW" about what happens after death, Billy says, "There'll be nothing else. The only thing I wish is that I could hear what people say afterwards. I'd really like that. You know, I'd like to be invisible watching what happens to people when I am not around" (83). Although he does not seem to expect to have a ghost's life after death, he seems to want one, not for religious reasons, but mainly to "watch" events and to "hear what people say" after he dies. Later in the interview, he is asked a related question: "do you think you will last in people's memories?" He answers, "I'll be with the world till she dies" (84). He wants to hear what people say about him; he expects to be remembered until the end of the "world" – these desires are associated with his state of recognition. Because he thinks that "[t]here'll be nothing else" after death, he cannot expect to become a ghost, but he can expect to be immortalized some other way: he expects to be famous, maybe legendary – known, as he says, throughout the world. His declaration about wanting to be invisible suggests, however, that he dislikes the visibility associated with a life of celebrity and having "Wanted" signs posted everywhere; his ghostliness is a symbol of his posthumous legend.

Although he does not expect his desire "to be invisible" to be satisfied, Billy is introduced to us as an invisible man: the first page of the book shows an empty square that represents "a picture [or a photograph, to be precise] of Billy" (n.p.). Because the title of the book suggests that Billy is the author of at least some of the "collected works," Ondaatje implies that Billy is trying to influence how readers will see him; the blank photograph reveals Billy as he would like to be shown: as a ghost.[7] In this initial instance of Billy's representation, Ondaatje suggests that Billy wants *not* to be shown – or known – except in the poems that he has supposedly written; he wants, especially, not to be shot by the camera, that crucial and gun-like tool of celebrity.[8]

The blank photograph is a significant challenge to its viewers; it encourages them to "see" Billy in their imaginations and to "shoot" him with their gaze. In his seminars on psychoanalysis, Jacques Lacan talks about the gaze as an awareness of "the presence of others" (84) who might be looking at the subject; it is, in that sense, social – not only a function of the eye (74). As the "underside of consciousness" (Lacan, *Four* 83), the gaze consists of the subject's nascent awareness of being a viewer and being viewed. When the gaze is returned, it is returned, at least in part, by the viewer looking at himself or herself.[9] Like Billy, the viewer tries "to adapt" to the gaze by "vanishing" (Lacan, *Four* 83), by trying to avoid being the object of someone else's desire. Lacan seems to associate this desire with death, as in his example of Hans Holbein's *The Ambassadors* (1533) – a double portrait and a type of *trompe l'oeil* now famous for also depicting an unrecognizable object that, when the viewer looks at the painting from its left and from above, takes the shape of a human skull in its normal proportions. Perhaps the uncanniness of the blank photograph of Billy, however, derives less from psychoanalytic relationships and more from the possibility that the image "captures" a ghost looking back at us. We should therefore be cognizant of our potential (though fictional) complicity in his fatal stardom and should consider who else is involved in scrutinizing Billy and telling his story – and what it means for him to run from us and them. He is confronted with a paradox of celebrity: in avoiding the gaze and its social implications, he dies, but in being "shot" by the gaze, he also dies.

Billy does not actually succeed in avoiding social implications; he is represented by several people (his society) in the book, and he thereby he avoids being monologically fixed by a single voice – even his own or that of Ondaatje, whose inclusion of *Billy the Kid and the Princess* proves that he is willing to invite other voices into his work. Ondaatje functions as the editor as much as the author of *The Collected Works of Billy the Kid*. He is also to some extent a handler who manages Billy's publicity. His decision to include other voices in a book supposedly authored only by Billy is necessary for his representation of Billy's celebrity; he needs them to show the tensions between Billy's privacy and his public. The implied editor includes prominent accounts about Billy by Paulita Maxwell (29, 96), Sallie Chisum (52, 87, 89), and to a lesser extent Sallie's husband, John, who tells the story of Livingstone's alcoholic dogs (59–62); these accounts are introduced with their names and establish Billy's social network.

Among the others in Billy's society, Garrett is special. Unlike the previous examples, the prose works of Pat Garrett (42–5, 86, 90) are not introduced by name, except in his first piece, which begins by announcing "MISTUH ... PATRICK ... GARRETT!!!" (42). The fanfare of this introduction is never repeated; subsequently, Billy's voice occasionally seems to become Garrett's, and vice versa, without remark, as if the editor included Garrett's views and then Billy unauthorized them (stripped them of their name) posthumously. For reasons I will soon consider, either Billy or the editor is interested in relegating Garrett to anonymity after what might be called his highly acclaimed, or exclaimed ("!!!"), initial appearance.

Now, however, I would like to suggest only that the editor manages not only Billy's visibility but also that of the other authorial figures in the text. The voice of the editor himself, for instance, seems to appear first in parentheses on p. 88 of the Anansi edition, and then without remark on pp. 92–3, 97, and 105. Together Billy and the editor (and to a lesser extent, Garrett) monitor Billy's polyphonic representation, haunting the collection as only authors can.

The significance of Billy's ghostliness in relation to his celebrity cannot be understood except through his relationship with Garrett. Prior to Garrett's first narration, he is introduced to readers by either Billy or the editor – probably the editor, given the seemingly editorial inclusion of Paulita Maxwell's first recollection (29). Garrett is described as an "ideal assassin. Public figure" (28), which immediately implies a connection between "assassin[ation]" and the "[p]ublic." Assassinations are secretive plots until they are executed, and they are not normally undertaken by sheriffs such as Garrett, but Garrett's pursuit of Billy is no secret. It is even sensational. The vaudevillian announcement of "MISTUH ... PATRICK ... GARRETT" reinforces this argument about him: he is the most direct symbol of the public's jurisdiction over stardom. Accordingly, Lee Spinks states that Garrett's "remorseless subordination of private feeling to public action makes a social virtue out of the most pathological behaviour" (73). The "social virtue" of murdering Billy, however, is also a betrayal of friendship, and that betrayal is one reason why Garrett has been "unauthorized," as I suggested earlier, by Billy or the editor. Readers can plausibly interpret Garrett as Billy's "unauthorized" biographer: the man whose control over Billy's life and death is inextricably associated with publicizing them.

Unlike Billy, Garrett knows how to live in public, how to maintain the necessary detachment from it. Billy, however, represents the private life of the star. Although the editor and Garrett offer substantial insights into Garrett's way of thinking, readers have no access to the most intimate aspects of Garrett's private life, such as his marriage: when his wife died, "[w]hat happened in Garrett's mind no one knows" (29). Conversely, Billy's thoughts are constantly on display in his poems, which Ondaatje once referred to as Billy's "mental shorthand" (qtd. in Solecki, *Ragas* 188). Because of Billy's notoriety – "I'd of course heard of him" (42–3), Garrett says – for much of the book Billy is running from the law and trying to avoid detection. He seems to want privacy; in one scene, he is relieved to stay in a barn "for a week," alone except for animals and insects that do not bother him: "The fly who sat on my arm, after his inquiry, just went away, ate his disease and kept it in him" (17). These descriptions show that Billy sometimes wants privacy over publicity; Ondaatje might also mean to imply that Billy, as a fictional poet, would not have been enthusiastic about publishing his "mental shorthand" in *The Collected Works*; his reluctance might account for the fictional editor's inclusion of other texts to supplement Billy's poems – a possibility that suggests that the editor and Billy might not be working together without disagreeing about how much to expose him.

What I have been suggesting so far is that Billy haunts the text in a posthumous attempt to manage his representation and his reputation; his tense negotiation between what can be made public and what should be kept private was, when he was alive, one reason for his conflict with Garrett. Their conflict begins almost immediately in the book with descriptions of how Garrett kills Tom O'Folliard and Charlie Bowdre in his pursuit of Billy. At the end of the chronology, he kills Billy in a dark room without giving Billy a chance to draw a gun. In the narrative, however, Billy does have a chance to confront Garrett: he responds to "MISTUH" Garrett's first and only authorized narration, the one that describes how Garrett met Billy and came to admire him. In that scene, Garrett's appreciation for him grows when Billy, at Sallie's request, pinpoints the exact location of a sick cat hiding under the floorboards and kills it with two quick gunshots. Garrett says, "I had a look I suppose of incredible admiration for him" (45); Angie appeared "terrified" (45). By countering some of the rumours about Billy's occasionally "cruel" disposition by also mentioning that he is "witty" and "charming" (43), Garrett presents himself as someone who is both attracted to Billy and a fair judge of Billy's character.

Perhaps the impression of Garrett's fairness and Angie's reaction bother Billy enough that he would want to object to them with a competing narrative. His response – a short, uncanny account on the following page – makes half an argument about Garrett, not Billy, taking cruel pleasure in killing. It is only half an argument because Billy's response initially seems strangely pointless; it merely describes (twice on the same page, with only a slight variation) a dog, Garrett, and two of Garrett's friends approaching the house where Billy is.

> Down the street was a dog. Some mut spaniel, black and white.
> One dog, Garrett and two friends, stud looking, came down
> the street to the house, to me.
>
> Again.
> Down the street was a dog. Some mut spaniel, black and white.
> One dog, Garrett and two friends came down the street to the
> house, to me. (46)

Later in the book, however, readers might notice *again* the "the dog" and Garrett with his two friends, "deputies Poe and Mackinnon" (92), approaching a house. The scene is described more fully this time: the house is Pete Maxwell's, and Garrett will enter it to murder Billy in the dark. The dogs and the two friends are the details that link these separate accounts of the same event. In the first account – Billy's response to Garrett's appraisal of him – Garrett "smiles" and "[t]he others laugh" when he enters the house, gun in hand. Rather cryptically, Billy adds, "All this I would have seen if I was on the roof looking" (46). Because he was not on the roof, his vision of the moments before his death is strange. Cooley argues that Billy has taken "the camera's position" (225) and that the repetitions are the "takes" in his film. The repetition is also a moment of repression: Billy omits "stud looking" from the second description, as if he wanted either to retract a compliment paid to the men who hunted him (i.e., they look like "stud[s]"), or to erase the suggestion that they were coming to him for sex (i.e., *he* is the "stud"). I agree with Cooley that Billy has appropriated the perspective of the technology that helps to produce stardom, but my interpretation emphasizes perspective over technology: Billy is a ghost who has risen out of his body (above "the roof") for a new vantage point.

Who gets the power of "looking," and then telling, is the question. Because Billy is the underdog in his conflict with Garrett, his statements about his power of sight can be interpreted as hypothetical: "All this I would have seen *if* I was on the roof looking" (my emphasis), though in this case I think that he means he was not on the roof and saw "[a]ll this" because he has a ghost's floating perspective. In a similarly hypothetical statement earlier in the book, Billy ruminates on what he would "say" "if [he] had a newsman's brain" (11). Other critics have argued that either he does (Lee 170) or does not (Barbour 47) have such a brain, but this debate seems to assume that Billy cannot change or learn; obviously, his ability to rely on his senses fails when Garrett murders him in the dark, and so, as a ghost, he learns how to *see* as if he had "a newsman's brain"; such detached sight might help him. Billy might benefit from trading places with journalists rather than remaining the object of their star-making gaze. When he begins to apply his newly acquired clairvoyance and objectifying power to the process of reinterpreting and representing his past, he imagines "[his] eyes / magnifying the bones across a room / shifting in a wrist" (39). He seems to combine this power of sight with an ability to "feel" (8) that Garrett, in his perpetually drunken state (28–9), could probably not match. In such passages, Billy reveals that he is learning to integrate his past life of the body with his ability to see as a disembodied ghost sees. Although Garrett does not have such insight, he does have an analogous detachment, "the ability to kill someone on the street walk back and finish a joke" (28), an aptitude for "study[ing]" (43) and "theoriz[ing]" (44), a clinical objectivity akin to that of a "newsman," and a related authority for telling stories.

Perhaps, however, as Billy acquires Garrett's "brain," he fuses their strengths to his own advantage. An important example of this fusion is in the second narration of Billy's death; this is the aforementioned third-person narration on p. 92 that names the "deputies Poe and Mackinnon" and specifies that the house is Maxwell's. The narrator initially appears to be neither Billy nor Garrett, because both are mentioned: "On some vague tip Garrett has come to ask Maxwell where he thinks Billy is hiding out" (92). Unlike the first version of the story, in which Billy makes Garrett appear cruel when he "smiles" in anticipation of the murder, in this second version Garrett discovers Billy by accident. He only knows that Billy is with him in the dark room because he "recognizes the voice" (92) when Billy, not suspecting Garrett's presence, asks Maxwell in Spanish about the identities of the men outside. Actually, it is the identities of Billy and Garrett that become uncertain. Readers might have difficulty in "recogniz[ing] the voice" of the narrator in this passage. The narrator's claim that he has written "a diagram" (92) of the scene indicates the "academic" (28) voice of Garrett; however, the strange "MMMmmmmmm" (92) that introduces the narration indicates the voice of Billy, because in an earlier poem Billy wrote "MMMMMMMM mm" to represent the characteristically sensual sound of his own "thinking" (11). The styles of the two men seem to add up – and in an uncanny coincidence in the arrangement of the death scenes, p. 92 is exactly the double of p. 46 in its page numbers: 46 × 2 = 92.[10] Corroborating Ian Rae, who argues that Billy gets revenge on Garrett "by absorbing Garrett's voice and narrative strategies" (115), I contend that the second narrative of the death scene is narrated by a fused Billy-Garrett, whom we might also think of as Garrett possessed by the ghost of Billy, who has returned from the scene of his future murder to ensure that Garrett, alone, does not have the privilege of the last word.

The darkness of the room where the murder occurs helps to make this fusion possible; it also hides – ineffectively – Billy's ambiguous sexuality. Nicholas Royle, in his analysis of Freud's essay on "The Uncanny" (1919), reminds us that "[r]epeatedly [Freud] evokes the uncanniness of moving about in the dark" (108); the effect of darkness on vision is uncanny because it both frightens and raises questions about what cannot be seen – in particular, about sexuality and identity. Cooley observes that, earlier in the narrative, Sallie put Billy in a dark room to protect him from the sun (214–15); on the occasion of Billy's death, "the dark room" (92) seems to be safe, but it becomes a place for questions that precede violence: Garrett enters the room to awaken Pete Maxwell and ask him about Billy's whereabouts; Billy enters the room to ask Maxwell about the two men outside, whereupon Garrett shoots Billy. The darkness partly accounts for Billy's confusion about what killed him (in his list of "the killed," earlier); it makes both Garrett and Billy into ghostly, invisible presences; and it also insinuates a very worldly, sordid affair. In Maxwell's bed, Garrett's gun is a phallic symbol. By shooting Billy, he symbolically penetrates him sexually, uniting them. The public and private come together in the dark room, but not equally; Billy, who elsewhere seems to possess Garrett, is ultimately killed for not entirely abiding by the other's norms.

The dark room in *The Collected Works of Billy the Kid* has its symbolic counterpoint in the book's "white rooms" (69) (which echo, differently, in *Coming through Slaughter*). No one would be surprised to realize that the homosexual implications of "the dark room" are negative in connotation, given the heterosexual imperative of cowboy culture. Thus, "the white rooms of Texas after a bad night must be like heaven" (69). Billy associates the "bad night" (69, 71; see also 105) with alcohol sickness (69) and with his memory of being captured by Garrett (he later escaped) long before Garrett found him again and killed him. On that earlier occasion, Garrett was transporting his prisoner to trial and decided to stop for a night at a hotel. Billy was at this point unable to walk "after the week on horses" and after his sunstroke, so he was carried into the hotel, where he would "share a room with Garrett and Emory" (79). Billy describes what Garrett said to him:

> Your last good bed Billy, he said, pick your position. I did, face and stomach down. He chained me to the bed. He taped my fingers so thick I couldnt get them through a trigger guard even if they gave me a gun. (79)

Billy nostalgically calls this his "last white room" (79), which is a comfortable place compared to where he has been and where he is going. It continues to imply the "heaven" he mentioned on p. 69. When offered a choice (however ironic it is), he takes the most sexually submissive "position" that a man can choose, re-enacting the passivity that he demonstrated in the earlier sex scene with Angie. His "taped ... fingers" mean that he cannot wield his "gun," a remarkable repetition of when his "fingers [were] paralysed" by Angie's vaginal secretions and he became "a crippled witch" (16): in neither case can he use his penis, nor does he have the "fingers" to use the gun that might symbolize his penis. Because the "white room" is a pleasant contrast to the disturbed safety of "the dark room," which is associated symbolically with the "bad night[s]," Billy might be suggesting that he wants his sexuality to come out of the "dark" – though he might instead be attempting to reverse Garrett's ridicule and to mock Garrett's sexuality. When Douglas Barbour indirectly supported my earlier argument by stating that Billy is outside the "law" of mortality (42), he could also have mentioned that Billy is also outside the "law" of masculinity that Garrett must enforce – and in contempt of the public's normative and perhaps hypocritical assumptions about male stars.

The question of who and what are exposed by Garrett's killing of Billy continues to preoccupy me. Initially, having noticed what Denisoff calls the "numerous descriptions" that confirm "[t]he homoerotic potential of a predominantly male society" (53), I assumed that Billy was a gay cowboy whose sex with women in the book was not an authentic sign of his desire; the homoerotic symbolism overwhelmed the literal descriptions. Denisoff also argues that no one should interpret the book's "decentring of heteronormative sexuality ... as the dominance of one version of social interaction over another or others" (63). This further argument remains in partial contrast with mine. The public dominates Billy's life as a celebrity; in the privacy of death and invisibility, Billy gains some power. Garrett, as the representative of the public, is not acting to expose Billy, but he *is* acting to eliminate the star who could draw attention to their homosocial desire. Among other possible motives, he kills Billy because ambiguous sexuality contravenes the "law" of compulsory heterosexuality among men in the Wild West. Garrett thereby keeps a secret of cowboy culture; in fact, he protects his own privacy.

My argument about Billy and Garrett fusing in a symbolic and punitive homosexual union indirectly corroborates other critics who have already shown how Billy and Garrett have close similarities and important differences. In the postscript to one of his essays in *Spider Blues* (1985), Stephen Scobie reflects on criticism that developed after his essay was initially published and argues that "to pass over the differences between Billy and Garrett is seriously to distort the book that Ondaatje actually wrote" (209). Although Barbour disagrees with Scobie on other issues, here he takes a similar position, arguing that too many critics assume that *The Collected Works of Billy the Kid* is "a form of realism" in which Billy and Garrett are "alike" (46). He states that the two characters are "complementary" and "necessary to each other [but] they are not inseparable" (Barbour 46). My argument is obviously not based in "realism," nor does it "pass over the differences," but it does propose that they become "inseparable." Billy is Garrett's "mirror image" (Nodelman 76) – both identical and opposite. They are drawn together in much the same way that opposing aspects of metaphor can approach each other and fuse; they are symbols of a metaphor's component parts, and they indicate Ondaatje's interest in metaphors of identity crisis as they are involved in identity politics. Writing about related issues, David Punter argues that "[m]etaphor is a crucial way in which we can apprehend the quality of the uncanny, considered as the process which establishes the inseparability of the familiar and the unfamiliar" (87). The uncanniness of Billy and Garrett involves their fusion, the confusion of *public* and *private*, and the resulting conflict of the values involved.

Billy is fascinated with symmetry, such as the hetero/homo relationship, and his associated social anxiety is even reflected in his poetic forms, which are in some cases uncannily symmetrical, repetitive, or temporally non-linear in their depiction of authorial sight and insight. My quotation of Billy's initial description of the moments before his death has already shown that he repeats himself ("Again"), partly because he needs to reassert and reiterate his narrative authority in his contest with Garrett. In other cases, the symmetry foreshadows the fusion of Billy and Garrett in the death scene, as in Billy's line-by-line palindrome about the death of Charlie Bowdre:

> His stomach was warm
> remembered this when I put my hand into
> a pot of luke warm tea to wash it out
> dragging out the stomach to get the bullet
> he wanted to see when taking tea
> with Sallie Chisum in Paris Texas
>
> With Sallie Chisum in Paris Texas
> he wanted to see when taking tea
> dragging out the stomach to get the bullet
> a pot of luke warm tea to wash it out
> remembered this when I put my hand into
> his stomach was warm (27)

In this palindrome (or poem-sized chiasmus), when Billy washes "a pot of luke warm tea" at Sallie Chisum's, he remembers the feeling of putting his hand in his fatally wounded friend's stomach "to get the bullet." Even more than the typically uncanny juxtaposition of the gruesome and the quotidian, the symmetrical form of Billy's poem simulates the uncanniness of this mnemonic association. The second stanza, in its backward progression to what we have already seen, produces a feeling of *déjà vu*. We usually think of *déjà vu* as the weird feeling of having seen something before, but perhaps even more disquieting is the possibility that what is *déjà vu* might also be an image of what will come, or the return of the repressed. Billy, revisiting his past as a ghost, has insight into the future in which he, too, dies from a gunshot wound. His fusion with Garrett is foreshadowed, even foretold, in this symmetrical poem: as Garrett did with a bullet, Billy reaches into another man's body, enacting a fantasy or confronting a fear of being penetrated; Billy seems to be unconsciously and compulsively suggesting – this scene is reflected on p. 48 in the Anansi edition – that bodily intimacy between men has deadly consequences in a heteronormative society.

Billy's self-reflective poem about Charlie is the first of two symmetrical poems in his *Collected Works*; in the second, the perspective changes and the symmetry is less exact – it is partly symmetrical and partly repetitive – but it is nevertheless another case of ghostly *déjà vu*. Royle tentatively argues that in addition to its usual meanings, *déjà vu* is "to be oneself *already seen*, watched (over)" (183). If he is trying to imply that the feeling of *déjà vu* is akin to the paranoia of being watched, then this new approach to *déjà vu* applies directly to my study of Ondaatje's representations of celebrity. If Billy is paranoid about being watched, he is probably justified, because his experiences of being exposed to the eyes of others tend to be painful or deadly. In the second (partly) symmetrical poem – what Royle might call the "ghost or double" (183) of the first – other narrators ("We" and "I") observe Billy's corpse after he has been shot. They are busy "clean[ing] him up" (104). Because of their higher perspective and their sense of responsibility for him – however insincere it is – they are "watch[ing] (over)" him. Significantly, their view of him coincides with his inability to see now that he is dead:

> Poor young William's dead
> with a fish stare, with a giggle
> with blood planets in his head.
> ....
> Poor young William's dead
> with blood planets in his head
> with a fish stare, with a giggle
> like he said. (104)

The narrators who refer to themselves in the lines between these ones (which begin and end the poem) could be any combination of Garrett, Poe, Mackinnon, Maxwell, and Celsa Guitterrez, who are all mentioned nearby on pp. 92–3. The imperfect symmetry of their poem might be the best that they can accomplish because they are too heterogeneous and too public to speak in a singular private voice like that of Billy the Kid. They represent the public because they "sold" the bullets – taken from Billy's corpse, I presume – "to the Texas Star" (13), where the newsmen "took pictures with a camera" (15). In contrast, Billy can write a perfectly symmetrical poem in a private moment of recollection.

The uncanny poems in *The Collected Works of Billy the Kid* give it a sense of double time as much as they give Billy what Rae calls a “double life” (107); we, as readers, get the story of his life and death superimposed with the story of his afterlife. Nevertheless, the other, partial reflections of scenes in the book suggest that Billy’s paranoia has driven him beyond doubleness to break the narrative into fragments that *we* have “already seen” (Royle 183); these fragments of symmetry help him to avoid being “fixed” (Barbour 42) or focused on by our gaze, which is complicit with that of Garrett – assuming that we as readers have also hunted for Billy, hoping to see (instead of a ghost) a man who escaped a photograph.

By manipulating the images, narrative, and the structure of poems in *The Collected Works of Billy the Kid* to produce uncanny effects, Ondaatje compels us to question the values that are most familiar to our society, such as heterosexuality. He also prompts us to reconsider the wisdom of allowing our private lives to become public, given that the public tends to be hostile to sexual ambiguity. The public seems to encourage paranoia about difference; even when Billy escaped scrutiny through death, “they buried him in leg irons” (97), still fearing him. He haunts his book to imply that celebrity dominates people and enforces problematic codes of conduct related to sexuality. Billy’s privacy is sacrificed to his public when his symmetrical relationship with Garrett becomes one of fusion equated with death; however, Ondaatje leaves the facts of Billy’s life open to question and open to legend. To save Billy from the law and from the “superficial pop immortality” of celebrity – which by definition would be too brief to be immortality anyway – Ondaatje assembles a collection of poetic texts that are not intended to produce Billy’s complete picture. Instead, they sustain the conditions that brought Billy through celebrity and into the “jungle sleep” (97) of legend – a death from which Billy might awaken into a more complex and secular immortality.

8 "A Razor in the Body": Ondaatje's *Rat Jelly* and *Secular Love*

Michael Ondaatje's interest in writing about the experience of being in a body might at first seem incompatible with his interest in celebrity, which partly depends on images that are less and less dependent on real bodies for their production.[1] In the previous chapter, however, we saw that Billy the Kid's stardom has little support from images,[2] and he is arguably very aware of his body and what he can and cannot do with it. He is a highly physical character, one who understands his world through the senses to such an extent that Lee Spinks has commented on Billy's "pre-personal mode" (74) of sensing, meaning that Billy perceives without much subjective involvement of his conscious mind. Ondaatje's representations of celebrity in *Rat Jelly* (1973) and the following decade are similarly phenomenological. Although they are concerned with the gaze, his representations are focused less on images than on celebrity's involvement in at least partially embodied conditions such as race, addiction, and insanity. He also implies, however, that stardom's effects on bodies can be understood as experiences of manifest and problematic social norms. Concerned with the interface of inner and outer worlds, in *Secular Love* (1984) Ondaatje allows his representations of celebrity to become more lyrical, even autobiographical, and his private persona comes forward, reflecting on his visibility, skin, size, vanity, and desire. Concerned phenomenologically with subjectivity, Ondaatje focuses on the harmful effects of publicity on the bodies of stars.

Ondaatje's own celebrity began shortly after *Leonard Cohen* (1970) with *The Collected Works of Billy the Kid* (1970) – two books that show that he had been thinking about careers and stardom. Until 1970, his publications were "known only to the few people who kept up with the Canadian poetry scene" (Jewinski 77). His book about Billy the Kid increased his recognition to the national level: "Ondaatje, who hated being in the public eye, suddenly could not seem to keep out of the newspapers" (Jewinski 82) – especially in 1973 when he was often in the *Globe and Mail* (see Table 3). The back cover blurb for its 2003 edition relates a now-familiar story about the book's reception: "When Michael Ondaatje won the Governor General's Award for Poetry in 1970 for [the book], [former] Prime Minister John Diefenbaker was publicly outraged ... and stated that it wasn't even about a Canadian."[3] Despite the book's American content, Ondaatje's celebrity remained "merely a Canadian affair" (Jewinski 130) after he won the award (until his international success with *The English Patient* in the 1990s), and he considered himself only "semi-known" (qtd. in York, *Literary* 129). His first experience of celebrity brought him to a national but not international level of recognition.

By the time of *Rat Jelly* in 1973, then, Ondaatje was visible enough in the media to be a national celebrity. He also seemed to be learning to accept his own public visibility, just as he had learned to accept "the poet as a public person" (qtd. in Sullivan 288) when he saw and heard Gwendolyn MacEwen read in 1972. In *The Collected Works of Billy the Kid*, the author's photograph is not much bigger than a postage stamp and shows Ondaatje (though he is not named) dressed as a cowboy when he was a child (Jewinski 67). In contrast, the back cover of *Rat Jelly* features a photographic portrait of Ondaatje that is almost half a page in height. The blurb states that he is so talented that the "power source [of his poems] is almost invisible." Calling Ondaatje's power "almost invisible" adds to his mystique, but some of his readers would know that part of the "power" of *Rat Jelly* is the star power that Ondaatje generated with *The Collected Works of Billy the Kid*. With his photograph on *Rat Jelly*, he distances himself from the pretence of his own invisibility, but in his poems he continues to imply that stars need to retreat from celebrity and the public without becoming images.

Ondaatje's work after 1970 is occasionally less subtle in its self-promotion but also more direct in appraising celebrity, often from the perspective of the fan; accordingly, *Rat Jelly* is the first of Ondaatje's creative publications to name *fame* and *celebrity* as forms of recognition that interest him in addition to *legend*. The opening section in *Rat Jelly* (entitled "Families") contains significant contributions from speakers who seem to be fans in imaginary dialogues with celebrities. Because of my detailed interpretations of *The Collected Works of Billy the Kid* in the previous chapter and of other individual poems that are obviously about stardom, this chapter has little room for thorough analyses of the topical but less symbolically interesting poems in *Rat Jelly*, though I will mention them: "War Machine," which seems to be from the perspective of a fan or a has-been celebrity who refers to "30 jayne mansfield stories" and "stories too bout vivien leigh princess margaret / frank sinatra the night he beat up mia farrow" (11); "Letter to Ann Landers," which suggests that people who think constantly about celebrities might not be emotionally secure or altogether rational; and "Postcard from Piccadilly Street," which describes the speaker having sex with someone while their dog "jumps on the bed and watches" – a practice of inviting voyeurism that encourages them to "open the curtains," shut the light, "and imagine the tree outside / full of sparrows / with infra red eyes" (19). Ondaatje was imagining celebrity from the perspective of symbolic fans, thereby reflecting indirectly on being the public, which is the other half of the role that he adopted by grandstanding as Billy the Kid (and, in 1976, as Buddy Bolden in *Coming through Slaughter*).

The poem that ends the "Families" section in *Rat Jelly* echoes throughout Ondaatje's work; "Letters & Other Worlds" is an autobiographical elegy about an alcoholic father, whose compulsion to drink was related – at least in this poem – to his celebrity. The poem introduces Ondaatje's private persona, which is evident in his reference to events that correspond with Ondaatje's biography and national heritage. Significantly, at the moment when Ondaatje's work becomes much more autobiographical, it also begins to suggest that stardom is a double bind that cannot be resolved by someone who seems unconsciously to encourage and even need it – as if it were an addiction, a complication of the body. "Letters & Other Worlds" also implicates Ondaatje's ethnicity in his own celebrity by describing the father's alcoholism as a response to an invasion of privacy, which – in a vicious cycle – occurred partly because his alcoholic behaviour was a public disturbance that led the public to notice his ethnic difference. In this context, even a minor degree of stardom draws attention to the embodied aspects of race and addiction, which Ondaatje also understands as social problems.

The speaker of "Letters & Other Worlds" explains that "two bottles of gin" (24) helped an aneurysm to kill his father, and he then tells some of the stories about what happened while his father was alive. In a scene that echoes in *Running in the Family* (1982), the speaker's father gained "instant fame" in Ceylon simply "by falling / dead drunk onto the street" (24) and stopping a ceremonial procession in a national religious festival. If fame is both "instant" and likely to pass quickly, it is more accurately described as celebrity (Rojek 9). The only unusual aspect of this alcoholism is that it is not a result of someone trying to forget the stress of celebrity; instead, it is one of the reasons the father becomes a celebrity, and, being located in the body more so than in society, it focuses blame on the private self. In this poem, celebrity is the result of his involving himself in public events such as "ceremonial procession[s]" and drawing attention to his status as an outsider at events of national and religious significance.

Ondaatje's private persona implies that his father's alcoholism and resulting celebrity have domestic and even national repercussions. The poem initially jokes that the speaker's father's "instant fame" was the "turning point" that "led to Ceylon's independence in 1948" – as when his father appears again in "the papers," drunk but described as "broken hearted" (25), and his mother insists that the editors print a correction. These jokes might distract readers from the implied divorce of his parents after their "14 years of marriage" (25); 1948 was also the year that Ondaatje's parents separated (Barbour 2). In the poem, the implied divorce is allegorical: Ceylon's "independence," its rejection of the "semi-official" and "semi-white" (25) colonial government that his father partly represents, is also a divorce. Indirectly, therefore, Ondaatje assigns responsibility for both domestic and national break-ups to his father's celebrity and, parenthetically, to his mother's:

> (My mother had done her share too –
> her driving so bad
> she was stoned by villagers
> whenever her car was recognized) (25)

In both the literal and figurative senses of this divorce, celebrity exacerbates the reasons – such as nationalism or racism – that motivate people to separate from each other.

The private persona describes this separation in "Letters & Other Worlds" as his father's increasing physical and emotional isolation, which was motivated in part by fear. Initially, the speaker says, "My father's body was a globe of fear" (24). Shortly thereafter, he says, "My father's body was a town of fear" (24). Eventually, his father is hiding in "a room" (24, 26) where he stayed "until he was drunk / and until he was sober" (26). The progression from "globe" to "town" to "room" implies that his father increasingly withdrew from society (not that the fear was shrinking) into the relative privacy of his own "body."[4] This withdrawal into solitude appears to have been voluntary but under psychological duress: he had "edged / into the terrible acute hatred of his own privacy" (26). As in *The Collected Works of Billy the Kid* and "Postcard from Piccadilly Street," the pleasures of privacy are destroyed by the fear of threats from outside: in this case, the danger of embarrassing the family in public and of being known as an outsider. He might also have been afraid of revealing a secret; the speaker claims that "[his father] hid that he had been where we were going" (24). The semblance of clairvoyance or prophecy here is the wisdom of having already imagined the downfall of his family. Having felt isolated or separated as a "semi-white" person in a South Asian country, he did not want to spoil the joy of life by predicting that his family or his nation would also separate. His letters to his family had "the most complete empathy" (26) and ignored his emotional turmoil because he wanted to spare them his pain. This flawed solution shows "the logic of his love" (24) but also the circular logic of self-fulfilling prophecy. His separation from society incites the "hatred of his own privacy" and of his own private self and fearful body; that hatred encourages his alcoholism, which, in turn, helps to cause the separation that he wanted to prevent.

Being a celebrity does not help him; it makes him into a symbol of colonial vices, such as alcoholism, and gives his society a reason to reject him and his "semi-white[ness]." Chris Rojek's argument about celebrity causing a crisis of "identity confusion" because of the "colonization" (11) of the private self by the public applies keenly to Ondaatje's father as he is described, but in his case, his celebrity countercolonizes him to identify him as an outsider and expel him. He seems to hate his own privacy because even in solitude he cannot change the public's attention to national and racial differences that constitute part of his identity.

The next poem in *Rat Jelly* that considers celebrity explicitly is "Heron Rex," which, like "Letters & Other Worlds," also engages in a figurative dialogue with a father-figure – or, more precisely, at least two father-figures: "Mad kings" and their "blood lines" (52). Even more than referring to lineage, these "blood lines" refer to the "introverted" veins that reverse the sanity of "the brain" (52) and cause madness. The difficulty is again, in part, bodily. The potential father of this poem is one of the "kings" in the "heritage of suicides," one of "the ones who went mad / balancing on that goddamn leg" (52). Balancing on one leg is the heron's distinctive way of standing, and balancing (especially on edges) is one of Ondaatje's themes. This image also seems to refer to Layton's "Whatever Else Poetry Is Freedom" (1958) and its poet, who assesses whether he is a mad "fool," compares himself to "King Canute," and "balance[s] on wooden stilts and dance[s]" (7). The poet in "Heron Rex," however, is not "proud" of the kings who succeed in the physical feat of balancing, possibly because he knows of bodily consequences to performances related to celebrity; instead, he or she is proud of those "whose eyes turned off / the sun and imagined it" (52).[5] The mention of "suicides" and "sacrifice" (53) also reminds me of Ondaatje's preoccupation with the figure of the saint in *Leonard Cohen* and suggests that the heron itself is a religious symbol. Regardless of whether Ondaatje was imagining Layton and Cohen while writing "Heron Rex," he is invoking some of their symbols of celebrity while developing his phenomenological concern about its ramifications.

Ondaatje seems to prefer Cohen over Layton as a model of celebrity; arguably, Cohen was the better representative of the culture of alienated youth that was significant in supporting celebrity in Canadian poetry in the 1960s and early 1970s. In "Heron Rex," the "suicides" that "they are proud of" are transgressions perpetrated by masochistic, alienated, enslaved, violent, insane people – the same kind of people who interest Cohen. Ondaatje simultaneously insinuates his sympathy for such people and his leadership of them by using the second-person "you," which is sometimes considered an indirect way of saying "I" in the first person:

> [you go mad] when you perfect the mind
> where you sacrifice yourself for the race
> when you are the representative when you allow
> yourself to be paraded in the cages
> celebrity a razor in the body (53)

The book's title – *Rat Jelly* – suggests that the "race" might be the proverbial "rat race" that the 1960s culture of youth resisted, but the "race" is also the lineage of "kings," and it vaguely implicates skin colour, as in "Letters & Other Worlds." Because they are "small birds" (53), they seem to be young kings. To remain willingly the "representative[s]" of this "race" is not to choose wisely. The "kings" ironically become slaves: "you allow / yourself to be paraded in the cages" (another echo of *The Energy of Slaves*). Despite its consequences, some people – typically young people – accept celebrity, even though this acceptance might be suicidal, "a razor in the body." This metaphor is essential to this chapter (and to this book) because it comments secondarily on metaphor itself. The metaphor of celebrity, too, can penetrate the skin, in the sense of its fusing of publicity and privacy, which are ultimately separated by the skin. Injury and madness are potential results. The poem closes with an image of the frailty of these "small birds," these heron kings: like "neon" and "glass," "they are royalty melted down" (53). This meltdown means, in terms of fusion, that the metaphor of celebrity has occurred; the public-private balance has not been maintained, and the culture of youth has been exposed and exploited ("paraded") to the point of its self-destruction.

Public exposure is in contrast with isolation, which seems to remind Ondaatje of the solitude of writing. With "White Dwarfs," Ondaatje concludes *Rat Jelly* with an homage to those "among [his] heroes" "who sail to that perfect edge / where there is no social fuel" (70). Dashiell Hammett is the only writer named as an example here: "And Dashiell Hammett in success / suffered conversation and moved / to the perfect white between the words" (71). The repetition of the word "perfect" implies that the "edge" is associated with "words," further suggesting that the "heroes" are star authors – such as Cohen, Layton, and his letter-writing father. "White Dwarfs" has obvious personal implications. Ondaatje is imagining Hammett, perhaps others, and perhaps himself resorting to "mouthing the silence" (70) after gradually retreating into seclusion and running out of inspiration in the form of "social fuel."

In the earlier poems, Ondaatje honored those whose balance dramatically failed, those who went *over* that "perfect edge," but "White Dwarfs" is different: passing over the edge is done not only with an explosive meltdown but also with a slow cooling. Whiteness reappears in this poem in the interior of the "room [made into] a fridge for Superman" (70). This "white room" is not the "heaven" that it was for Billy, but it is a similarly cool place of relief from the heat of scrutiny.[6] A refrigerator is ideally a cool place of stasis, and the fridge is associated with the white dwarf, a star that is gradually cooling to become a stellar remnant known as a black dwarf ("White Dwarf Star"). The star symbolism in "White Dwarfs" implies, then, that star authors are not always deliberate in retreating into seclusion; sometimes, their stardom cools and their lack of popularity means they are eventually ignored.

The ambition of such authors deserves some of the blame for their need to escape and for the potential overexposure of celebrity. Ondaatje refers to releasing "sandbags / to understand their altitude" (70), as if his star were not yet off the ground and he needed help from a hot-air balloon – though from the balloon he has some heat to counteract the coolness of the "fridge for Superman." The reference to Superman puts Ondaatje's literary heroes in the sky,[7] perhaps with the ambitious *Übermensch* that inspired Layton in his poems about celebrity. This Superman, however, is "burned out" (71): he has "exhaust[ed] costume and bones that could perform flight" (70). Even the "bones" of his supposedly invincible body have been defeated by his stardom; the mention of "costume" and "perform[ance]" also places the writer in the theater of public situations that focus on the persona or the "costume." Because "flight" is not possible now, the writer is trapped on that stage, at least until his evident failure leads him to be ignored.

The ultimate consequence for the writer is not only to be ignored but also to suffer, even to suffer bodily. Although the public temporarily elevated the star author above his peers, their approval and devotion are not without a sense of irony. The public's role in his "success" is torture to the writer, and this torture is implied in the allusion to the crucifixion of Jesus Christ:

> that silence of the third cross
> 3rd man hung so high and lonely
> we dont hear him say
> say his pain, his unbrotherhood (70)

The emphasis on martyrdom and the yearning for brotherhood recalls major themes of Cohen's work from the mid-1960s to the early 1970s; the appearance of Christ in a poem about stars also grimly reflects upon Billy the Kid's excruciating (and tragicomic) description of sunstroke. More stars, the classic symbols of celebrity, conclude "White Dwarfs":

> there are those burned out stars
> who implode into silence
> after parading in the sky
> after such choreography what would they wish to speak of   anyway (71)

This final line recalls the similarly long final line to "Letters & Other Worlds," in which the speaker's father dies, "the blood searching in his head without metaphor" (26). The obvious conclusion to both poems is that a body's death leaves it without any need to express itself further, but the less obvious conclusion is that metaphor itself is the vital force that sustains the body. Here, the final line conveys the speaker's admiration for an ultimately expressive "choreography," which translates from the Greek *khoreia* and *graphia* as the writing of dance (or the dance of writing) and thereby metaphorically refers to literary performances that seem to say everything and thereby satisfy the need for more literature.

However, "parading in the sky" is also akin to being "paraded in the cages" as in "Heron Rex" (and in the parade scenes in *Coming through Slaughter*), but with questionable relief from bodily confinement. The final line expresses both admiration and sympathy for literary celebrities and the various silences and other physical punishments that they both produce and endure. All of these details of the poem – allusions to a patriarchal lineage of celebrity, to performance, and to pop culture, in addition to an ironic religious pretence – make "White Dwarfs" an almost perfect stereotype of representations of literary celebrity, but with the addition of physical imaginings (e.g., bones, torture, dancing) of the bodies of the star authors.

Despite its ambivalent ending, the penultimate stanza in "White Dwarfs" is seemingly positive in general. It proposes that the whiteness of the page and the associated fridge might also preserve a latent fecundity – a subtly sexual inspiration for the long term, as long as privacy and private spaces remain available to the writer:

> This white that can grow
> is fridge, bed,
> is an egg – most beautiful
> when unbroken, where
> what we cannot see is growing
> in all the colours we cannot see (71)

In "White Dwarfs," Ondaatje implies that legendary writers pass through a phase of celebrity that might lead them "to die in the ether peripheries" (70); the isolation related to celebrity in "Letters & Other Worlds" is also a problem in "White Dwarfs," which can end with optimism because of "what ... is growing." Whatever it is, "we cannot see" it, and it is invisible thanks to the "beautiful" and "unbroken" shell of an egg, where a body and its mysteries can develop in a privacy that will never again be so perfect. Stardom is its antithesis.

In this poem and others in *Rat Jelly*, celebrity and isolation are serious concerns that are linked to bodily consequences such as addiction. The fans in the book seek to communicate with celebrities to alleviate their own sorrows; in turn, celebrities sometimes indulge in the performance that seems to open their private lives to the view of the fans. Instead of bringing people together, however, celebrity separates them. In poems such as "Letters & Other Worlds," it provides an excuse that seems to legitimize an audience's rejection of a prominent but unwelcome person, such as Ondaatje's father in Ceylon. The imperial lineage of celebrity in "Heron Rex" has status, but Ondaatje seems to prefer those "whose eyes turned off / the sun and imagined it," as he did by partly rejecting celebrity and choosing to "imagin[e]" it instead. That "sun," becoming a "White Dwarf," casts no vital light; the only recourse that Ondaatje proposes is to be invisible and beyond publicity despite the isolation.

Ondaatje's next book happened to be his first novel, or at least a much more novelistic narrative than *The Collected Works of Billy the Kid*. In 1976, Ondaatje published *Coming through Slaughter* and retained many elements of his poetry despite the change in forms. *Coming through Slaughter* is explicitly concerned with what its narrator calls "the twentieth century game of fame" (136), and as Lorraine York proposes, it is "Ondaatje's definitive treatment of fame the destroyer" (*Literary* 140). Nevertheless, although *Coming through Slaughter* contributed significantly to my thinking about Ondaatje's representations of stardom, and although it is a highly poetic novel, I eventually decided not to include extended analyses of novels in this book about poetry. Had I included *Coming through Slaughter*, it would have shown that celebrity and race exert their power on Buddy Bolden by publicizing the private and domestic spaces in his life.[8] Without the racial component, a similar argument can be made with Ondaatje's *Secular Love*, a book published in 1984 after – and possibly in response to – the approximate end of the era of celebrity in Canadian poetry.

Despite the risk of further exposing his private life after his memoir *Running in the Family*,[9] Ondaatje's *Secular Love* is partly about the break-up of his first marriage and the beginning of the relationship that would lead to his second (Jewinski 107–12). Although the collection's emphasis is on relationships, Ondaatje considers not only relationships but also the question of how people are relational – as seeing, speaking, listening, touching, and creative beings. He writes about relationality itself, representing the written word and the nearby space as some of the private body's phenomenological extensions.

Secular Love's long poem *Tin Roof* (which was published separately in 1982) is a meditation on escaping from publicity and using the body to enlarge its own privacy. As does the seventeenth-century diary that Francis Barker analyses in *The Tremulous Private Body* (1995), *Tin Roof* describes an autobiographical return to (or, in the case of Barker's Samuel Pepys, an initial turn to) privacy. Pepys is for Barker a definitive figure in the early modern separation of private and public realms, and this separation – which came together at least for stars during our era of celebrity – can be partially regained in solitude and isolation.[10] There, writing mediates between privacy and the public that the text might ultimately reach. In much the same way that the diary of Pepys is "the record of a terrible isolation" (Barker 7) and an "inner history" (Barker 8), *Tin Roof* is a record and history of bodily desire suppressed or sublimated through writing. Its speaker and his lover are "hungry / for everything about the other" (34), and he "[writes his] hunger out" (38). Writing expresses his "hunger" and pushes it "out" into the world of readers who can share his desire and appreciate the intimacy of the text.

As usual, Ondaatje's willingness to engage with the public through writing means that he is on the symbolic edge of privacy and publicity. In the epigraph to *Tin Roof*, one of Elmore Leonard's characters says, "I'm trying to tell you how I feel without exposing myself" (n.p.). Sam Solecki, reviewing *Secular Love*, claims that "[t]he speaker in most of the lyrics seems to be Ondaatje but he's rarely interested in enacting or describing his darkest and most problematic emotions and situations" (126). Instead, Solecki explains, Ondaatje's laconic attitude and highly controlled style "hint at repressed or displaced experiences and aspects of the self the writer is unwilling or unable to deal with" ("Coming through" 126). In the beginning of *Tin Roof* the speaker says, "This last year I was sure / I was going to die" (24), but this is probably the most direct personal statement in the book. Indeed, Ondaatje avoids "exposing [him]self" by indirectly expressing his feelings, but his private persona is also obviously engaged in publicity through writing.

All writers who publish are so engaged, but Ondaatje in *Secular Love* adds direct and affectionately elegiac references to famous authors and celebrities. *Secular Love* contains over a dozen references to people of considerable fame or celebrity, mostly American movie stars and popular musicians of the 1940s and 1950s, when Ondaatje was a boy. The speaker exclaims, in *Tin Roof*, "I was brought up on movies and song!" (40). This statement and the references to celebrities contribute to a feeling of nostalgia for the end of an era, such as the

Golden Age of Hollywood. Humphrey Bogart is one of the many famous people and stars in *Secular Love*. Authors such as Rilke, Yeats, Lorca, Cervantes, Neruda, and Shakespeare mingle with stars such as Bogart, John Wayne, Frank Sinatra, Burt Lancaster, Tony Curtis, Billy Holiday, Billy Graham, and Bessie Smith. Although none of the authors is American, all the performers are – a fact that shows Ondaatje's affinity for American pop culture and his interest in relating to an American audience not entirely comprised of the literati. As usual in the discourses of famous literature and American fandom, the authors need only a single name, whereas the celebrities are usually referred to by both first and last names.

The exception is Bogart, who is granted an authorial status that brings him closer to Ondaatje's own status as an author – even though Ondaatje had not yet been, like Bogart, an internationally recognized star. In *Tin Roof*, Ondaatje imagines what could have happened to Bogart after the film *Casablanca* (1942). The speaker states, "I could write my suite of poems / for Bogart drunk / six months after the departure at Casablanca" (40).[11] As fans often do to celebrities, Ondaatje's private persona has conflated Bogart with his character, Rick – suggesting that Ondaatje is aware that he might be conflated with characters that he has invented or personas that he has adopted. One question he raises is whether he is willing to be understood through Bogart. In the film, Bogart plays Rick, an apolitical businessman who finally makes a decision to choose a side in the Second World War by sending his former lover, Ilsa, to safety with her husband in America. The speaker of the poem ultimately claims that his writing is motivated by "pain loneliness deceit and vanity" (43), and he could easily have imagined that Rick might have felt such things after sending Ilsa away without telling her in advance about his plan to help the French Resistance. In "Late Movies with Skyler" from *There's a Trick with a Knife I'm Learning To Do* (1979), Ondaatje writes that

> In the movies of my childhood the heroes
> after skilled swordplay and moral victories
> leave with absolutely nothing
> to do for the rest of their lives. (97)

In the case of *Casablanca*, having "nothing / to do" also means having no one to love. Because the speaker has conflated Rick and Bogart, readers are implicitly asked to imagine what Ondaatje might have perceived in himself to justify his identification with the unhappy hero Rick as played by Bogart. The obvious answer is the "pain loneliness deceit and vanity" of having lost the girl – motives that also inspired *Secular Love* in general.

The less obvious answer comes from Ondaatje's perception of himself as having endured emotional and at least symbolically physical problems that are similar to those of his favourite stars. Ondaatje was born only a year after *Casablanca* was released. He draws attention to his age at the end of the Bogart passage, when the speaker asks, "What about Burt Lancaster / limping away at the end of *Trapeze?* / Born in 1943. And I saw that six times" (40). *Trapeze* was released in 1956 when Ondaatje, born "in 1943," was thirteen.[12] He seems to have negatively reinterpreted Rick's heroic actions as regrettable, and he now identifies Rick with "Lancaster / limping away." The physical injury related to "limping" is a representation of an emotional difficulty associated with celebrity, which – like Bogart's alcohol – seems to have consequences on the body. He seems to assume that movie stars endure physical and psychological injuries related to their acting and celebrity. My suspicion is that these associations also relate to the end of the era of celebrity in Canadian poetry; the weariness and sense of pause in *Tin Roof* suggest that Ondaatje, like Lancaster and Bogart as he imagines them, barely survived a time of intense strain, such as a personal crisis or the frenzy of activity in Canadian poetry in the 1960s and 1970s. The themes and mood – the sense of an ending – of *Tin Roof* are as ambivalent and uncertain as in Cohen's *Death of a Lady's Man* (1978), which marked, as I argued in previous chapters, the approximate end of that era. Ondaatje's identification with other celebrities in *Secular Love* suggests that he was an audience – *and* a celebrity – who had gone along for the exhausting ride and was trying to imagine what "to do" next, and how.

To help with pondering this question, the speaker uses the main setting of *Tin Roof* – a "small cabin" (24) in Hawaii – as an extension of his body and a reminder of his privacy. It is a site where the body becomes familiar once more with privacy. Billy the Kid has similar locations (such as the barn), as does Buddy Bolden (such as Webb's cabin), but figures of publicity (Garrett and Webb) are always potential intruders in those spaces; the sense of being truly sheltered and intimate with a small space is much more acute in *Tin Roof*. Seeming to think of our bodies as sensing fields, Maurice Merleau-Ponty writes that the body "combines with" and "includes" space and time (140). The speaker of *Tin Roof* wants to know his "small cabin" through senses other than that of sight, such as touch and spatial memory, which help him to internalize a history of his own grieving and reflection; he projects, and as a writer inscribes, these emotional and cognitive experiences onto the space of the cabin. He says that he knows the cabin so well that he "could rise in the dark / sit at the table and write without light" (24). This image recalls dark rooms from *The Collected Works of Billy the Kid* and *Coming through Slaughter*; however, partly because writing in the dark is hypothetical (he "could" write that way), the speaker is not actually replaying scenes from those earlier works. He seems to have retreated from sites of visibility and stardom, as Buddy did when he went to Webb's cabin and heard the mysterious radio broadcast. The speaker of *Tin Roof* wants the reassurance of his bodily reality, possibly to help him reduce publicity's distorting effect on relationships.

The star-fan relationship itself appears symbolically in *Tin Roof* along with a phenomenological concern for the interface of the inner and outer worlds of the speaker. In *Tin Roof*, the speaker has little human company but does have an audience represented by geckoes (small tropical lizards that can climb smooth surfaces). The speaker notes that "[g]eckoes climb / the window to peer in" (24); they prevent him from being totally secluded, but they are also akin to the sparrows with "infra red eyes" in "Postcard from Piccadilly Street," which I mentioned near the beginning of this chapter. He seems to be worthy of some attention, and the geckoes are not unlike fans or members of the paparazzi in their spying on him. Thinking later about the geckoes looking in through the window, the speaker states, "There are those who are in / and there are those who look in" (29). Initially, the speaker is in, looking out. Solecki argues that Ondaatje is both in and out ("Coming Through" 128).

One sign that Solecki is correct is that the private persona sometimes has the same posture as the geckoes and thereby adopts the role of the symbolic fan (possibly also a fan of himself). For example, in a nested poem in *Tin Roof* called "Rainy Night Talk," the speaker remembers watching cheerleaders and Miss America contestants. He wonders what such faraway women living in "a city of suicides" (38) were thinking while he

> put [his] hands
> sweating
> on the cold
> window
> on the edge
> of the trough of this city ... (39)

The speaker is still inside, looking out, but his position against the glass is like that of the geckoes and suggests that, regardless of the degree of his celebrity or the visibility of his private persona, he is also an audience remembering these distant women – one of whom is "from Kansas" (38), whence came Ondaatje's second wife (Jewinski 107–8). With his "sweating" hands on the "cold / window," possibly causing condensation that would mingle sweat and water, the glass becomes an extension of his body – a new and larger skin that might sense the thoughts of the Miss America contestants from many kilometres away. He is, of course, doing the opposite of what fans are assumed to do. He is as far from the stars as he can be – living for a time in what might be called "guilty secrecy" (Barker 9), trying to receive thoughts while also projecting his desire for at least one of the women through the surface of the glass (and the surface of the text, as Pepys does in the diary entry that Barker analyses in *The Tremulous Private Body*).

The "secrecy" and privacy in *Tin Roof* have further phenomenological meaning because of the small size of the geckoes combined with the smallness of the cabin. Although the glass might symbolically enlarge the speaker's body and increase his sensitivity (though perhaps not so much that his skin can receive messages from other minds), the geckoes reverse the sense of scale. The cabin is small but bigger than the man, who is bigger than the geckoes – a sliding scale that recalls the intensifying privacy of the globe-town-room progression in "Letters & Other Worlds." In *On Longing* (1984), Susan Stewart argues that miniatures (or in this case geckoes and the cabin) can signify "interior space and time," whereas gigantic things stand for "the collective, public, life" (xii). She claims: "The body is our mode of perceiving scale ... We can see the body as taking the place of origin for exaggeration and, more significantly, as taking the place of origin for our understanding of metonymy (the incorporated bodies of self and lover) and metaphor (the body of the other)" (xii). The speaker and the geckoes are not in contact physically (i.e., "incorporated"), but they are metaphorically united through identification and through the glass, a symbolic skin that dramatically sensitizes Ondaatje's private persona.

The senses of privacy and scale help to create the mood of quiet contemplation and timelessness in *Tin Roof*. The cabin is without question a relatively private space, and a sense of privacy develops when someone spends time alone. If a human could perceive time while also experiencing life as a gecko does, the passage of time would probably seem different, at least if any given minute were thought of in the context of a gecko's shorter lifespan. In *On Longing*, Stewart remarks on an experiment in a school of architecture in which five minutes seemed like thirty to adults who were playing with miniature figures in miniature spaces: "This compressed time of interiority tends to hypostatize the interiority of the subject that consumes it in that it marks the invention of 'private time.' In other words, miniature time transcends the duration of everyday life in such a way as to create an interior temporality of the subject" (66). Reading *Tin Roof*, I am not certain if time seems faster or slower, and it could be either or both, depending on whether time is experienced through the bigger or the smaller figures (i.e., Ondaatje's speaker or the geckoes) – both are possible because the speaker and gecko are fused, both in and out. The sense of pause, however, can be clear, and this "private time" is partly an effect of Ondaatje's choice of setting and his juxtaposition of differently sized spaces and bodies.

With an altered perception of time and space because of his identification with at least one of the geckoes, Ondaatje's private persona comes to understand his body transcendentally. Presumably talking about himself, he says that

> He focuses on the gecko
> almost transparent body
> how he feels now
> everything passing through him like light. (28)

The speaker shares some degree of this "transparent" quality with the gecko and the glass. Because "everything" passes through him, he is imagining himself as someone insubstantial; he is reminded perhaps of how small and delicate (like a gecko) a human body really is, and perhaps he also alludes to the invisibility of Billy the Kid, who rejected his celebrity by refusing to be pictured in a *photograph* – written in light, according to the Greek etymology. Identifying with an "almost transparent body" is also partly a denial of the human bodies whose images promote most types of celebrity. Because we have bodies, we have fantasies of transcendent connections with others, and even though celebrity has its own designs on transcendence, Ondaatje's speaker does not want to block those connections. Regardless of whether Ondaatje wanted to invoke physics with the reference to "light," the poem affirms the meaningfulness of subjectivity and relationality – not Newtonian physics, but maybe Einsteinian.

The subtle indications of physics and biology here are, at most, figurative, but they help the speaker to understand himself and his work. Notably, he "gazes / through gecko / ... / into sea" (25), which is an earlier symbol of his poetry (43). He is staring through his own weak symbolic body into his comparatively strong symbolic poetry, which has taken precedence as the object of his attention. Despite the appearance of his photograph on the back cover of *Secular Love*, Ondaatje is like his speaker: transparent or invisible to readers. His public cannot see him, or they can see through him by reading him.[13] The speaker later writes about himself that "[i]n certain mirrors / he cannot see himself at all. / He is joyous and breaking down. The tug over the cliff" (28). Although he is "not happy" (37) elsewhere, here he is "joyous," possibly because he *wants* the "[break] down" of his visible self and the compulsion to go over the "edge" of the "cliff" – another edge that signifies the fine line between privacy and publicity. On that edge, he discovers a sense of selflessness that counterbalances the narcissism and self-reflexivity of any celebrity. The star poet regains a private life while remaining open to the world.

Although the author contemplates his symbolic death by learning to see himself from the reader's perspective, the speaker of *Tin Roof* is definitely alive, even if his invisibility in "certain mirrors" hints that stardom is vampiric. He was "sure [he] was going to die" but did not, and, for that reason, *Tin Roof* is more concerned with life than with death; he is not concerned with legend – that typically posthumous type of public recognition – because he knows that his death is probably not imminent. Given Ondaatje's prior use of characters who symbolize him to some extent, and given the especially personal and even autobiographical content of *Secular Love*, the speaker's visibility only in *some* mirrors probably means that Ondaatje understood that he was still in a state of liminal or incomplete celebrity – and ambivalent about a closeness to the public that made him feel the ironic "joy" of breakdown or crisis.

Like *Running in the Family*, *Tin Roof* is set in an exotic locale where the star seems not entirely comfortable and where self-reflection seems to be a function of the place. Throughout the poem, the process of self-reflection encourages the celebrity to think not only of himself but also of others – particularly his audience.[14] Because they are symbolically visible to each other, a reversal of positions or a fusion of identities becomes possible: the speaker becomes like the gecko; Rick becomes Bogart, and the speaker, to some extent, becomes Bogart too. As a fan, Ondaatje suggests that the social function of celebrity as religion depends on this illusion of mutual identification – a "secular love" between the star and the fan. Understanding his own writing as a symbolic extension of his body, he accepts a degree of publicity while maintaining the sanctity of private space, pondering his willingness to develop such love, especially when it might drive him into isolation from the public and away from the romantic and familial relationships that are becoming more important to his poetry.

In his own life, and not only in his creative writing, Ondaatje continued to think about stardom. He even helped to edit *Brushes with Greatness: An Anthology of Chance Encounters with Celebrities* (1989). He could occasionally treat celebrity lightly and see its positive aspects, even when his own recognition became international with the success of *The English Patient* as a novel (it won the Booker Prize and the Governor General's Award) and a film (it won nine Academy Awards) in the 1990s. Despite insisting on his privacy, he admitted that his celebrity did have some perks. In her interview in 2007 with Ondaatje in the *Globe and Mail*, Johanna Schneller asked him if the "movie-level fame" generated by *The English Patient* is different from "novel-writing fame," and he responded, "Oh yeah, a lot of people have seen the film. It helps me going across the borders. If you want to get to someone [for research], that can be a way in. ... But I tend to keep a low profile when I'm talking to someone" (Schneller R5). He responds in terms of quantity ("a lot") and not quality, but his remarks are nevertheless interesting. In contrast with the English patient in his novel, Ondaatje can cross borders more easily *because* he is recognized. Contrary to his representations of celebrity in his poems, in his life, celebrity has occasionally extended his freedoms of mobility and association.

The prominent image of being on the edge in Ondaatje's poetic texts is his way of expressing a desire for *some* celebrity – neither total exposure nor total privacy, because both would be fatal, as the experiences of Billy and Bellocq (in *Coming through Slaughter*) suggest. Ondaatje consents to being interviewed, but according to predetermined rules. He promotes his novel and its film, but refuses access to materials that are now in a public archive. He writes about himself, but usually with characters who mediate between his privacy and the public.

In his poetic texts – which express far more about his thinking than he is willing to divulge in interviews – Ondaatje is extremely critical of celebrity. Having identified with Billy and perhaps more fully with Buddy, Ondaatje ultimately realized that to call celebrity disappointing would be a dramatic understatement: "There are no prizes" (*Coming* 160). He represents celebrity as a cause of numerous crises: of bodily problems like addiction and other forms of self-destruction; of the body undergoing a transformation into something insubstantial, transparent, or invisible to escape the public; of the fusion of public and private (and their uncanny symmetry); of the imposition of national, racial, and gendered values on individual artists; of the compulsion to continue to write even when his writing makes him vulnerable to the public; of the transition from the pretended religious roles of Layton's prophet and Cohen's saint to the secular spirit of the ghostly Billy the Kid.

In *Rat Jelly*, Ondaatje began to depict celebrity far more literally, naming it and considering relationships between fans and those they adore. This relationship, he suggests, persists because of an illusion of closeness. As it was for Ondaatje's father, this closeness is evidently problematic when celebrity calls attention to difference and results in stars being exiled from their own culture and driven to addiction and other bodily problems. As with his father and with Buddy in *Coming through Slaughter*, this problem is related to the racial biases of the public and its false promise of wholesome inclusiveness. Himself critical of celebrity and willing to question his racial position and national origin, Ondaatje nevertheless promotes his exotic persona in *Running in the Family* and *Secular Love*. His exoticism, however, becomes a way for him to reflect upon himself. Like his more and more frequent allusions to the popular culture of movies and music, his willingness to be an outsider in his own country helps him imagine himself outside the culture of celebrity, as in *Tin Roof*, where he finds a private space and time. He seems capable of sharpening the edge of privacy and publicity, suggesting through metaphor that a razor in the body is a risk of stardom and of metaphor itself.

9 The Magician and His Public in the Poetry of Gwendolyn MacEwen

The previous chapters identify various figures of stardom in Canadian poetry, but the most overtly performative of these figures belong to Gwendolyn MacEwen, who initially represented the artist's relationship with her public through magicians and other potential stars who work on stage. Like Irving Layton and Leonard Cohen, MacEwen was intrigued by the pretence of religious significance that gives stardom some of its cultural power. Although she suggests in her first novel, *Julian the Magician* (1963), that celebrities fake their religious significance but then sometimes begin to believe that they are sacred figures, she also suggests that a celebrity's overconfidence (e.g., grandstanding, standing in for a bigger man, even a god) can be a response to the pressure of audiences. Her magicians are users of metaphor, and through metaphor they sustain their own illusions but also attempt to understand their own genders and other aspects of their identities. Regardless of their questing for self-knowledge, however, they ultimately think that celebrity is a status to escape; the public's expectations are too restrictive, even punitive, and the public itself seems demonically cruel. Her magicians and their relative, the escape artist, are figures of divine vision and inspiration, alchemical experimentation and charlatanry – and performative exhilaration that the public eventually snubs or mutes.

Myth, magic, and mysticism were the unorthodox trinity of important themes in her work from the beginning of her career, and these three preoccupations are also relevant in the context of her limited celebrity and her representations of performers. When MacEwen said, in her oft-quoted statement, "I want to construct a myth," she was referring specifically to the myth of "that joy which arises out of and conquers pain" (qtd. in Bartley 2). This is also among other things a fine explanation of the feeling that inspires religion. Although MacEwen was not a devout believer, she was compelled by spirituality in general, such that "[t]he frustrations of the mystic quest are a major theme of MacEwen's prose" (Bartley viii) and, I would add, of her poems about magicians and related figures. In *Invocations* (1983), Jan Bartley uses the language of metaphor (e.g., "marriage," "integration") to explain at least Julian as a not quite religious figure:

> The young magician has nothing but contempt for shallow exploration and mere manipulation; yet he retains a reverence for the marriage of opposites, the transcendent unity. The union is transcendent in the sense that a higher level of spiritual wisdom and self-knowledge is attained: a level of being that rises above the material level of existence. This self-knowledge, made possible by the integration of opposites, is often referred to by MacEwen as a secondary level of reality and is a central concern in her writing. (17)

In terms of similar "opposites," MacEwen said, "In my poetry I am concerned with finding the relationships between what we call the 'real' world and that other world which consists of dream, fantasy, and myth. I've never felt that these 'two worlds' are as separate as one might think ... " (qtd. in Bartley 8). Bartley realizes that "Julian himself is seduced by his own craft. He begins to wonder at his own lack of limitation; he confuses illusion and reality; and he recognizes that he is dependent on the audiences whose worship creates him over and over again" (19). This worship eventually becomes "suffocating and destructive" (Bartley 19). MacEwen's use of metaphor to reconcile myth, magic, and mysticism with the "real" world can result in self-knowledge, but in the context of potential celebrity it is, again, a threat.

The most obvious star in MacEwen's work is Lawrence of Arabia in *The T.E. Lawrence Poems* (1982), but, given that she was aware of Lawrence as early as 1962 but did not write about him until "some twenty years later" (as she states in the foreword), she had him in mind even as she invented other characters to represent celebrity prior to *The T.E. Lawrence Poems*. Her earlier celebrity characters fit into categories that accord with the titles of some of her works. The first is the magician, a prominent and explicitly Christian figure in *The Rising Fire* (1963) and, in the same year, *Julian the Magician,* the first two of her books to follow her chapbooks. The second is the escape artist, who extends from the magician in *A Breakfast for Barbarians* (1966). The third could be the king, who egotistically reduces a polytheistic society to monotheism in *King of Egypt, King of Dreams* (1971), but I will refer to him only to note his narrow view of religion and the irony that his disfigurement led him to a life of solitude that made him unrecognized by his people.[1] In *Invocations,* Bartley brings the characters of the magician and the king together under the rubric of MacEwen's "Muse" (8), whom Margaret Atwood had identified (already in

1970) as a male figure, contrary to traditional representations. Because *Julian the Magician* is more poetic and more focused on celebrity than *King of Egypt, King of Dreams,* and because I can use it to set up the remainder of the chapter in only a few pages as I could not with *Coming through Slaughter* (1976) in the previous chapter, I will include some analysis of *Julian the Magician.*

In chapter 2, I argued that poetry was losing prominence relative to novels and other arts and diversions by the 1970s; no new Canadian poets would become celebrities – not while remaining mostly committed to poetry as a form – beyond the end of the 1970s (Messenger 944; Hošek 939–40). Some of those who had already established their celebrity extended it, as Cohen did, by committing themselves to forms other than poetry. MacEwen did not develop into a career novelist; her two novels were both published relatively early and did little to extend her celebrity. Her biographer Rosemary Sullivan states that MacEwen hoped *King of Egypt, King of Dreams* would establish her in "the international élite of historical novelists – she could write novels and make enough money to sustain the poetry. MacEwen had once said: 'I don't call myself a poet, I call myself a writer'" (qtd. in Sullivan 193). Sullivan insists, however, that MacEwen "had a poet's vision" and that, by the 1980s, "poetry was dying" (385). It would be more accurate to claim that MacEwen chose to remain generally a poet during the "dying" of *celebrity* in Canadian poetry, a decision that had a major effect on the content and tone of her later work. There is no direct evidence that MacEwen knew the era of celebrity in Canadian poetry had ended (though she probably knew she was living through it), but the novelistic *T.E. Lawrence Poems* – modelled partly on the historical Lawrence's highly linear *Seven Pillars of Wisdom* (1926) – is uniquely teleological among her poetry and is implicitly concerned with being at the end of a line. In contrast, when *Julian the Magician* was published in 1963, she had confidence in her potential. Citing various signs of MacEwen's enthusiasm then, Sullivan argues that "she must have felt she was on the edge of fame" (98).

As with others writing during the era of celebrity in Canadian poetry, however, MacEwen's excitement disguised a suspicion that such an "edge" was the precipice of celebrity, a fate worse than fame. The negative connotations of celebrity are impossible not to notice in her representations of the magician and the related escape artist. MacEwen's first novel, as its title suggests, is about a nineteenth-century magician, whom MacEwen calls a "celebrity" (21) and represents as a pseudo-religious entertainer, and possibly as a writer, confused by the effect of celebrity on his spirituality and on other aspects of his identity, such as his sexuality. Whereas the nonheterosexual inclinations of Ondaatje's Billy the Kid are suppressed or repressed by the normative heterosexuality of the Wild West (and possibly of celebrity during its era in Canadian poetry), Julian openly declares his bisexuality. Similarly but without an explicit statement, Manzini the escape artist – an extension of the magician – rejects his masculinity in a performance that promotes his celebrity even though his only audience besides the speaker of the poem is the brute that ties the ropes around him. The limited freedom of self-definition that these characters share is one cause of their literal and symbolic deaths.

Although death is not always negative, *Julian the Magician*'s arresting and highly poetic opening line describes the sound of applause in terms that seem to threaten death: "Bulls up out of their rushes, bats' wings, bulls up out of rushes, bats' wings, bull's blood" (3). The concussive alliteration is like an assault, and the sound of a crowd cheering "like a skipping-rope chant of devils" (3) reinforces the depiction of celebrity as deadly and hellish (also childish). Julian's sleight of hand inspires the crowd to "hideous worship" (3) of him. He assumes that they think he is "divine" (3), thereby initiating the ensuing contrast between the fearsomely hellish crowd of batty, bloody "devils" and his explicitly "christlike" (40) representation. As in representations of celebrity by Layton, Cohen, and Ondaatje, he is a pseudo-religious martyr sacrificing himself to an audience that is, in this case, terrifying and dangerous.

The religious pretence that surrounds Julian is never really more than pretence, but his actions lead one or two people to put faith in his divinity. He does, for a while, insist that he is "a simple trickster" (40) and a faker of miracles, yet he constantly acts to convince others of his candidacy for the role of the New Messiah. He seemingly makes clay into sparrows (8) and cures a blind man (55). He later fails to resurrect the formerly blind (and formerly living) man, whom he calls "Lazarus" (65), but he invokes the transubstantiation of his body and blood when offering a cup of deer's blood to his apprentices (73). Finally, the townsfolk crucify him, and "three days later the sun rose" (106) – though Julian's second coming is not described until *Noman* (1972), which features a short story about him returning to earth in 1970. As with the image of the doffed halo in Layton's "A Tall Man Executes a Jig" (1963), "[Julian's apprentice] Peter noticed that the moon was directly behind Julian's head. Julian's head was haloed; a silver aura. When he moved on ahead the halo slipped" (69). Peter's view of Julian is shared with few people, but to one of the elders of the nineteenth-century town, Julian says, "My audience creates *me*, sir – over and over – ... I do not force belief, I *let* them believe what they will" (49–50, original emphasis). No "force" is necessary. According to Julian, his "audience" simply believes in him.[2]

MacEwen's eventual emphasis, however, is that Julian becomes a believer in his own religious significance. The townspeople endorse Julian's divinity only so that they can later reveal him to be a fraud and use him as a scapegoat for their latent violence. Before healing a man and also seeming to cause the man's death, Julian "himself began to wonder" (8) about whether he was a religious figure. He later says, "I don't want to be divine ... I don't want them to make me divine ... they force it, they force it" (29–30). He "[does] not force belief"; the *audience* does, and its members "force" it upon him, not each other. The audience increases the degree of his celebrity to heights that expose his charlatanism to almost everyone but him; ironically, the disbelieving audience makes him believe in his own access to God.

Julian's confusion about what to believe leads him to articulate – though not always clearly – the identity crisis related to his status as a celebrity. He writes in his journal: "A secondary logic has overtaken me. An enclosed genius has come out of my skin and rules me, a genius and a will so sharp, so complete I cannot recognize it as my own. It is not my own. Things I know, deeds I do, miracles I perform, all stem from this foreign genius who is not me" (140). The mysterious "foreign genius" is partly a confirmation of the "invasive reconfiguration" (Latham 110) of identity caused by celebrity. "Genius" is not necessarily the positive condition that we are accustomed to admire; it can be a spirit that can possess a person to do evil (*OED*). Given my argument in the next chapter, that MacEwen's critique of celebrity is partly postcolonial, the "foreign" quality of Julian's genius is surprising to me; MacEwen never feared foreignness but invited it into her life instead. *Julian the Magician*, however, has much less to say about nationality than *The T.E. Lawrence Poems* does. In the context of *Julian the Magician*, the foreign genius is the audience that forces its "will so sharp" upon Julian. It makes him question what is "[his] own." He defines it in opposition to himself; it is, he says, "not me." Bartley's aforementioned argument is that MacEwen seeks "self-knowledge" made possible by "the integration of opposites" such as the ones that Julian observes. If those opposites – what Northrop Frye called "this" and "that" (11) in his definition of metaphor – are "me" and "not me," native and foreign, self and other, private and public, then MacEwen might have intended to discover herself partly through the insight of her audience, which can help metaphor to achieve its full but always risky potential. If the members of that audience are indeed the "devils" that the narrator of *Julian the Magician* describes, then trusting the audience for insight is a dangerous mistake – or a risk MacEwen is willing to accept – in the search for self-knowledge. The audience creates a new but less self-determined identity for the star, who welcomes it at first because of the promise of self-knowledge, only to find it inflexible.

The character of the magician reappears in *précis* in MacEwen's immediately subsequent publication, *The Rising Fire*, to reflect on her criticism of being possessed or owned by the audience. "The Magician: Three Themes" (30) is a three-stanza poem subtitled at each division. The first stanza ("One: The

Magician") begins: "odd that the people want to own you / and produce you like a black poodle / at fatal teaparties" (30). The speaker's musing about the audience's desire to "own" and "produce" is a musing about what aspect of the self can be grasped and controlled. In the second stanza ("Two: The Magician as Man"), this aspect is the body, not the mind. The speaker, speaking as the magician, complains about needing to do basic sleight-of-hand "when my real love is the mind / moving as sailboat through the days, / the whiteness and the freedom of it" (30). Unlike Julian, whose mind was impressionable and easily muddled by the ironic devotion of his audience, the magician here is at least thinking clearly about how "mind" and body interact. The body, not the mind, gives the audience something to possess; however, the work the body must do constrains the "freedom" of his mind simply by requiring his attention to the coordination of his performances.

In the final stanza ("Three: The Magician as Christ"), the poem's argument concludes by showing a surprising interest in the well-being of minds other than that of the magician. Julian was never more than self-centred, even in his actions that seemed helpful. In contrast here, the magician is concerned about members of his audience and about what or in whom they believe: yet like penicillin from a mould

> his pretence breeds wonder
> at the throat of their belief
> like fingers or a strange bacteria [*sic*]
> holds the hard mind screaming ... (31)

This "pretence" that "breeds wonder" is religious, as the subtitular reference to "Christ" and the later reference to "churches" (31) suggest. The poem does not resolve the question of whether the religious pretence is helpful ("like penicillin") or harmful (like strangling "fingers") to the "hard mind," but the emphasis on the hard mind is what makes this stanza important to MacEwen's view of celebrity. The hardness of the mind means, first, that it is unsympathetic or overly rational; second, that it is embodied and not wholly intangible. The magician overcomes the hardness of the mind and inspires it, through wonder, to a strong emotional and bodily reaction (the scream). It is screaming because it can be affected and even controlled – a rapture, perhaps. Although some scenes in *Julian the Magician* raise questions about the goodness of Julian's influence on his audience, "The Magician: Three Themes" is the first of MacEwen's texts to represent the audience as an embodied mind – a being capable of "wonder," of being healed, hurt, and "[held] screaming." In this poem, MacEwen invokes the usual religious pretence of celebrity, but she also seems to be thinking about the audience as if its members were worthy of attention and compassion, and not the devils that they were in *Julian the Magician*.

Compared to Julian, who has a didactic and even condescending view of his audience ("I *let* them believe what they will"), the magician here seems genuinely worried that his audience might not be fulfilled by living only in a body or a mind so rational that it has no soul. He is not, however, worried only about the members of his audience. He wonders

> ... how
> much of him is theirs, how much of him
> do they re-create in the vast thunderous churches
> of their need ... (31)

The enjambment after the initial "how" creates the following declaration: "much of him is theirs"; in other words, they substantially own him. The enjambment does not wholly ruin the integrity of the question, however. The speaker's only certainty seems to be that the audience has a "need" for "churches." As superficial as the "crust and context of his act" might be, it has the effect of "hypnosis" (31) on the audience. The magician's power over the audience here is stronger than in *Julian the Magician* because the audience needs not a scapegoat but a freeing of the mind or spirit. MacEwen suggests that, illusory or otherwise, the magician's "act" is what the audience needs, but she recognizes that the act also gives the audience the means of eventually using the performance against the performer.

As a representation of celebrity, the magician did not disappear but did change between *The Rising Fire* in 1963 and *A Breakfast for Barbarians* in 1966, when MacEwen's nascent celebrity became much more intensely realized. Since 1963, she had been occasionally broadcasting her verse plays and poetry on CBC Radio's *Anthology* program at Robert Weaver's request (Sullivan 191). In 1964, MacEwen supposedly "was sent on a poetry tour with Irving Layton and Leonard Cohen" (Sullivan 179). That same year, Layton and Cohen toured with Earle Birney and Phyllis Gotlieb under the aegis of McClelland and Stewart, a publisher that never represented MacEwen. If she had indeed joined Layton and Cohen on tour,[3] it was a coup for her and Macmillan, which had published *Julian the Magician* in Canada. MacEwen had only two books, but youth in that era was newly fascinating to the media, and she had already established an exotic mystique that made her seem ageless, both girlish and wise. Known through radio, readings, and her books, MacEwen was becoming a celebrity and, as the next chapter will argue, had personal reasons for becoming distrustful of such status.

In 1966, MacEwen returned to the magician to extend her thinking about poetry in the context of her celebrity and its limits. In *A Breakfast for Barbarians*, "The Magician" (not to be confused with "The Magician: Three Themes") is set "on stage" (36) during a magic act that involves both the magician and the poet. Although allusions to performance often accompany poems about stardom, the audience is conspicuously absent in "The Magician," thereby suggesting that the magician is only practising (not performing) or that his time in the spotlight either has not begun or has come to an end. The only spectator seems to be the poet, who watches the magic act and then responds to it with her own poems; this representation of the poet as a fan later becomes a crucial aspect of the politics of writing *The T.E. Lawrence Poems*. In "The Magician," MacEwen states that her art is "more a lie anyway / than the lie of these illusions," but she later asserts that "to believe or not believe / is not the question" (36). This assertion helps put to rest the debate about celebrities believing in their own divinity in *Julian the Magician* or the audience believing in the divinity of celebrities in "The Magician: Three Themes." Instead of belief, the new concern, which concludes "The Magician," is a different question posed as an archaic declarative statement:

> finally then do all my poems become as crazy scarves
> issuing from the fingers in a coloured mesh
> and you, magician, stand as they fly around you
> silent as Houdini who could escape from anything
> except the prison of his own flesh. (36)

The poet wonders whether her poems "become" superior to the magic act by making the "magician" realize that he is trapped in "the prison of his own flesh" as Harry Houdini was and as poetry is not. Magic acts need the presence of a performing magician, but poetry does not require the author to read it aloud. Both forms, however, need some kind of audience. Here, the magician's general lack of an audience is associated with his need to "escape ... his own flesh." In *Julian the Magician*, Julian had stated: "Poets, I think, are simply magicians without quick wrists" (128) and, in "The Magician," poets are magicians without the need to perform with their bodies. As I suggested of Ondaatje in the previous chapter, here MacEwen suggests that poets can escape their flesh by publicizing their work in writing. She seems to be thinking that the requirement of presence is a limit to celebrity that poets can surpass.

MacEwen's magicians tend, in sum, to be duped by their own craft, and later, despite the various threats of their audiences, they wonder about the extent to which their faith in themselves is justified. This wonder involves their own consideration of how body and soul define identity – and of whether performances such as poetry can function as magic and thereby change the world for the benefit of both the magician and the audience. MacEwen seems to suggest, however, that transformative magic – as much as it is desirable – is dangerous, and so one of the characters for whom she expresses the most enthusiasm is almost, but not quite, a magician.

Implicitly commenting on "The Magician" on the next page in *A Breakfast for Barbarians* is "Manzini: Escape Artist,"[4] which suggests that the escape from the flesh means abandoning one's "sex" (37) and thereby freeing oneself from the expectations about sexuality associated with stardom. Gender and sexuality were not new topics for MacEwen; Julian had declared: "It is possible I am a woman – I have long debated it. However, my gender is no matter – my mind is decidedly bi-sexual; thus I can navigate in both female and male territory as freely as grass" (121). His comment suggests that MacEwen was not distinguishing between sex and gender, which are now commonly understood by scholars to be distinct but related concepts. Julian means that, although his body is presumably male, he sometimes thinks of himself as a woman and is not worried about such categories. In contrast, "this boy, Manzini" is defined by "his sex" and "struggled" (37) to escape it. Manzini's sexuality, however, is not clearly defined. He stands "with black tights and a turquoise / leaf across his sex"; the "tights" and "turquoise" are campy and suggest a degree of gender-bending that might discomfit the speaker, who repeats three times that he is a "boy" (37). The speaker – a spectator as in "The Magician" – is obviously impressed, however, by Manzini's ability to escape the "bonds" of the "flesh," which are made literal in the "drenched / muscular ropes" that appeared

> as though his tendons were worn
> on the outside –
> as though his own guts were the ropes
> encircling him. (37)

These gut-ropes are "muscular" and, because of their shape, seem phallic. The "boy, Manzini" appears to be struggling to escape pre-emptively from his future manhood.

Fascinated by this struggle for freedom, the speaker imagines what Manzini might be thinking, and also makes an implicit connection between Manzini's gendering and people who might be better known than he is. The speaker imagines Manzini "inwardly / wondering if Houdini would take as long" (37) to escape similar bonds. Houdini, the most famous escape artist in history, is represented not only as Manzini's precursor but also as the male model against which he defines himself. This representation reinforces Harold Bloom's concept of a competitive and masculine lineage between poets (or performers, in this case). Bloom's theory, articulated in *The Anxiety of Influence* (1973), problematically excludes women almost completely and has become unfashionable for this and other reasons; however, it should be mentioned in the context of Houdini and Manzini because Manzini's performance is a factor in his freedom from both Houdini's precedent and his own masculinity. Imagining Manzini as "inwardly / wondering," the speaker presumes to have knowledge of Manzini's interiority; perhaps the speaker is problematically assuming that whatever is external (phallic guts) simply represents what is internal (the self-concept, including gender), but MacEwen is arguably engaged in a critique that, to some extent, pre-empts Bloom's argument. She suggests that Manzini is purging himself of internalized concepts of masculinity while retaining his outwardly male body, though the most emphatic trope in this poem full of similes is a related synecdoche: "he / was suddenly all teeth and knee" (37) – body parts that are not gendered, suggesting that even his maleness was altered or transformed through performance. In any case, he partly rejects his precursor and assumptions about his sexuality, whether inside or out or both, and contrary to my previous argument about Cohen symbolically inheriting Layton's celebrity, the unexpected result is that Manzini does not inherit Houdini's celebrity or fame.

Instead, Manzini performs only for the speaker of the poem and for "the big / brute [who] tied his neck arms legs" (37) – an obviously male observer whose job involves restricting Manzini's movements, whereas the speaker (whose sex is never specified) is interested in seeing Manzini return to freedom. As in "The Magician," the escape artist is not much of a star and the speaker is, in effect, the only promoter, enthusiastically and repeatedly insisting that readers "listen" (37) to tales of the performer's exploits. The need to repeat so insistently suggests that the speaker, too, has not much of an audience that would listen. The general suggestion is that the typical audience of celebrity is not interested in performances that question the status quo; performers who make a priority of freedom, such as freedoms of expression or sexuality, risk being ignored by those who could grant them widespread recognition.

A possible source of "Manzini: Escape Artist" is Eli Mandel's poem "Houdini" (1967), included in the posthumous selection *From Room to Room* (2011), which is worth considering because this earlier poem represents the escape artist as a figure of the poet – a writer who is trapped, specifically, in metaphor. Referring to Houdini's mysterious ability to escape locked containers, Mandel writes: "I suspect he knew that trunks are metaphors" (20). He then describes Houdini's ability to "distinguish between the finest rhythms" (20), which indicates Houdini's poetic sensibility as he is represented by Mandel (a sensibility MacEwen seems to expect in magicians). Mandel continues:

I think of him listening to the words
spoken by manacles, cells, handcuffs,
chests, hampers, roll-top desks, vaults,
especially the deep words spoken by coffins

escape, escape ... (20)

In his afterword to Mandel's *From Room to Room* (2011), Andrew Stubbs argues that "[t]he Houdini of the poem is eventually the voice of the poet, which is why the various traps, gadgets, and toys ... Houdini plays with are, finally, words. Poetry is a game, where the object is to escape from language itself; but, ironically, this is only in order to return to the very verbal constructs, chains ('metaphors') he left behind" (60).

Except by implying in her enthusiasm that the escape artist is also a stand-in for the poet, MacEwen does not use metaphor in "Manzini," though the aforementioned synecdoche is closely related to metaphor and especially metonymy.[5] His transformation is not as complete as it would be in metaphor; he becomes "all teeth and knee," which are parts of his own body, not something totally different. MacEwen might not want to be as emphatic as Mandel because she expects her Manzini to struggle more than her magicians need to do; they have the advantage of magic in their transformations. Perhaps the absence of an audience and the related irony of stardom in "Manzini" also discourage the metaphor of celebrity from affecting the escape artist with a potentially threatening fusion of selves, and perhaps for this reason the end of the poem can be "beautiful" (37) despite the symbolic death.

Thus, Manzini's eventual "victory" (37) is ambiguous and ambivalent. The speaker explains that Manzini, "finally free, slid as snake from / his own sweet agonized skin, to throw his entrails / white upon the floor" (37). His ensuing "cry" (37) might be victorious but it is also tortured; Manzini might be like a moulting "snake," but he also seems to be in the act of gutting himself, which would surely mean his very painful death. MacEwen's use of the "snake" as a symbol of transformation and possibly death is much like Layton's use of the snake at the end of "A Tall Man Executes a Jig." In that poem and in "Manzini," the potential star is tortured to the point of accepting self-destruction as an escape. Freedom, therefore, is bittersweet. When MacEwen's poem ends – "*now there are no bonds except the flesh,* / but listen, it was thursday, there was this boy, / Manzini" (37, her emphasis) – the crucial "but" suggests that Manzini did escape the "flesh" and surpassed Houdini (though not as a celebrity) as the poet did in “The Magician.” As an extension of the magician, the escape artist also represents the poet and celebrity, and so the speaker of this poem believes “it was beautiful” (37) to see someone convert even the worst of experiences – such as death – into something artistically meaningful and into an important freedom from social norms.

The transition from the magician to the escape artist was a critical development in MacEwen’s representation of celebrity in the first half-decade of her career. In *Julian the Magician*, she suggests that celebrities are charlatans but that the impression of approval from an audience might lead celebrities to believe in their own religious pretence. The star’s belief in the religious pretence might also be a way of coping with an intimidating audience such as the “devils” that Julian faces. The question of belief leads MacEwen to suggest, in “The Magician: Three Themes,” that celebrities *do* respond to an audience’s religious “need,” but a few years later she revises her suggestion in “The Magician” by arguing that belief is not the issue.

Instead, she stops worrying about audiences and – coincident with the emergence of her anticipated celebrity – begins to propose that the challenge of celebrity is to “escape” the “flesh” and remain free. Manzini, her escape artist, struggles against the limitations of his body; in a similar way, celebrities struggle against the expectations related to sexuality and gender that the public has of their bodies. MacEwen’s contact with Layton and Cohen – she had supposedly participated with them on tour and had certainly corresponded with Layton (Sullivan 95–6) and dined with him and Cohen at Layton’s house (Sullivan 332–3) – probably suggested to her that celebrity among poets in Canada was going to be patriarchal; Atwood had the same rueful suspicion. MacEwen’s substantial focus on gender-bending in these texts is the necessary beginning of her eventual adoption and adaptation of Lawrence’s voice – her ultimate critique of the era of celebrity in Canadian poetry.

When that era was reaching its peak intensity around 1968 (the year Cohen’s *Selected Poems* proved that poetry of celebrity in Canada had a maximum altitude that could be increased only in the slipstream of other popular forms, such as music), MacEwen “was giving a great number of poetry readings all over the country” (Sullivan 232). Nevertheless, Macmillan initially would not publish her *King of Egypt, King of Dreams* until a “foreign co-publisher” (Sullivan 240) for the novel could be found. Three companies in New York and one in London had rejected it, an outcome that moderated MacEwen’s hopes of becoming “financially independent” (Sullivan 241) as a writer. Despite her having been originally published by Corinth Books in New York, MacEwen’s Canadian stardom did not have an international currency. This disappointment did not seem to be eased by the coming peak of her literary celebrity in Canada.

Instead, MacEwen began to have personal problems that sometimes manifested themselves when her celebrity put her in stressful situations. Although they had lived together for only five months, she divorced Milton Acorn in 1966 (Sullivan 198); after breaking up her subsequent relationship in 1968 (Sullivan 222), she began – usually in secret (Sullivan 321) – to drink alcohol, a drug that she had avoided because of her father's addiction (Sullivan 250). Coincidentally, she developed a fear of traveling by airplane. Atwood, who was then teaching at the University of Alberta, invited her to do a reading in 1969, but on short notice MacEwen decided against the trip, blaming her phobia and exhaustion after her "eighth or ninth poetry reading of the month" (Sullivan 252). When her celebrity peaked with her winning of the Governor General's Award for *The Shadow-maker* (1969) in 1970, she discreetly asked Weaver to ensure that if Acorn was also a winner her prize would be given to someone else; she feared "even slight publicity" (qtd. in Sullivan 269) that might bring her and Acorn into the same room again. Regardless of whether these developments were mere coincidences, MacEwen's personal problems and her celebrity were emerging around the same time in her life – partly inspiring *The T.E. Lawrence Poems*, which is the subject of the next and final chapter.

MacEwen's celebrity was real, though relatively minor, and she anticipated many of its problems even early in her career. The related figures of the magician and the escape artist have audiences that ignore them or control them – but the magician's public is also worthy of compassion, and MacEwen expresses concern for the public even as she grows wary of it. The question of whether she gained insight into herself through her own public or her publicity is one that I will return to in the next chapter, but I have shown through "Manzini" that she was not always ready to enact metaphor and fuse with her public in order to understand herself through others. Gaining new relevance in the context of her celebrity, Manzini and her other performers illustrate a process of introspection that plays out in her themes of magic, mysticism, and myth, leading ultimately to her figure of Lawrence of Arabia.

10 Passing and Celebrity in MacEwen's *The T.E. Lawrence Poems*[1]

In 1993, Michael Ondaatje said that watching Gwendolyn MacEwen read to an audience "was the first time [he] had a sense of the poet as a public person. ... She was giving herself to the public. She was ... the poet who took all risks for poetry" (Sullivan 288). That reading was around twenty years earlier; she was promoting *Armies of the Moon* (1972), and her celebrity would never again have such promise. Although her celebrity did not reach a height comparable to that of Margaret Atwood or Leonard Cohen, she was known about as widely as Ondaatje during the latter half of what I call the era of celebrity in Canadian poetry. That era began around 1955, when Irving Layton was appearing on television and his poetry was becoming increasingly popular, and it ended around 1980. At a time when poets were no longer becoming stars in Canada, MacEwen wrote *The T.E. Lawrence Poems* (1982), which implicitly compares her own limited celebrity to that of T.E. Lawrence, who had gained "world notoriety" (Aldington 24) as Lawrence of Arabia. Choosing and modifying phrases for her book from his *Seven Pillars of Wisdom* (1935) and other texts, MacEwen imitated his voice but never lost her own. More than any of her other books (even 1983's *The Honey Drum,* her translation and invention of Arab tales), *The T.E. Lawrence Poems* complicates her voice, invoking celebrity to raise questions about her cultural standing, identifications, and other aspects of her identity.

Needing a way to explain the complex identity politics – personal, racial, and national – of *The T.E. Lawrence Poems,* yet acknowledging Graham Huggan's concern in *The Postcolonial Exotic* (2001) about "what we might call the ethics of artistic passing" (176), I have ultimately chosen to adapt the concept of passing as an approximate but usefully political term to encompass the grandstanding, impersonation, and ventriloquism that MacEwen enacts in her literary imitation of Lawrence. In the poems analysed in this chapter, MacEwen speaks convincingly in Lawrence's voice, which is stylistically restrained and precise compared to what Frank Davey calls the "inflated poetic language" (*Surviving* 65) of her earlier books. She passes as Lawrence to imagine herself as a man, to experiment with her identity, and to appropriate his stardom. This passing is a critique of Lawrence's imperialist acculturation into Arab society, and yet she does not entirely denounce him for orientalism. Her Lawrence struggles to define himself against the normative values of celebrity that were more readily accepted by many other poets of her era, such as heterosexual masculinity and religiosity; she also struggles against those values, and for a critical distance from him. With an uneasiness that Lorraine York has found to be typical in Canadian texts that represent stardom (*Literary* 4), MacEwen comments upon the debt that Lawrence's stardom owes to his imperial presence in the Middle East, and she thereby critiques her own appropriation of Middle Eastern fashion, language, myth, and religion – aspects of her own identity that helped her to appear exotic and be recognizable as a celebrity.

Although MacEwen's career benefited from her exoticism, which was of interest to readers long before postcolonialism was at work in Canadian literary studies (Slonim *passim*), she implies in some of her poems that Lawrence's celebrity was partly in service of imperialism. In *The Postcolonial Exotic*, Huggan argues that the glamour of celebrities "shares several features with other, better-known variants of exoticist discourse, among them the creation of a commodified mystique that veils the material conditions that produce it" (209). Today, we can see that celebrity is in the vanguard of the international cultural and economic promotion that is a form of colonialism. When MacEwen first read Lawrence's *Seven Pillars of Wisdom* as a teenager (Sullivan 340), she was doubtlessly attracted to his exoticism and worldliness among other characteristics. Lawrence's imperialism was culturally colonial, affecting not only the Middle East but also the imaginations of people around the world – including her own in Canada. Only after her career and financial problems began in the late 1970s did she choose to represent exoticism and celebrity as problems in themselves.

Identifying with these features of Lawrence both as a fan and as a celebrity in her own right, MacEwen understood that becoming too public can have tragic consequences, in addition to the other results of stardom. The scene of Lawrence's death at the end of *The T.E. Lawrence Poems* is in close proximity to poems that reveal his hatred of his celebrity (i.e., "The Desirability of El Aurens" and "There Is No Place To Hide"). MacEwen's biographer Rosemary Sullivan suggests that MacEwen's early enthusiasm for celebrity was soon tempered; Sullivan argues that MacEwen chose Lawrence as her symbolic "twin" to express her frustration with her Western culture (338). By writing his life from beginning to end, by implicating celebrity in his death, and by passing as Lawrence to involve herself in his narrative, MacEwen imagines herself dying through him. She thereby comments on her own ambivalent experience of celebrity and on the end of the era of celebrity in Canadian poetry – specifically, on the cultural standing of female poets in the 1970s. The end of this era had serious consequences for MacEwen's career as a poet. Her representations of celebrity suggest that she was thinking personally and fatalistically about its ramifications. All the celebrities in her works die, figuratively if not literally. Their "passing" is crucial to their meaning, especially in the case of Lawrence.

In the context of the decline in the popularity of poetry relative to the novel – the "passing" of the era of celebrity of Canadian poetry – that I explain in chapter 2, MacEwen could not have been encouraged, given that her own experience of celebrity was mainly the result of her poetry. It began when she was barely out of her teenage years and peaked in the late 1960s and early 1970s. After MacEwen travelled from Toronto to Montreal to read to the public from her chapbooks in 1961, she exclaimed in a letter: "best reception ever – sold 50 books!! Am being treated like a national celebrity by these people ... Maybe I'm God" (Sullivan 126–7). MacEwen's prospects rapidly improved, and Sullivan argues that, by 1965, the two leading players of Toronto's poetry scene were Atwood and MacEwen (185). Ondaatje had not yet published his first book, though he was on the scene as a spectator; Sullivan relates that "Ondaatje remembered how important it had been to the young writing community at Queen's University when [MacEwen] came to read in 1965. She was the poet people most wanted to hear" (190). Also in 1965, she began "using her sister's address for most of her professional correspondence, because, she said, she needed to guard her private life very closely" (Sullivan 188). MacEwen had become a wary celebrity in the field of literature in Toronto and, by the 1970s, would have national public recognition.

After the peak of MacEwen's success in the late 1960s and early 1970s, the alcoholism that led to her early death began to affect her public life. She "was giving a great number of poetry readings all over the country" (Sullivan 232), and she was more recognized than ever after winning the Governor General's Award for *The Shadow-maker* (1969) in 1970. By 1973, MacEwen's alcoholism was interfering with her poetry readings, which she often missed, and by 1978, "her books weren't making any money" (Sullivan 312). She had an episode of psychological stress and alcoholism that put her in hospital in December 1980 and again in February 1981 (Sullivan 321–2). Around this time, she began writing *The T.E. Lawrence Poems*, which is notably the most biographical and historical of her characterizations of others (not excepting

1971's *King of Egypt, King of Dreams*), and which cannot easily be separated from her own biographical and historical contexts.

The T.E. Lawrence Poems is involved in these contexts as a reflection of MacEwen's stardom, which rose only as high as the proverbial glass ceiling. MacEwen's lack of financial success near the end of her career was arguably related to her decision to remain committed mostly to poetry rather than to write another novel, and yet men were much more likely than women to be successful as poets in Canada. In 1993, Atwood explained: "You found yourself at the centre very fast in those days. The writing community ... was welcoming to any newcomer with talent, including women"; however, she also noted that "[c]reativity in those days was seen as ejaculatory" (qtd. in Sullivan 109, 111). In a different context, Atwood wrote that men "dominate[d] poetry publishing and tend[ed] to exclude women" ("Introduction" xxix). Thus, Layton supposedly discouraged women from writing, and his biographer Elspeth Cameron relates an anecdote about Layton's outrageous contempt for Atwood specifically (441). Indeed, according to Faye Hammill, female writers who became celebrities elsewhere and earlier in the twentieth century often contended with "various forms of hostility toward women's writing" (21) including what Aaron Jaffe calls a "restrictive promotional system" (165).

Although there is no direct evidence that MacEwen was writing to expose either discrimination against women in Canadian poetry or the constraint on the degree of her own celebrity,[2] these possibilities are suggested by her difference from Lawrence. The simple contrast between the degree of their celebrity begs the question of why MacEwen chose to write in his voice when, for example, Atwood chose Susanna Moodie, who was comparatively obscure despite being the "best known of Canada's early pioneers" (Staines x). The answer involves sex and gender among other factors. Gender is noticeably contrived because it must be performed over and over again to persuade us that it is natural, and other performances can therefore subvert it (Butler 138–41), at least partially. MacEwen's imitation of Lawrence is not especially parodic, but it is subversive. Lawrence was more than her symbolic twin. If the most obvious difference between MacEwen and Lawrence is sex, perhaps the most obvious of her implicit goals in reimagining him is to critique masculinity and, symbolically, to take from Lawrence some of the power that men, rather than women, often have. Her grandstanding – performing as a man of much greater celebrity, her "standing in" for someone more "grand" – draws attention to a notable disparity while also enabling her to take various risks with her own identity.

In these historical and biographical contexts, MacEwen's passing as Lawrence has other implications, but first the term *passing* should be explained in more detail, especially as I am relating it to celebrity. Sinéad Moynihan explains that "[a]lthough the term *passing* is increasingly used to denote a wide range of performative practices, from its origins it referred most commonly to 'passing as white'" (810). Passing is racial; it is an illusion of racial sameness that goes undetected. Race is implicated in the public personas of MacEwen and Lawrence, but it is not a factor in their relationship to each other. Although MacEwen and Lawrence both dressed as Middle Easterners at times, they were both white. He was a British soldier in the Middle East who was often photographed wearing the garb of an Arab prince; she was a Canadian traveller to the Middle East who was often known for wearing the kohl eyeliner of an Egyptian icon (Aldington 169; Sullivan 107). She was obviously not visibly identical to Lawrence; she does not pass as him in that sense.

By imitating his voice, however, MacEwen begins to pass as Lawrence. Without their images in mind, a reader could easily be persuaded that the historical Lawrence wrote *The T.E. Lawrence Poems*. In fact, MacEwen annotated and corrected a copy of her book, which is now stored in the archives at the University of Toronto, and she underlined phrases that she had copied directly from various texts by the historical Lawrence. There is underlining in forty-five of the sixty poems. She describes four of them as "found poem[s]" that are composed mostly of the historical Lawrence's phrases. These inclusions are not remarked upon in the published book. One might say that she speaks Lawrence's voice invisibly or that she silently *incorporates* his voice into the book. His voice becomes his body. In that sense, she passes as Lawrence.

Although passing cannot actually gain her more celebrity, it raises questions about identity in general and MacEwen's in specific. Anna Camaiti Hostert argues that passing – as the historical activity of black people posing as white people for "social promotion" – is too often assumed to be only the recourse of victims of oppression who have learned to hate themselves. Passing is a sign of a "crisis of identity" (Hostert 11–12, 33), but it is also a tactic for overcoming the crisis by redefining identity according to chosen identifications, however problematic they might be. In *Identification Papers* (1995), Diana Fuss argues that identities are formed by people's identifications with others: "Identification is ... a question of *relation*, of self to other, subject to object, inside to outside" (3). Passing is a both personal and political use of identification – and is subversive especially because it can be undetectable, even enabling what Hostert calls *disidentification*, "a free fluctuation of identity" (91). This intense freedom to be anything or nothing is arguably what MacEwen wanted from celebrity.

Celebrities can sometimes define themselves however they want, through performance, but sometimes their frequent performances become a habit in their private lives, and their public and private selves become increasingly difficult to separate. This is the identity crisis that the figure of Lawrence (not Lawrence himself) can be said to experience when MacEwen speculates about his private life and writes his autobiography in poems. The experience of celebrity has been called, in coincidentally postcolonial terms, "an invasive reconfiguration" (Latham 110) of identity. Fans change themselves through their identification with celebrities, and celebrities are also changed by the experiences of celebrity – such as their creation of personas and the public's invasion of their privacy. We can think of MacEwen as a fan of Lawrence who is involved in the public's invasion of his privacy. By writing in Lawrence's voice about his life, from start to finish and often in a confessional mode, MacEwen changes him. Never seeming vindictive, she countercolonizes and even penetrates the male imperialist whose celebrity helped to draw her away from Canada, and alter her thinking about Canada, when she was a young woman.

She also changes herself, redefining herself through an identification with Lawrence, whose questionable status as a role model did not prevent her from reflecting on his crises and understanding herself through them. In the only book-length study of MacEwen's work, Jan Bartley argues that the "central concern" of MacEwen's poetry is "self-knowledge" (17). In *The T.E. Lawrence Poems,* MacEwen passes as Lawrence to create a new identity, possibly by destroying her old one and certainly by adopting and adapting that of the historical Lawrence. By passing as Lawrence, she could experience or at least imagine the identity crisis that celebrities of higher degree might have felt. Few people would want such an experience except the most devoted artists (often method actors) – those willing to take, in Ondaatje's words, "all risks."

As a fan, MacEwen might have identified too closely with Lawrence as a celebrity. Sullivan claims that MacEwen "found in Lawrence precisely the persona she needed to explore what she herself had been through" (341), though MacEwen also evidently wanted to go beneath the "persona" and discover something more personal. Surveying other scholarship, Ellis Cashmore in *Celebrity / Culture* explains that fans can develop imaginary relationships with celebrities and, seeing them as role models, might adopt their attributes, values, and behaviours. This is sometimes called "over-identification" (Cashmore 81, 89). In rare cases, fans might even imitate dangerous behaviours. Among other reasons for her untimely death is the possibility that MacEwen was imitating, consciously or not, Lawrence's reckless endangerment of himself.

My suspicion is that MacEwen's readers and critics often wonder about that possibility and others,[3] but no one makes explicit claims; they are reluctant to speculate because speculation might be not only false but also an invasion of MacEwen's privacy – the very invasion that fans indulge in when they begin to assume they know the celebrity. The individual fan is usually characterized as an "obsessed loner" (Jenson 11), but a critic's persistent work in solitude often verges on obsession. Fans and critics are not always that different from each other: Ondaatje, who wrote a critical book about Cohen, was late for the launch of his own *Coming through Slaughter* (1976) because he was delayed by the many encores at a Cohen concert (Rae 133). Although critical reservations about biographical speculation are serious and worth constant reiteration, such reservations did not overly influence MacEwen, who engaged in very personal speculation while remaining critical about Lawrence's flaws and the limits of what she could know about him. She was able to produce a book that comments on Lawrence and herself from the perspective of both a fan and a critic. Arguably, *The T.E. Lawrence Poems* has value as criticism that would be reduced almost to nothing if it were disconnected from the life of its author. Knowing that it was written by MacEwen – a woman, a poet who had been a celebrity, a student of the Middle East, at a time of crisis in her life – is highly important, even essential.

Studies of celebrity should account for biography because celebrities have learned to use their private lives to promote their careers. Sometimes, this accounting will appear to be the irrational or invasive inquiry expected (sometimes with little justice) of fans. Joe Moran in *Star Authors* (2000) explains that "the audience's relation with the star is a compulsive search for the 'real' – an attempt to distinguish between the 'authentic' and the 'superficial' in the star's personality" (62). Given what little bearing the "real" usually has on celebrity, Moran also states that "any attempt to distinguish between the 'public' author and the 'private' self [is] a deeply problematic exercise" (23). In fact, it is likely to be impossible, both for critics and even for celebrities themselves. Nevertheless, the uncanny array of similarities between MacEwen and Lawrence, which Sullivan and Brent Wood have noted, provokes curiosity about MacEwen's willingness to associate her biography with his. The historical Lawrence died at forty-seven, MacEwen at forty-six. He died in a fatal crash after a series of increasingly injurious motorcycle accidents (Aldington 387). She died of metabolic acidosis caused by a complete refusal of alcohol and food after a period of binge drinking (Sullivan 408–10). This coincidence raises the admittedly disturbing question of whether MacEwen was writing about Lawrence's possibly suicidal death while self-promotionally foreshadowing her own.

Not all critics have shied away from similar possibilities. Thomas H. Kane introduces the concept of "automortography" in his essay on the celebrity of four authors who wrote about their own deaths while they were dying of cancer. MacEwen might not have expected to die early, but her father had died at the age of fifty-six from a heart attack associated with alcoholism, and she had initially avoided alcohol because of her father's addiction (Sullivan 83, 250). She knew a similar fate was possible for her. Kane, referring particularly to Raymond Carver and Charles Bukowski, argues that their "scripting and directing" of their own deaths "enhances their literary celebrity," partly because their automortography "elicits feeling" in the reader (410). Combining and literalizing two ideas from Roland Barthes, Kane implies that readers get more pleasure from a text if they know it is about the death of its author. Critics need to consider tactfully the possibility that MacEwen wrote *The T.E. Lawrence Poems* with special attention to Lawrence's celebrity, among various aspects of his biography, and conceived of her own potential death – her passing as he did – as the ultimately ironic promotion. If that is the case, then an additional irony is that her promotion extends to Lawrence, whom she ultimately criticizes for his imperialism.

My interest in MacEwen's decision to write poems in Lawrence's voice is motivated as much by the poems themselves as by the provocative questions that they raise. The quite different remainder of this chapter concludes my argument about her passing as Lawrence – both in giving evidence that MacEwen herself was unsure of how to differentiate her impersonating voice from Lawrence's voice, and in considering how her poems quote Lawrence without disclosing their sources. To understand MacEwen's criticism of Lawrence, we need to know when and how she refuses to identify with him, despite the powerful draw of his celebrity. The extent of her identification with him can be gauged when she modifies Lawrence's phrases, sometimes to assert her differences from him and thereby to involve herself in "disidentification."

MacEwen's sources for *The T.E. Lawrence Poems* were several; her aforementioned underlining of her otherwise undocumented quotations in her annotated copy at the archives adds evidence to some of my earlier arguments about her identity. Her handwritten notes at the University of Toronto's Thomas Fisher Rare Book Library reveal that she was reading various texts by and about Lawrence, such as his *Seven Pillars of Wisdom*, his translation of *The Odyssey of Homer* (1935), his posthumous *The Mint* (1955), his published letters, and John E. Mack's *A Prince of Our Disorder: The Life of T.E. Lawrence* (1976). The archive has her copy of *Seven Pillars of Wisdom*, and a small number of its pages are folded to indicate where she found some of her inspiration (as in the case of "There Is No Place To Hide"). It is otherwise mostly unmarked, despite the high number of phrases (at least twenty) that she found in it and used in *The T.E. Lawrence Poems*. The annotated and corrected copy of her own book contains, as I reported earlier, underlining in forty-five of the sixty poems, and her handwriting in a note at the beginning of the book indicates that the underlined phrases "are Lawrence's."[4] The question is, for whose information did she underline those phrases in her book? A thorough examination of her archived correspondence might yet reveal the answer, but there are two noteworthy possibilities. The first is that MacEwen wanted to reassure her editor and publisher, for reasons of copyright, that she had not used too much of Lawrence's texts. (His phrases amount to a little less than 20% of the book.) The second is that she wanted to remind herself whether a phrase was hers or Lawrence's; indeed, her handwritten question marks beside the underlining in four poems – "Excavating in Egypt," "Thunder-Song," "Apologies," and "Visual Purple" – suggest that she was not always certain. Her own handwriting attests to the fact that her voice can be indistinguishable from that of Lawrence.

Two poems near the end of the book explicitly demonstrate that her impersonation of Lawrence's voice is involved in, and possibly motivated by, his celebrity. In "The Desirability of El Aurens" ("El Aurens" approximating the way that some Arabs pronounced his name in David Lean's 1962 film *Lawrence of Arabia*, which MacEwen had evidently watched because she mentions one of its scenes in the title story of her 1972 book *Noman*), Lawrence is ostensibly frustrated that he was accorded the respect due to a *sherif* (a Muslim ruler, often a religious authority). He is therefore a public figure, and he complains that he was

> all dressed up in [his] Sherifian regalia,
> looking like a perfect idiot, posing
> for the cameras, and hating it
> all the way to Damascus. (66)

Later in the poem, MacEwen involves herself self-reflexively in such "posing" when her Lawrence says, "A discharged mental patient / with the face of a wrinkled monkey / is reported to be impersonating me" (66). MacEwen was obviously not seeking to flatter herself by associating herself with Lawrence; instead, she identifies with him or "apes" him. The poem is sceptical of her authenticity and his. Referring to herself as a "discharged mental patient," she also implies that celebrity – at least for a fan – can have psychological consequences.

The potentially inauthentic mutual performance of Lawrence's celebrity appears again in the next poem, "There Is No Place To Hide," whose title attests to Lawrence's impression of the public's invasion of his private life. He says, "Here is a famous world; I'm standing on a stage / With ten spotlights on me, talking about how I detest / publicity" (67). Ironically, MacEwen's Lawrence is openly critical of his celebrity in this way only when he is in public. As Sullivan's biography of MacEwen shows, she also expressed some frustration with "publicity," at least after the phase of her initial excitement. MacEwen's own experience helped her to imagine how celebrity of much higher degree must have affected Lawrence.

At the end of "There Is No Place To Hide," MacEwen's Lawrence reflects upon his celebrity and implies that madness and self-inflicted injury are possible results of being known as an image. (The poem has the staggered indentation that is common to the book, and which MacEwen probably chose because of similar formatting in the poem "To S.A." that serves as the epigraph to *Seven Pillars of Wisdom*.) Her Lawrence says,

> Outside my window, a small tit bird bashes itself
> against the glass. At first I thought
> it was admiring itself in the window.
> Now I know it's mad. (67)

Wood interprets the bird "as MacEwen the poet looking through her imaginary window at the imaginary Lawrence inside" ("No-man's" 158), but the bird initially symbolizes Lawrence, who is "talking about" himself; the bird behaves with the same narcissistic self-reflexivity as Lawrence in looking at its own reflection and going crazy by "bash[ing] itself" against its own image. Wood is correct to suggest that MacEwen imagines herself in that maddening situation.

MacEwen evidently appreciated the negative assessment of celebrity reported in *Seven Pillars of Wisdom*, which is one source of "There Is No Place To Hide." Parts of eight lines in "There Is No Place To Hide" are underlined, and one of her sources is the chapter entitled "Myself" in *Seven Pillars of Wisdom*.[5] The aforementioned page (583) in MacEwen's copy of that book, indicated by a fold, includes the source of the line about the "court martial," which is less interesting than other statements in the same paragraph by Lawrence. His awareness of celebrity's threat to identity and the self is evident in this statement: "The self ... was forced into depreciation by others' uncritical praise. It was a revenge of my trained historical faculty upon the evidence of public judgement, the lowest common denominator to those who knew, but from which there was no appeal because the world was wide" (*Seven* 583). He is complaining of the baseness of public opinion that results in the "depreciation" of the self, which MacEwen transforms into a tit bird whose interest in or admiration of itself becomes damaging.

The superficiality of the star's image in "There Is No Place To Hide" is in contrast with a genuine religious concern that helps to create the mystique of MacEwen's public persona. Her passing as Lawrence is a representation and even enactment of her quest for mystical emptiness or transcendence. As I have shown, celebrity involves a pretence of religious significance, and MacEwen was both earnest and ironic in adopting such a pretence. Wood states that numerous critics have remarked on the spirituality of MacEwen and her poetry ("From *The Rising*" 67)[6] but that "MacEwen herself belonged to no specific community of belief" ("No-man's" 147). She was a curious but not devoted student of actual religion who was self-taught in mysticism from a wide range of Judeo-Christian, Islamic, and Hindu sources in addition to her knowledge of Greek myth. Although Sullivan thought that MacEwen once "intended to train herself to be a visionary" (74), Wood has not enough evidence to suggest that MacEwen had actual "visionary experience" ("From *The Rising*" 41); nevertheless, MacEwen's passing as Lawrence is a metaphoric process, and metaphor can create what J. Christopher Crocker describes as a "mystical sense of union" (62) between a writer and audience – or a celebrity and fan. The risks here – bad faith, identity confusion, and overidentification – were ambivalent to MacEwen because the politics involved were so complex.

In "Apologies," those politics are ambivalently postcolonial and are associated with MacEwen's desire for a mystical emptiness – arguably an absence of desire for attachments and identifications. Both the historical and fictional Lawrences suggest that they occupy or even personify a "void" (*Seven* 30; MacEwen 64) that is the result of being always between worlds, Western and Middle Eastern, or trying to enter one world from the other as the tit bird at the window tries in "There Is No Place To Hide." To have an internal void is almost to be *empty* – another key word from "Apologies" – which is, in effect, the transcendental condition of selflessness that some mystics experience (Underhill 318). Quoting the historical Lawrence's claim that Arabs are "children of the idea" (*Seven* 41), MacEwen writes,

The Arabs are children of the idea; dangle an idea
In front of them, and you can swing them wherever.
        I was also a child of the idea; I wanted
        no liberty for myself, but to bestow it
Upon them. I wanted to present them with a gift so fine
        it would outshine all other gifts in their eyes;
        it would be *worthy*. Then at last I could be
Empty. (29)

In "Apologies," the void is unwanted, whereas emptiness is desirable – both for MacEwen's Lawrence and in *The Mint*, where the historical Lawrence describes the "ecstasy" of "go[ing] suddenly empty" (105) when listening to music at concerts. The void is a condition of being between wanted things, whereas emptiness is a similar space but without desire – in these cases, desire for identifications with other people or cultures. MacEwen might have felt the void and wanted to feel, as her Lawrence did, "how beautiful it is to be empty" (29).

She seems to have understood that sentiment and his ambivalence about the imperialism that underlies his celebrity. The historical Lawrence wrote that his acculturation into Arabia was "an affectation only": "I had dropped one form [of faith and of appearance] and not taken on the other" (*Seven* 30). MacEwen's Lawrence is both postcolonially apologetic and defensively orientalist when he claims that his "mind's twin kingdoms fought an everlasting war" (29). He does not treat these "twins" equally: the Bedouin are "reckless" and he is "civilized" (29), and his presumed ability to have assimilated an Arab way of life into his "mind" is itself colonial. He realizes that the religious pretence of his celebrity, and his celebrity itself, is irrevocably tainted by his imperialism: "I, whatever I was, / Fell into a dumb void that even a false god could not fill, / could not inhabit" (29). Reconfigured by his celebrity, he cannot describe himself except as "whatever" – or as the aforementioned mirage. Whereas he suggested in "Water" (the book's first poem) that he would be able to transform to fit into Arab culture, here he is a "false god" who could neither "fill" nor "inhabit" (i.e., fit into) that culture. With the emphasis on the "false[ness]" of his religiosity, MacEwen's Lawrence sees himself as a "soiled Outsider" (29) who would be happier without identifications across cultures.

Although MacEwen seems devoted to Lawrence through her identification with him, at a crucial point later in the book she separates herself from him and sides with the women who have been massacred during the Arab Revolt. Her passing as Lawrence is detectable when her Lawrence refers to his own work as poetry (in "Tall Tales" or "The Void," for example); it is also detectable in "Tafas," where the description of violence against women is more graphic than Lawrence's account of his rape in "Deraa." In "Tafas," MacEwen's voice and that of Lawrence cannot be distinguished by style, except that the politics of their descriptions generate noticeably different tones. Liza Potvin argues that "MacEwen may not be interpreted as a feminist poet in the typical application of the term; certainly she did not call herself one, and her poetry offers no overtly feminist statements or objectives; on the contrary, she writes [in *Armies of the Moon*] that 'all ideologies enrage me.'" Potvin adds, "she nonetheless reserves a great deal of criticism for dualism and sexism as exclusive and excluding modes of thought" (18, 19). Nowhere is this more obvious than in "Tafas," especially compared to the historical Lawrence's account.

Lawrence's version in *Seven Pillars of Wisdom* is as horrifying and nearly as moving as MacEwen's in *The T.E. Lawrence Poems*, but he points no finger at men, as men, for their crimes in war. In fact, the only individual man that Lawrence mentions is a sympathetic character. Lawrence's description of finding the bodies of Arab women killed by Turks involves one of his Arab companions, Abd el Aziz, whose grief and outrage make him inarticulate:

> It was a child, three or four years old, whose dirty smock was stained red over one shoulder and side, with blood from a large half-fibrous wound, perhaps a lance thrust, just where neck and body joined.
>
> The child ran a few steps, then stood and cried to us in a tone of astonishing strength (all else being very silent), 'Don't hit me, Baba'. Abd el Aziz, choking out something – this was his village, and she might be of his family – flung himself off his camel, and stumbled, kneeling, in the grass before the child. His suddenness frightened her, for she threw up her arms and tried to scream; but, instead, dropped in a little heap, while the blood rushed out again over her clothes; then, I think, she died. (*Seven* 652)

Some of these phrases appear in "Tafas," too. Lawrence then explains that his company moved along through the village and discovered many women murdered by the retreating Turks:

> I looked close and saw the body of a woman folded across it [a sheepfold, a low mud wall], bottom upwards, nailed there by a saw bayonet whose haft stuck hideously in the air from between her naked legs. She had been pregnant, and about her lay others, perhaps twenty in all, variously killed, but set out in accord with an obscene taste. (*Seven* 652)

Lawrence's response to the massacre is to seek vengeance: "I said, 'The best of you brings me the most Turkish dead'"; "[b]y my order we took no prisoners, for the only time in the war" (*Seven* 652, 653). He responds as a male warrior traditionally does, with general brutality.

MacEwen's Lawrence has the same reaction – "We went after the Turks / And killed them all" (52) – but he blames men more specifically than does his historical counterpart, and the result is that the poem's tone, compared to that of *Seven Pillars of Wisdom,* is more accusatory. In "Tafas," MacEwen decides that the wounded girl's mother is the woman found impaled on the bayonet, but the historical Lawrence makes no such claim. MacEwen thereby accentuates the pathos of the scene and forms a connection between the girl and woman that parallels her connection to them as a person of the same sex. Her Lawrence notices that

> Death's little silver cock was stuck
>   between her mother's legs;
> She sat on the tip of a saw
>   bayonet. And a pregnant woman
> Was bent over a sheepfold ... (52)

All of these atrocities are perpetrated by men against women; they make sexual symbolism real (though they are, in this poem, imaginary). Cohen, in *The Energy of Slaves* (1972), wrote that poems were "lying down in their jelly / to make love with the tooth of a saw" (117). Ten years later, MacEwen transforms Cohen's metafictionally abstract image into a highly visceral image of rape and murder "on the tip of a saw / bayonet." Here, MacEwen intervenes in the otherwise extraordinarily male texts of both Lawrences (and possibly that of Cohen); her voice has a feminist urgency that Lawrence's does not.

MacEwen's intervention in "Tafas" is closer to ventriloquism than impersonation or passing; this intervention is the crucial moment when MacEwen implicitly refuses to pass undetectably as Lawrence. In *Gendered Persona and Poetic Voice* (2004), what I call "passing" is what Maija Bell Samei would call "*non-ventriloquistic cross-dressing* or *transvestism*," which is evident when the persona is "apparently ... unitary" (31). In almost all of *The T.E. Lawrence Poems*, MacEwen's voice passes as the historical Lawrence's voice. Although "Tafas" uses four of his phrases, it is an exception to MacEwen's usual passing as Lawrence. For the aforementioned political reasons, her difference from the historical Lawrence can be detected in "Tafas." Samei "use[s] *ventriloquism* [as the term] for those cases in which the persona of the poet is allowed to surface alongside that of [the poem's speaker]" (31). Samei argues that any "entering into the persona of another, this impersonation, need not be so permanent nor so well-concealed; a ventriloquist, for example, allows the props of his impersonation to be displayed before his audience and moves in and out of the persona of the puppet, returning to his own character in the interim" (29–30). In "Tafas," MacEwen finally exposes "the props." She reveals herself behind Lawrence, her puppet, and figuratively speaks with him – not only through him – in a voice that is more her own than his. She partly withdraws from her identification with him. Although MacEwen might be grandstanding by speaking in Lawrence's voice, she does not believe him to be the bigger man; his complicity in war crimes means that he, too, is an agent of death, and "Death's ... silver cock" is "little."[7]

What the historical Lawrence did not say explicitly enough, MacEwen does say: men make war – and she says so not by changing *how* Lawrence expresses himself, but by changing *what* he says to agree with a more feminist view. The style of the voice continues to be different from that of MacEwen's previous books and is passable as that of Lawrence, but the content becomes subtly incompatible with his biases, and so MacEwen's identification with him is evidently not total. Her criticism of Lawrence's imperialist war and of his celebrity is from the perspective of a woman sensitive to her difference from him as a poet and as a celebrity of lower degree. By standing in for Lawrence in poetry, she draws attention to the unlikelihood of a female poet having such cultural standing in the reality of her time and place: Canada after the 1970s. (She is probably also implying that Canadian writers in general never have status comparable to that of Lawrence – but how many English writers anywhere have both military and cultural power?) Ultimately, her passing as Lawrence is both wishful thinking and a study in contrasts that exposes unfairness related to sexuality on levels historical, political, and personal.

A celebrity of low degree compared to some of her contemporaries, MacEwen imagines in *The T.E. Lawrence Poems* the appropriation of the power of a celebrity who was more widely recognized than any Canadian poet. Partly because she is too late – at the end of an era – to use that power for social promotion as a star and female poet, she uses it against itself, interrogating the imperialism that was essential to Lawrence's celebrity and, to a lesser extent, her own. She arguably became critical of the affectations that Arab robes or Egyptian eyeliner on Westerners might indicate. Disillusioned, perhaps, by the limitations of both her stardom and the spiritual development that she had sought in Eastern mysticism, she criticizes – through Lawrence – her own "posing" (as in "The Desirability of El Aurens") and the postcolonially regretful but orientalist yearning of her desire for mystical emptiness (which Lawrence expresses in "Apologies"). Lawrence's status magnifies these issues so that they can be seen more clearly by her public, including her readers – and by MacEwen herself.

Although MacEwen's passing as Lawrence is ultimately incomplete, their closeness is also evident: in her own potential confusion about whether she wrote certain phrases or whether she found them in Lawrence's texts, in her deep empathy for Lawrence's psychological and physical trials, and in her understanding of the relational and performative basis of identity formation. By choosing to write in the voice of a man of such celebrity – a status threatening to identity especially at such a high degree – she gambles with her own sense of self. Her experiment was critical and ironic but also spiritual and possibly fatalistic. She once asked Layton in a letter to explain "how you personally have survived ... how to guard oneself against the intensity of one's own vision," and she added, "I fear my own poetry. Fear the actual strength of the voice" (qtd. in Sullivan 96). Regardless of whether she anticipated her own death in *The T.E. Lawrence Poems*, she understood that her devotion to more than one strong voice would push her to the limits of her art.

Conclusion: Public, Nation, Now

The common representation of celebrity that emerges from the poetry in the previous chapters is complex but ultimately negative, even distressing. Suicide, murder, slavery, oppression, and repression are all variously and symbolically blamed upon celebrity. The public – represented by photographers, interviewers, lawmen, mythic punishers, variously unwholesome crowds – seems generally ready to invade the privacy of the star and to assimilate or reconfigure the identity of that private self. The identity crisis resulting from the fusion of selves that underlies the metaphor of celebrity – *privacy is publicity* – is the star's theoretically total confusion in looking at the mirror's image and recognizing the public. But why should a vision of the public be so menacing rather than welcome?

Most of my answers so far have implicated star poets themselves in the identity crisis, real or imagined, that they reflect on. Their distorted vision of the public and of themselves is not the fault of the public itself as much as the result of publicity or their condition of being too public. The metaphor of celebrity is one of the reasons why so many celebrities appear to worsen their own identity crises: their strategies of self-promotion, such as grandstanding, are also processes of identity formation (e.g., the adoption of personas) that depend on metaphor. The typical authorial concern with publication and publicity becomes more serious when one of the most versatile techniques, metaphor, impinges upon the authors' versatility and free thinking by obliging them to the expectations of the public. The obligation is not actually total, but metaphor is totalizing, and when it is self-promotional it gives an undue power to the public.

Although Irving Layton, Leonard Cohen, Michael Ondaatje, and Gwendolyn MacEwen do not usually represent the public realistically, its threat to stars is real: an experience of being watched, questioned, gossiped about, followed – and, in some cases, worse. For MacEwen to represent Julian the magician's audience as a horde of demons, however, or for Ondaatje to represent Billy the Kid's audience as the crew of an assassin, is to overstate the physical threat to account for the psychological risk. Someone might reasonably ask why celebrity in Canadian poetry would inspire these poets to respond to it – perhaps disproportionately and without much regard for its boon to their art and their industry – and reinforce Canadian literature's long-standing stereotype of celebrity as a "destroyer" (York, *Literary* 42).

Part of the answer is that these authors, writing in the era of celebrity in Canadian poetry, were keenly and collectively aware of what could be gained or lost through stardom, on individual and national levels. I have refrained from concentrating on nationalism partly because *the public* as a term does not necessarily indicate the nation, but the nationalistic celebrations of the late 1950s and 1960s could not have been ignored by the aforementioned poets, who probably realized that they were being encouraged to ignore the odds of a bust after a boom. Their culture of stardom would later be described as modest and minor (Cohen, "Leonard"; Dudek, "Committed" 8). At the time, however, they played along, helping celebrity to become a major creative and cultural issue – while refraining from writing optimistically about the future of Canadian poetry as an enduringly popular art. The evidence of their pessimism and concern is in their representations of celebrity. They often characterize it not only through their fictionalized protagonists but also through their equally imaginary audiences, which have little national significance in the examples in this book. Their choice of subjects – all their non-Canadian stars – is what creates the national and transnational significance, which reflects obliquely upon the not especially Canadian public that they have imagined. Is it horrible because it isn't Canadian? Foreign or otherwise, real audiences are neither so homogeneous nor so cruel, so it is ironic that the demonization of the public in the previous chapters is partly the result of stars thinking and acting similarly, as crowds are assumed to do.

More than thirty years later, have Canadian poets changed their ways of interacting with the public? Do they continue to represent it in their work? These two are relatively easy questions to answer in the affirmative, because technological changes in the mass media necessitate new interactions, and the public as a category is big enough to include many aspects of society commonly described in poems. But have Canadian poets shifted their attitudes to publicity and privacy, and to what extent are these terms opposite or identical now? Has celebrity emerged in poetry again, and, if so, what supports it? What is its scope – the number of stars, their geographic distribution, their relative stardom, and the evidence of their popularity?

Canada still has authors who have recently published bestselling books of poetry. Cohen is one of them again, partly because of the financial scandal involving his management that motivated and promoted his *Book of Longing* (2006), and because of the musical comeback that he began in 2008. Another is Christian Bök, whose *Eunoia* (2001) sold twenty thousand copies by 2009, only eight years after its publication – at a time when a tenth that many sales is considered a success in Canada ("Calgary Poet"). His book's popularity might be an indication of the open-mindedness of a reading public delighted by its formal ingenuity and Oulipian experimentation. I have also heard it described as a gimmick. The differing opinions help to create controversy, and, as Layton knew, controversy is promotional. Canadian poets in general might be more popular if more of them were writing experimental texts that were as curiosity-provoking and controversially entertaining as Bök's *Eunoia* – but, as Carmine Starnino observes, "poets who can bring off this sort of thing aren't exactly thick on the ground here" (135). Although Canadian poetry is supported by contests, awards, and festivals that produce instances of celebrity on a yearly schedule, there is no general excitement in Canadian poetry today – few signs of a critical mass of poets, successful for any reason, who are widely known and whose presence attracts new readers (or other audiences) to them and to other poets.

The critical mass that once existed was concentrated in a small number of media – print, radio, and television, which could be mutually reinforcing – but now the media have another dimension, the Internet, which has changed the relationship between artists and their audiences. Today, a successful slam or spoken word poet can recite poetry for large crowds and appear online on video-sharing websites without needing to get anyone's attention in print – Shane Koyczan and Kaie Kellough being recent examples. Kellough and Koyczan also work with musicians, and some of their recordings are increasingly available partly because of increasing bandwidth online. The multifunctionality of the Internet and its enormous virtual space have allowed poets and almost anyone else to have a presence. It is, however, diffuse. Not only is there the Internet, but the number of television channels and radio stations is also growing so big that significant cultural trends are not easily created or predicted, and the proportion of these media that encourages the language arts (excluding popular music) is relatively small. Poets and poems online can go viral, but they are likely to remain more obscure than they would be if a publisher were promoting them. Finding a niche is still their best hope.

Recently developed software on the Internet has allowed poets to delineate their niches as they involve themselves more directly and personally in the promotion of their work. Bök, Margaret Atwood, Sina Queyras, derek beaulieu, Alison Pick, rob mclennan, Michael Lista, and others have created online personas on various popular sites, such as Twitter, which lets users send very short messages to their websites and to others who follow their tweets. This service enables some of the publisher's usual tasks to be reassigned to the author. As Lorraine York argues in *Margaret Atwood and the Labour of Literary Celebrity* (2013), a star author's adoption of new technologies of communication is part of the work of maintaining celebrity today, and this should help critics and other readers to recognize that self-promotional efforts can be individual accomplishments that evince sophistication in public outreach (126, 131). The online activities that poets have chosen to share have probably not often created celebrity, but they are one more way for poets to build their networks of readers and supportive others. As I write this, Bök has 5,852 followers on Twitter. Atwood has 388,760. To promote themselves and their work, contemporary poets use tweets and blogs to narrate their supposedly personal reactions to cultural events and texts. These technologies create a newly public form of diary and correspondence that raises questions about activities that are usually thought of as private, such as reading and writing to each other one-to-one. Of course, the traditions of reviewing and of writing open letters have long raised these questions, but now the technologies are more accessible, and so a public (e.g., the culturally specific readership of a little magazine) can quickly and easily grow bigger, more diverse, and full of strangers: *the* public – one that authors can interact with more spontaneously and influence more directly.

Such an influence in new media can then be applied to book readerships. One of the aforementioned tweeters, Queyras, has even decided that her next book will be composed almost entirely of her Twitter feed. (Her 2009 book *Unleashed* was partly an experiment in blogging.) The rationale that she stated at the 2012 Public Poetics conference at Mount Allison University is that if you want your poetry to be public, it should begin in public (Queyras). Wanting to be heard as a critical voice, but knowing that public speech can have consequences if it is radical, Queyras explained in her address that she has an "alter ego" online. This persona might have helped her to overcome her admitted reluctance to contribute to public discourse, because an online persona or alias offers at least a semblance of privacy, and it can help to restrict the number of readers who are "in the know" to a literary circle or clique even if the texts are widely available.

Although we are beginning to understand privacy and anonymity as fictitious, especially online, we can still snoop around (at least, it can feel like snooping) and read any number of tweets and blogs for which we are obviously not intended or ideal readers. We are then members of the public, but the messages that we read often encourage us to join a more specific, restricted, somewhat more private public – such as Bök's 5,852 – by returning often. Much of our activity online is a negotiation with others who want us to identify less with the public than with a public, because we will then have accepted another social role, one that identifies us to them ideologically or culturally even if they do not know our names or Internet Protocol addresses. All of these allegiances and secret but ultimately discoverable identities suggest that espionage might be more apt than surfing as a metaphor of Internet activity.

In fact, a remarkable example of a metaphor of espionage or spying in Canadian poetry has recently appeared in the poetry of Wendy Morton. Her metaphor of the poet is of titular significance in her books *Private Eye* (2001), *Undercover* (2003), and *Gumshoe* (2007), which reflect some of the experiences in her career as an investigator for an insurance company. Most of the authors in the previous chapters used metaphor for the exposure of their own private concerns, and they chose highly recognizable figures as public personas. By her own account, Morton tends to write about and expose the concerns of relatively anonymous or unknown others, and to insinuate herself into this exposure through sympathy or empathy.

Her figurative espionage and real activities as a private investigator coincide with the extraordinary publicity of both her poems and herself. In her memoir, *Six Impossible Things before Breakfast: Taking Poetry Public across Canada* (2006), Morton describes her almost incredible success, through corporate sponsorship, in gaining publicity in newspapers, on radio, and on television. Many of her poems have contrastingly private and even secret origins. One poem included in *Six Impossible Things* describes the death of the son of a lawyer Morton was working with. Another, "Spanking with Cabbage," is about her investigation into insurance claims filed by two people "who were running an S&M bed and breakfast" (Morton 17). Others are about personal details of people she met on flights with her sponsoring airline: a dream, a hope, a wedding, a vacation with the family. In these cases, she is a corporate author whose writing about the personal details of others is publicity for the benefit of herself and the corporation, and, significantly, for the person whose feelings and thoughts she is trying to express or acknowledge. Morton states that "poetry is the shortest distance between two hearts" (71) and that her poetry is about "connection" (99). Far more openly than in any other book I have read, her poetry uses intimacy and privacy to publicize corporations, develop brand loyalty in consumers, and promote the author for material gain. Her work is the prime example so far of the metaphor of celebrity – *privacy is publicity* – in Canadian poetry (at least since the turn of the millennium and maybe of all time), but her intentions seem to be very different from those of the star poets during the boom years of the 1960s and 1970s.

Layton, Cohen, Ondaatje, and MacEwen all had some interest in celebrity as a status that could develop into fame, legend, or myth; in contrast, Morton seems to want more immediate results, through instant relationships with members of her audience – whether the results are cathartic or commodified. Many of her poems could be described as "occasional verse," written for special occasions and often to be read aloud to audiences who are surprised and unprepared to be audiences. Sponsored by several companies, including WestJet and DaimlerChrysler, she has integrated marketing and poetry for the short-term gains associated with celebrity rather than fame. Although she has worked to popularize poetry in her community, her poetry in this context seems not to be interested in the grand statuses of fame, legend, and myth, which often favour supposed universality over particularity, and longevity over significance on demand.

Integrating the stories of the people she meets, she creates poetry of and for the public whom she encounters in her travels, and she writes of this public with enthusiastic appreciation. Her relentless optimism about the potential of poetry to connect authors with readers, with corporate help, is partly the result of the perks and of her audience's appreciation for her highly personalized type of literature: texts that would probably be enduringly meaningful only to the listeners and readers – arguably clients – who had accepted them. Her work aims to please rather than trouble her audience. It is popular, not elitist. Reportedly thrilled to have had the attention of a poet, her audience reciprocates her appreciation, but whether her work will *appreciate*, in the sense of gaining value over time and relative to other cultural products, is questionable.

York prompts this question in her recent article about a vineyard in the Niagara region that has licensed the printing of poems by Morton, MacEwen, and others on their wine-bottle labels. York demonstrates through interviews with some of the winemakers and poets that fine wine and poetry are thought to be mutually beneficial in this arrangement, and she notices that not all the poets represented on the labels are canonical ("Viticultural" 69); thus, poetry seems to have its own cachet regardless of its authorship, while the noncanonical poets might nevertheless gain attention thanks to the prestige of fine wine. So, can fine wine, which is supposed to appreciate, confer similar distinction upon the poetry? Morton's poetry is also associated now with Chrysler cars, which appreciate even less often than do wines, and with an airline that has a reputation not for class but for economy. Her poetry's uses are many, and they show that stardom can transcend cultural and material divisions, but the pop cultural examples outnumber the elite examples, and this imbalance might prove restrictive – not in Pierre Bourdieu's sense, as "selective" (338), but in the sense of creating an undesirable limit.

And yet she is measurably on par with another writer who would be acknowledged without reluctance as a celebrity who can be called "literary." In the ProQuest library database called Canadian Newsstand Complete, a search for "Wendy Morton" returns 394 results from newspapers since the year 2000, compared with 444 for "Christian Bök" (including "Bok"); 9,811 for "Leonard Cohen"; and 14,351 for "Margaret Atwood." The qualitative difference in these numbers is that Morton was not simply mentioned but focused on in proportionally more articles. That she is in the same range as Bök is notable. Her success might mean that the sexism and perhaps the ageism of star poetry circles did not outlive the 1970s, though I doubt that they have vanished.[1] Furthermore, almost no one I know has heard of Morton, whereas many have heard of Bök. In literary and academic circles a poet's familiarity tends to be the result of literary fame (i.e., canonicity), nascent or established, not celebrity in its nonliterary sense. But perhaps it is remarkable that Bök has garnered as much attention as Morton in the newspapers, where poetry that illustrates and develops experimental literary theories is rare indeed.

Morton's celebrity is quantitatively similar to that of Bök in the newspapers, but it is qualitatively different because of how she is recognized. Her poetry is not yet likely to become canonical, one reason being that she has not won a long-standing or lucrative literary award – though in 2010 she won Lorna Crozier and Patrick Lane's inaugural Spirit Bear Award and the Golden Beret Award of the Calgary Spoken Word Society ("Wendy"). In contrast, Bök won the big purse of the Griffin Poetry Prize in 2002 ("Christian"). In *Prizing Literature* (2011), Gillian Roberts notes that major awards indicate precanonicity or canonicity (34); they are written into the record books that literary scholars and historians cite as one kind of evidence of a writer's importance over time. Even with major prizes, however, the winners outnumber the canonical authors, which is further reason to distinguish between celebrity and fame. This distinction is also upheld for critics who believe that Morton's writing cooperates too directly with capitalism; some readers still want to believe that literature is or should be untainted by corporate money. The Griffin Prize is funded by corporate money, but it has an individual's name (in much the same way that the Governor General's Award has an individual's title) that grants it a prestige associated with a person's achievement or entitlement. The impression of fairness created by the juries of the major awards has the same effect. A critic might therefore wonder if Morton is a pure celebrity: someone whose occasional works, spin-offs, and many appearances in the mass media will not generate long-term interest. Morton is the celebrity; Bök is the literary celebrity en route to fame.

Morton is not the only poet to have recently attempted to reach out to the public with occasional works. Ondaatje and Margaret Atwood were recently back on the poetry scene in an unexpected way: as contributors to a trust fund. They were not promoting an individual poet as much as what Richard Dyer would call a "star text" (qtd. in York, *Literary* 12). The publication of *The Al Purdy A-frame Anthology* (2009), edited by Paul Vermeersch, was intended to generate a profit and donations that would allow the Al Purdy A-frame Trust to buy the late Al Purdy's house, restore it, and preserve it as a retreat for writers – a star text serving fame.[2] The story of the trust fund appeared in major newspapers and other media, and the publisher, Harbour, created a promotional page on its website that offers several ways to contribute financially to the fund. Among other supportive authors, Atwood and Ondaatje were evidently hoping that their status would publicize an effort to maintain a house, a history, and a life's work that have arguably become a public good. Ultimately, Cohen was among the major donors and the house was saved from likely demolition ("Poet"), but only after Purdy's wife Eurithe decided to sell it for much less than the market value that was originally reported (Jackson). Fundraising continues so that the house can be readied for visitors, and its seemingly incremental progress is a sign of a resistance to any literary *cause célèbre* in Canada today (and to any philanthropy during recession times), especially in poetry, even when some of the people involved are widely recognized in Canada and abroad.

Would Morton's more direct approach to corporate sponsorship help the Al Purdy A-frame Trust? Imagine Ondaatje and Atwood in a Chrysler sedan with Purdy decals driving around on a tour in support of the anthology and of the trust: comic, partly because their readers might think it beneath them to promote literature and culture in this way. Morton, however, has experienced some of the same recognition and promotion that Atwood and Ondaatje have, and all of them, in fact, have corporate sponsorship if we accept that their presses are corporations that operate for profit. The main economic and cultural difference is that Morton's promotional funds come from corporations not usually involved in literature. As in politics, the source matters. Although Morton's sponsors seem open and not prejudiced against women and older people, there are literary and other institutional biases that might negatively affect the perception of her corporate sponsorship, regardless of how progressive it is. One reason, which is not merely a bias, for being reluctant to ask for corporate sponsorship of Purdy's Trust is that its supporters want Purdy's house and work to be valued as a public good, believing that art has a value similar to that of land that has not been laid claim to. This might seem foolish to anyone who has accepted that more privatization would benefit our arts, culture, and heritage, and in fact capitalism and globalization increase the difficulty of preserving national heritage as national. I would not want to see Purdy's house branded by a major corporation, but corporate money *could* have helped to save the house (and indeed might have been involved behind the scenes). It would require that the trust's supporters agree to a separation of nationalism from Purdy's canonicity (i.e., literary fame). Robert Lecker, however, argues throughout *Making It Real* (1995) that such values cannot be separated. We would have to abandon some of the significance that makes the house worth saving. Imagine – and this is not as funny – the WestJet Purdy Museum and Retreat (or the Griffin Purdy Museum and Retreat, less likely because Scott Griffin's patronage of the arts is not as direct as WestJet's patronage of Morton). In an era when poetry is obscure compared to other arts, and when much more public money is distributed to questionable economic causes than to questionable artistic and cultural causes, Morton might have one answer – one that needs its own solutions – to the dilemma of what to do for Purdy's house.

Representations of celebrity in Canadian poetry today involve different attitudes toward stardom, star texts, and related commodities that apply to this dilemma. The promotion of the trust through a star text might in itself be an impediment to a solution, because stardom – with its ability to cross borders – might be seen as nonnational, transnational, or – with its Hollywood connotations – even imperialistically American, which would be objectionable to Purdy's nationalism. In the last several years, poets in Canada have refused the 1960s and 1970s trend of writing about non-Canadian stars and have written about Canadian stars or stars in the Canadian milieu. In Steven Price's *Anatomy of Keys* (2006), the internationally recognized escape artist known as Houdini comes to Canada, where he is fatally wounded backstage in Montreal by a young man disturbed by Houdini's reputation for invincibility. *Anatomy of Keys* supports the claim that some Canadians (not necessarily Price) are hostile to foreign models of stardom, even though these models are the obvious basis for celebrity in Canada.[3]

Other recent books, however, represent the celebrity of *Canadians*, and they do so with a degree of appreciation not seen in the poetry of the 1960s and 1970s. By the 1950s and 1960s, Canadian stars such as Glenn Gould and Terry Sawchuk were emerging on the national stage, but poetic representations of these stars did not appear until around half a century later, in Kate Braid's *A Well-mannered Storm* (2008) and Randall Maggs's *Night Work* (2008), respectively. The delay partly suggests that their celebrity needed to be validated over time, perhaps as fame, before they were interesting to poets or justifiable as objects of fandom – implying that Canadian literary readers and writers today would rather appreciate historical stardom than current popular culture.

(Ondaatje and MacEwen had the same preference; Layton and Cohen did not.) This sense of *appreciation* is, as earlier, related to distinction as a judgment that has financial and institutional values that need to be acknowledged; these books are invested in Canadian stardom. The delay also suggests that stardom – then and now, and especially after it has aged – can be understood as a phenomenon that is involved in producing the complicated identifications and affect that poets want to write about and be associated with.

Although the authorial personas in *A Well-mannered Storm* and *Night Work* are evidence of an appreciative fan culture, Braid and Maggs exhibit the familiar wariness of the public when they stand in for their chosen stars. In *A Well-mannered Storm*, Braid assumes a persona known only as *k*, a self-confessed "groupie" (106), and writes a series of poetic and increasingly personal fan letters to Gould, the Canadian pianist famous for his interpretations of music by Johann Sebastian Bach and for his eccentric public engagements. Her imagined Gould indirectly responds to the letters with lyric poetry that attempts to explain his muses, processes of artistic creation, and fears: "Celebrity lashes me like a whip. / I am slave to it" (60). Her Gould also says, "yesterday someone said I am an 'iconic' figure – / another appalling variation on a life in public, / the shackle of it" (97). In *Night Work*, Maggs writes about Sawchuk, the National Hockey League goalie whose face was severely scarred throughout his career in front of the puck – "Four hundred stitches in his face alone" (61) – a man whose face and mask were both real and symbolic aspects of his public recognition. Like Braid, Maggs maintains distance from his subject while also offering suggestive glimpses into the private life of a very public person – glimpses that ultimately help to fuse the personas and the private selves of these performers in the public eye of the author. Maggs, Braid, and Price also associate their chosen stars with injury or illness, continuing a Canadian literary tradition of linking stardom to negativity but focusing more obviously on homage.

This ambivalence that tends toward homage might in itself be a result of the relative obscurity of Price, Maggs, and Braid, none of whom can be described as a celebrity whose public recognition extends beyond the literary field of cultural production. Morton's celebrity is less literary in the sense that she *has* reached beyond that field, and her attitude toward celebrity is comparatively positive – because of the material benefits but also because she is not concerned with literary traditions of promotion and the related expectations. But Morton has not evidently promoted herself on the Internet, unless she does so undercover, leading me to think that these contemporary poets have no realistic hope of achieving celebrity of high degree. Although the continuing integration of mass media, the development of social networking technologies, and viral celebrity create the potential for at least momentarily widespread stardom for poets, the field of celebrity in poetry today is much smaller than it was in the boom years of the 1960s and 1970s. This lack of public pressure might have affected their attitudes toward popular culture: Morton could be positive; Maggs and Braid could write about Canadian stars. There might be less pressure because nationalism in the arts culture today is not as intense as it was in the 1960s and 1970s. Now, literary celebrity in Canada can be understood as a phenomenon, however rare, that is nationally significant but increasingly separate from nationalism in the sense that it is not only a by-product of nationalistic arts funding programs.

Ironically, under less pressure to conform to nationalistic ideals, Braid, Maggs, and Price focus on Canadian stars and places and, as authors, are farther from each other geographically – spanning the country – than the Quebeckers and Ontarians of the previous chapters. Today, in the absence of centennial-era nationalism, our poets can be somewhat more nationalistic, identifying through homage with a hockey player and a CBC Radio personality. This irony seems to verify that the Canadian star poets of the 1960s and 1970s wrote about non-Canadian stars partly to disapprove of narrowly nationalistic views of popular culture.

All this is to say that the era of celebrity in Canadian poetry was a special time in Canadian literature, and that the four poets of the previous chapters were and are significant commentators on Canadian and popular culture. MacEwen, Ondaatje, Cohen, and Layton engaged in risky identifications and metaphors that had personal and political ramifications – not least of which was the imagining of a public that was not a nation. They all sought a degree of international renown, and celebrity can oblige. Material conditions, however, and social norms partly determined how far their stardom could move them, in spite of their hope; meanwhile, the metaphor that was realized through their publicity then created for them the impression of a public that was too immersive. From a broadly cultural vantage point, the era of celebrity in Canadian poetry was a "minor whirlpool" (Dudek, "Committed" 7–8). But from a perspective within that whirlpool – regardless of its actual size – it was both heady and disorienting. If the era of celebrity was in itself a "destroyer," it was not a social but a personal destroyer. There is some evidence that for MacEwen it was, and that for Cohen it almost was. It affected all concerned. For these poets, the era of celebrity in Canadian poetry was a time of crisis, but it was also a time of opportunity for their art and for their reflection upon themselves. Looking in the mirror is not in itself hazardous. What they saw there was sometimes a threat from outside and sometimes a portrait of looking inward – an image of their own wondering.

Acknowledgments

Many people helped me with this book. I owe Brian Trehearne a tremendous debt for the many hours he spent reading and commenting incisively upon drafts of my chapters, and for all our conversations about literature, academia, and life. I am also very grateful to Robert Lecker for his generous mentorship and the years of important experience I gained working with him as a teaching and research assistant. To Monique Morgan, whose graduate seminar introduced me to additional theories of figurative language, I am thankful.

Others at McGill University and beyond had occasion to offer their ideas about my work. Tom Mole is foremost among these for his expertise on celebrity. I thank him and Will Straw and Allan Hepburn for their clarifying questions. At McMaster University, Lorraine York has been encouraging, cheerful in all her help, and altogether welcoming in the field of Canadian literary studies. I feel similarly lucky to have worked with Peter Stoicheff at the University of Saskatchewan, where I also got honest advice from Francis Zichy, Ron Cooley, Susan Gingell, and Paul Bidwell.

Some of my friends kindly read some of the chapters or sections in this book at various stages: Margaret Herrick, Michael Parrish Lee, Caroline Z. Krzakowski, Robin Feenstra, and Naben Ruthnum. Others helped in other ways, Cléa Desjardins with custom brain-warming and heart-warming tuques, Jordanna Comeau with optimism and assistance during the indexing, and Norah Franklin with a timely work-life preserver. I hope to be able to repay the favours and continue the conversations, including book talks with Liisa Stephenson, later chats with Benjamin S.W. Barootes, and exchanges with Julie Peters, Owen Percy, and Paula Derdiger.

Other conversations with people enrolled in my recent course at McGill on Westerns and the West in Canadian literature helped to improve my understanding of Billy the Kid – thanks especially to Francesca Bianco, Nicholas

Cameron, Lana McCrea, Rebecca Babcock, Charlotte McGee, Giles Ayers, Zev Steinlauf, and Meggie Stainforth-Dubois.

Concerned about listing and thereby diminishing the importance of each person, I nevertheless want to acknowledge a group of people from the 2012 Public Poetics conference at Mount Allison University: first, the organizers, Bart Vautour, Erin Wunker, Travis V. Mason, and Christl Verduyn, who arranged everything so well; and second, the participants whose enthusiasm was so energizing as I revised this book for the second-last time: Robert David Stacey, Dean Irvine, Katherine McLeod, Ian Rae, J.A. Weingarten, Karis Shearer, and Will Smith.

Earlier and more direct support came from Davorin Ciković, at the CBC Radio archives in Toronto, who gave me access to a database of broadcasts that was essential to my chapters on media and the era of celebrity in Canadian poetry. I also received funding from the Social Sciences and Humanities Research Council of Canada that enabled me to focus for a while on this work, and a subvention from the Aid to Scholarly Publications Program enabled its completion at the press. Finally, the living poets, the representatives of the late poets, and the publishers of the creative works cited in this book all granted permission for the block quotations, which I appreciate.

My parents, Lloyd and Mary, were both directly and indirectly supportive during the many years of study and work, academic and artistic, that led to the present publication. I owe them an unconditional debt of gratitude. This book is for them.

Finally, I thank my editor, Siobhan McMenemy, for her interest in this book and for her plentiful advice, crucial expertise, and patience in response to my many questions.

Appendix: Four Tables

Table 1. Number of Appearances per Year of Four Poets on CBC Television, 1955–80

Year	Layton	Cohen	Ondaatje	MacEwen
1955	0	0	0	0
1956	1	0	0	0
1957	0	0	0	0
1958	1	0	0	0
1959	0	0	0	0
1960	3	0	0	0
1961	0	0	0	1
1962	1	0	0	0
1963	1	0	0	0
1964	0	0	0	0
1965	0	1	0	1
1966	1	3	0	0
1967	3	2	1	0
1968	0	0	0	0
1969	0	0	0	0
1970	0	0	0	0
1971	0	0	0	0
1972	1	0	0	0
1973	4	1	0	0
1974	1	1	0	0
1975	0	0	0	0
1976	2	0	2	0
1977	2	0	0	0
1978	5	0	0	0
1979	2	0	0	0
1980	3	3	0	0
Total	31	11	3	2

Table 2. Number of Appearances per Year of Four Poets on CBC Radio, 1955–80

Year	Layton	Cohen	Ondaatje	MacEwen
1955	1	0	0	0
1956	1	0	0	0
1957	2	1	0	0
1958	6	3	0	0
1959	10	1	0	0
1960	4	2	0	0
1961	3	3	0	0
1962	0	1	0	0
1963	6	5	0	0
1964	0	0	0	0
1965	4	5	0	0
1966	7	13	0	1
1967	6	9	1	0
1968	5	6	3	0
1969	7	7	0	0
1970	8	3	1	1
1971	8	8	7	0
1972	6	4	3	0
1973	7	3	3	0
1974	3	4	2	0
1975	10	8	1	0
1976	6	3	0	0
1977	9	3	3	2
1978	6	8	1	6
1979	6	5	3	3
1980	7	13	6	1
Total	138	118	34	14

Table 3. Number of Pages of Mention(s) per Year of Four Poets in the *Globe and Mail*, 1955–80*

Year	Layton	Cohen	Ondaatje	MacEwen
1955	1	0	0	0
1956	3	1	0	0
1957	0	0	0	0
1958	0	2	0	0
1959	4	0	0	0
1960	0	0	0	0
1961	7	1	0	0
1962	2	2	0	0
1963	5	0	0	0
1964	4	1	0	1
1965	4	0	0	0
1966	13	7	0	0
1967	3	8	0	0
1968	6	9	0	0
1969	2	27	0	1
1970	18	26	0	1
1971	8	5	1	0
1972	10	13	0	1
1973	23	39	17	1
1974	11	5	2	0
1975	12	12	0	2
1976	18	16	2	1
1977	12	6	2	0
1978	19	22	1	3
1979	16	4	4	1
1980	25	16	6	0
Total	226	222	35	12

* A page with either one or more than one mention of a poet is recorded only once.

Table 4. Number of Texts per Year by and about Four Poets in the *CPI*, 1955–80*

Year	by Layton	about Layton	by Cohen	about Cohen	by Ondaatje	about Ondaatje	by MacEwen	about MacEwen
1955	2	0	0	0	0	0	0	0
1956	8	0	0	0	0	0	0	0
1957	2	0	0	0	0	0	0	0
1958	18	1	4	1	0	0	1	0
1959	4	1	4	0	0	0	1	0
1960	22	0	0	0	0	0	0	0
1961	17	0	2	0	0	0	5	0
1962	14	1	0	0	0	0	6	0
1963	10	0	0	0	0	0	5	0
1964	13	0	0	0	0	0	12	1
1965	0	2	0	1	0	0	2	0
1966	19	2	0	2	6	0	1	0
1967	11	1	0	2	6	0	1	0
1968	12	0	0	3	4	0	3	0
1969	1	0	1	3	7	1	4	0
1970	10	0	0	2	6	0	3	1
1971	13	3	0	0	0	0	1	0
1972	10	0	0	1	2	0	1	0
1973	0	0	0	0	6	1	1	0
1974	9	3	0	1	0	0	1	2
1975	3	1	0	1	0	0	9	2
1976	11	2	0	1	0	1	0	0
1977	6	2	1	2	0	4	0	1
1978	11	5	0	5	2	2	0	0
1979	1	5	0	5	6	3	0	1
1980	8	2	0	0	3	5	0	1
Total	235	31	12	30	48	17	57	9

* After 1975, the index's coverage increased by 65%, though this increase would affect the proportion of pre- and post-1975 numbers only if new periodicals that published these posts were added, and, most likely, none were.

Notes

Introduction

1 Perhaps the most instructive argument about the conceptual rather than verbal or written basis of metaphor is *More than Cool Reason* (1989), by George Lakoff and Mark Turner, who show how metaphor "deals with central and indispensable aspects of our conceptual systems" (215).

1 The Metaphor of Celebrity

1 If this implied definition of publicity seems to call for an alternative term such as "publicness," consider how the mere act of being in public is for so many people an occasion of publicity in the sense of advertising, e.g., wearing branded clothes or using distinctively styled devices such as iPods that have both a corporate and individual use value. For celebrities especially, the condition of being public is inseparable from publicity in this sense.

2 The various uses of the personas examined in the following chapters suggest that a persona is an imagined self; it might also be understood as a performed self – a self auditioned and sometimes considered to be worth integrating into the behaviour of the self assumed to be real. The debate about the term *persona* itself is explained in *The Literary Persona* (1982) by Robert C. Elliott.

3 This and some of my other writing in this chapter also appear in a different context in an article about Ingmar Bergman's film *Persona* (1966) and various superhero movies in *The Journal of Popular Culture*. It should appear in print around the same time as this book, or shortly thereafter.

4 With a further psychoanalytic insight, David Punter writes that "we make sense of the world only by perceiving likenesses and differences between things and other things; thus, metaphor becomes itself a metaphor for the continuing encounter with the other which makes up most of our mental life" (81).

5 Ted Cohen calls this "a special example of metaphorical personal identification, peculiar, perhaps, but common, in which the person one identifies with is oneself. This happens when one tries to gain a sense of oneself at a future time" (*Thinking* 67). The example is "special" partly because it helps to show that metaphor is involved in our contemplation of our motivations, actions, and their potential consequences, which affect who we are and want to be.

6 The use of the term "continuum" here might prompt some readers to wonder if I am actually describing metonymy rather than metaphor, because metonymy is often explained in terms of contiguity. Following the work of Roman Jakobson, David Lodge in *The Modes of Modern Writing* (1977) explains with impressive clarity that metaphor and metonymy are significantly different types of figurative language. Our brains seem to control language based on two different operations: selection and combination. Lodge writes that "[s]election involves the perception of similarity ... and it implies the possibility of substitution (*blouse* instead of *teeshirt, boats* instead of *ships*). It is therefore the process by which metaphor is generated, for metaphor is substitution based on a certain kind of similarity. If I change the sentence, 'Ships crossed the sea' to 'Ships *ploughed* the sea', I have substituted *ploughed* for *crossed*, having perceived a similarity between the movement of a plough through the earth and of a ship through the sea. Note, however, that the awareness of *difference* between ships and ploughs is not suppressed: it is indeed essential to the metaphor" (75). (The type of metaphor in use here, I would add, is implicit rather than explicit; the expression "I am someone else" is explicit as stated, though rarely does anyone state it as such.) Also following Jakobson, Jane Hedley in *Power in Verse* (1988) convincingly argues that "[m]etaphor and metonymy are antithetical figures" (5): "Metaphor proposes that *X* be taken for *Y*, whereas in language and experience they usually belong to different spheres of activity or being [i.e., contexts]. If, then, a metaphor occurs in a discourse whose procedure is according to the axis of combination, it will rupture the fabric of contiguities that discourse is weaving, by importing an element from out of context" (5). Although the public and private realms are contiguous, an implicit declaration such as "I am someone else" cannot be only metonymic; it asserts an often irrational identification between those realms.

7 The private and public selves of stars cannot ever be totally distinct, and some critics have been cautious about attempting to differentiate those selves (Moran 23). The quotations from Grant, Gabin, and Hope say nothing explicit about the private experiences of celebrities; instead, they express impressions of public desires. Nevertheless, in the following chapters I am attentive to the signs of different personas operating in poems. I admit that this is problematic to the extent that it helps me only to refine our understanding of how inaccessible authors are in their texts; however, knowing the difference between the personas can help us to notice the author's ways of thinking about himself or herself in relation to the audience.

8 Similarly, David Punter claims: "Metaphor, of course, consists of comparison, but perhaps these comparisons can never be quite equal; perhaps they always also serve some purpose of aggrandisement or belittlement" (51).

9 Jürgen Habermas has a similar suggestion, arguing that the public can engage in a critique of the nation that could not be accomplished from within government (Fraser 110–11). Robert Lecker refers to this suggestion and other ideas about publicity and academia in his article "Privacy, Publicity, and the Discourse of Canadian Criticism" (1993). On a related but other topic, that of the multiplicity of publics in the context of Canadian mass media, Robert Weaver gives various examples in his "Broadcasting" address at the 1955 Canadian Writers' Conference (106–7).

10 Although my concern is with selfhood, privacy arguably guards not only an aspect of the self. The use of social media by a culture of youth who are not often concerned about privacy and who are using this media to organize protests against capitalism (e.g., the Occupy Wall Street movement) raises the question of the involvement of private property in the concept of privacy. Is privacy a value of rich people who want to hide some of their wealth and thereby protect it? Or, given conspicuous consumption, is privacy a value of a middle class that has just enough money to want to keep it from view – and not enough to be confident in flaunting it and being able to replace it?

11 Metaphors indeed can be examples of bad logic or wishful thinking, but George Lakoff and Mark Turner argue that metaphor is not "completely unconstrained" (200); "[i]t is not the case that anything can be anything" (203). Metaphors are meaningful even if they are illogical. Because they are conceptual, they can never be interpreted as pure nonsense. If I am correct in understanding Lakoff and Turner, a nonsensical (as opposed to illogical) statement cannot be a metaphor. Jacques Lacan has a statement germane to this: "metaphor is situated at the precise point at which meaning is produced in nonmeaning" (150), but whether he means "nonmeaning" as "nonsense" is beyond my ken. He also writes about metaphor in the context of metonymy, but David Lodge is much less ambiguous on this topic.

12 Mandel expressed this tension more directly in a poem that precedes the foregoing 1969 quotation. In "The Meaning of the I CHING" (1967), he writes: "one cannot be another, I cry, / let me not be crazed by poetry" (*From Room to Room* 17). Here, he acknowledges the emotional and irrational aspects of metaphor (and identification), which he purports to fear. Mandel's poem ends as "one becomes another / I am crazed by poetry" (18), in agreement with Layton's occasional representation of poets (users of metaphor) as madmen.

13 The distinction between the public and the audience is under consideration in Alan M. Thomas's "Audience, Market and Public – An Evaluation of Canadian Broadcasting."

14 Robert Lecker, too, has linked privacy with literariness but in a different context; he argues that literary critics in Canada have nearly lost their "public function" ("Privacy" 32) since the 1950s because of their increasing engagement in an academically specialized, culturally exclusive, and ultimately private discourse.

15 This is a funny example: Irving Layton on a T-shirt is a sign of celebrity; Al Purdy on a road sign is a sign of fame. *The Al Purdy A-frame Anthology* (2009) reproduces a photograph of Purdy by the road sign for Purdy Lane, so named in recognition of his significance to the local culture of Ameliasburgh. The lane is "the steep gravel road that ends down at the village cemetery" (Heinricks 71), an ironic location. In the image, Purdy is wearing a T-shirt on which a portrait of Layton is recognizable. The significance of this gesture is multivalent, implying not only attitudinal, commercial, cultural, and temporal distinctions but also contiguity between celebrity and fame.

16 Some of us appreciate the failures, however, and sometimes failure can be performed – the performance being a feat in itself. My analysis of the literary works in the following chapters appreciates that the authors of those works were fascinated by celebrities who failed to deal with their success. On the topic of failure, see "Fame Damage," the introduction to the final section of Su Holmes and Sean Redmond's *Framing Celebrity* (2006).

17 What is the political position of wanting fame, legend, or myth instead of celebrity? Douglas Grant argues that *radical* is the term to describe the poet and *conservative* for the public (34); the poets in this book are radical in the sense that they reject some of the norms associated with the public, but they are conservative in the sense that they distinguish between celebrity and other types of more enduring recognition that they seem to prefer. I hope that my position is appropriately neutral; as Grant also suggests, the critic has allegiances on both sides.

18 In *The Society of the Spectacle* (1995), Guy Debord claims, similarly, that "[t]he spectacle is essentially tautological, for the simple reason that its means and its ends are identical" (15).

19 The aforementioned (note 15) "Fame Damage" section in *Framing Celebrity* suggests that celebrity is often interpreted and represented as a destroyer, or in the context of destruction, in other countries, too.

2 The Era of Celebrity in Canadian Poetry

1 I would consider adding Robert Service to the smaller list of early star poets partly because of his remarkable late-life cameo in an A-list Hollywood movie (Osborne 13), which acknowledged his earlier popularity.

2 Ways of seeing Canadian literature were, however, beginning to change in the mid-1950s. A collection of poetry and fiction called *Canadian Anthology* (1955),

edited by Carl F. Klinck and R.E. Watters, was the first to organize its contents according to "major" and "minor" authors. T.S. Eliot discussed those categories in "What Is Minor Poetry?" (1944); Canadian anthologists had rarely inquired about such categories. Robert Lecker, in *Keepers of the Code* (2013), argues that *Canadian Anthology* was the first to prefer biography and theme to technical merit and other values. With this anthology, "[t]he history of Canadian literature becomes a history of personality writ large" (Lecker, *Keepers* 202). Lecker notes that the anthology contains forty-seven authors but only fifteen writers of prose fiction; "'[m]ajor' seems to involve poetry more than prose" (*Keepers* 202). *Canadian Anthology* helped to open the canon to celebrities – defined by "personality" – after the mid-1950s.

3 Today, interviewers on television and in other media ask celebrities about national politics, religion, evolution, and many other topics without any concern for the expertise of the celebrity. Layton's status as a poet might have been relevant to his celebrity, but celebrity often needs no such justification.

4 Dudek's remarks about television and the culture of youth are biased by his feud with Layton, which began when Layton gained recognition from various American poets in the early 1950s (Cameron 273) and which culminated with a printed exchange of insults in the late 1950s (Cameron 287) when Layton's celebrity itself was peaking.

5 Delores Broten defines a medium-sized publisher as "[a] firm producing 5 to 19 titles per year, 1970 to 1972 ... [c]orresponding to sales of $100,000 to $500,000 per year" (3); a large publisher would have published an average of "20 or more new titles per year in 1970 to 1972 ... [c]orresponding to sales of over $500,000 per year" (3). I presume that McClelland and Stewart, Macmillan, Oxford University Press, and Ryerson were large. During the era of celebrity in Canadian poetry, the writers under consideration in this chapter tended to publish their novels with the first three of these publishers. Their poetry tended to be published by what I presume were small or medium-sized publishers, such as Contact Press and Coach House Press. With the exception of his first book, Cohen has always published with large publishers.

6 "By the end of the 1980s, among the large publishers only McClelland and Stewart regularly published poetry; among the smaller nationalist presses House of Anansi had become a literary division of General Publishing, and Press Porcepic had discontinued poetry publication" (Davey, *Canadian* 85).

7 Stardom itself is not necessarily countercultural. Most of the representations of celebrity in Canadian poetry are of the public's use of it to affirm social norms. In contrast, most of the representations of celebrities themselves – such as Ondaatje's Billy the Kid or MacEwen's Lawrence of Arabia – are of men who question their widespread recognition and the values of the public.

8 No market supports the equal growth of all modes of production. To increase the size of a small market, producers with limited means must often concentrate their investments in one area more than another.

9 My suspicions about a backlash against poetry of celebrity are slightly beyond the scope of this study, though I hope to return to this topic in the future or see it investigated by others. The backlash, if there was one, was certainly associated with what Davey calls the collapse of the Canadian poetry canon. Davey suggests that cultural diversity, literary regionalism, and the growth of smaller publishers divided the national canon into canons; the so-called "death" of Canadian poetry was "more a cry that the lyric poem [and its ideology of humanism and individualism] is in difficulty" (*Canadian* 98) and that "Canadian poetry may only be in crisis to the extent that the national federation is in crisis" (*Canadian* 99). Because nationalism is not my focus, I have raised it only transitionally as an issue; however, Davey's remark significantly contextualizes the focus of this chapter: the era of celebrity in Canadian poetry coincides with the rise and fall of nationalism in Canadian culture in general. Celebrity had a role in canon formation, which can be described as the production of literary fame.

10 I doubt, however, that Atwood could have sold, overall and in a comparable amount of time, what Grisham sold in the 1990s: the sixty million books that I reported in the previous chapter.

11 When necessary, I have accounted for name variations in my searches; Purdy's early publications were sometimes under the names "Alfred W. Purdy," and MacEwen's were initially under "Gwendolyn McEwen."

12 Another caveat is that I am not a statistician, nor do I have any expertise in statistics or quantitative methods.

13 Purdy and Ondaatje each appeared three times between 1955 and 1980, and MacEwen twice (1961 and 1965).

14 On rare occasions, the website's optical character recognition software misrecognizes a character. For this reason, and because the software does not count names that are hyphenated at the end of a line, the statistics I report from the *Globe and Mail* are probably not exact. As with my other statistics, they are useful mainly as an indication of the relative name recognition of the poets in this chapter. I have also tried to ensure that other people with coincidentally the same names (e.g., other men named Irving Layton) have been excluded from this study, but I cannot guarantee that my searches have excluded them entirely.

15 In fact, despite its reputation, the *Globe and Mail* does not provide much information about lesser (e.g., local) degrees of celebrity. MacEwen appears in the *Globe and Mail* only twelve times between 1955 and 1980, whereas a box in her archives at the University of Toronto (Box 32 OVS) contains a little more than eighty

newspaper clippings from various Toronto newspapers throughout her relatively short career.

16 When a name appeared more than once per article, letter, or advertisement, I counted that name only once. In the cases of Atwood and Purdy, I did not confirm the count by viewing every page on which one of their names appeared. In the cases of the other four poets, whom I am studying closely, I viewed every page. I did not count the frequency of their photographs appearing, but that would obviously be another indication of celebrity.

17 An article in the *Globe and Mail*'s "Report on Business" on 19 August 1969, refers to MacEwen, in addition to Layton and Cohen, as "an international figure" (B3), but she is rarely acknowledged as such in that newspaper, and I have no other evidence to suggest that she was internationally well known.

18 This lack of information is not a serious problem because Layton was the only poet under consideration besides Purdy who was publishing in some of those periodicals in those years (and not often). If he published a poem in 1956 in a magazine that was not counted that year, the omission from the statistics would have little effect on the comparisons between the four main writers in this study.

19 I have not tracked, from year to year, the publications in which these poets usually appeared to determine whether these publications were indexed consistently in the *CPI*, though I expect that they were.

20 Of the many periodicals that had not appeared in association with these six writers before 1971, *Quill & Quire* is the only one to have represented one writer dramatically more than the others between 1971 and 1980; that writer is Atwood, who was written about eleven times, compared with four publications about MacEwen, three each about Layton, Purdy, and Cohen, and one about Ondaatje.

21 The useful website *The Leonard Cohen Files* (http://www.leonardcohenfiles.com) includes interviews with Cohen conducted during the era of celebrity in Canadian poetry from *Melody Maker*, *New Musical Express*, and *Sounds*, which were published in the United Kingdom. In 1967, and for at least a few years thereafter, his songs would probably have been broadcast often on the radio, thereby making him much more widely recognized than any other Canadian writer in those years, including Atwood.

22 For instance, the *Globe and Mail* shows that in some years Atwood, Layton, and Cohen were being mentioned in that newspaper two or three times per month, which is relatively often. Furthermore, Layton was the recipient of nearly six hundred fan letters, which survive in the Concordia University archives (Camlot); Cohen had phenomenal book and album sales; Ondaatje felt he had to protect his privacy by asking York University (his employer) to withhold information about him (Jewinski 134) and by denying my requests (and those of others) to see his

archival materials; and MacEwen was mentioned a little over eighty times in Toronto newspapers during her career, as clippings in her archives reveal. They all experienced celebrity, but not in the same ways or to the same extent.

23 These numbers, especially those recorded in the literary magazines in the next paragraph, often refer to more than one poem or other work appearing in a single issue of a magazine. For example, Purdy's one hundred-plus publications in *Canadian Forum* included several occasions when he published more than one poem in a single issue. Although such a case would increase his public exposure compared to other writers featured in that issue, it does not increase his public exposure in general any more than if he had published a single poem in that issue. These numbers, therefore, are only indications of celebrity; Purdy had around twice the number of publications than Atwood had in *Canadian Forum,* but that does not qualify him as having generated twice the celebrity.

24 In 1964, the company had arranged for Layton, Cohen, Earle Birney, and Phyllis Gotlieb to tour from place to place, together, to promote their recent books.

25 Anachronistically, I am referring to Cohen's photograph on the cover of his album *I'm Your Man* (1988).

3 Becoming "Too Public" in the Poetry of Irving Layton

1 Notably, his American publisher did not share the Canadian publisher's qualms about his material. Ryerson Press was associated with the United Church and had religious reasons for objecting to Layton's poetry. Layton might have speculated that the bigger, diverse American market was much more conducive to literary celebrity than the Canadian market because of the religious beliefs at Ryerson, which was one of Canada's only major publishers. He exploited what might have been a national difference, using the same conditions that made celebrity unlikely for Canadian poets to establish post-war literary celebrity in Canada; he was also lucky that Jack McClelland, in Toronto, was willing to take risks for Layton and in general, even when the censorship of his publications was a possibility – as in the case of Cohen's *Beautiful Losers* (1966). See also chapter 4, on controversy and the media.

2 Layton gives the poem a less sensational title, "Existentialist," in *The Black Huntsmen* (1951), surely not knowing that he would eventually have had five wives and a reputation not so incongruous with the tabloids. Attesting to the media's later interest in his personal life, his marriage to Harriet Bernstein was announced in the *Globe and Mail* on 24 November 1978, with the headline "Poet Layton Marries Movie Publicist" (Cherry 11). The story included a large photograph of Bernstein and Layton.

3 Another of men's responses was to bond with other men, and recent studies of poets who experienced some degree of widespread recognition have shown that men form homosocial groups that consolidate their power and help to counter the supposed feminizing of male poets. Aaron Jaffe writes about the former situation throughout *Modernism and the Culture of Celebrity* (2005). Michael Davidson writes about both in *Guys Like Us: Citing Masculinity in Cold War Poetics* (2004): "even within the most progressive communities – whether homosexual or heterosexual – forms of misogyny and homophobia are often necessary to their continuation" (48). He suggests that "only male community could serve as protection" against "reciprocal objectification – and feminization" (Davidson, *Guys* 48) potentially resulting from men's expression of supposedly feminine interiority in their lyric poems. Layton's mentorship of other poets – usually younger men, such as David Solway and especially Cohen – confirmed his authority as paternal, and it also helped to validate and strengthen a community of men who felt the need to respond to social changes that were seemingly not in their interests.

4 Nietzsche appears in the MA thesis that Layton wrote at McGill University in 1946 (Cameron 158–60).

5 The sun-god of Greek myth is actually Helios (Hamilton 31), and Apollo, not Dionysus, is the god of light whose other name, Phoebus, means "brilliant" (Hamilton 30). Nietzsche thought that Apollo and Dionysus created inspirational tension when brought together; he eventually focused on Dionysus, and the symbol of the sun became associated with him, which partly accounts for Layton's use of it (Francis, "Layton" 46–7).

6 As Elspeth Cameron suggests, the title also refers to his "revolutionary past" (294) as an advocate of "red" communism, and it comes directly from his 1958 poem "For Mao Tse-Tung: A Meditation on Flies and Kings." In "For Mao Tse-Tung," Layton aligns himself with the dictator Mao and dismisses the forgiving attitude of Jesus; nevertheless, he says that he "pit[ies] the meek" (42) and appears less stereotypically Nietzschean (i.e., pitiless) than the figure of Mao would suggest. The book also announced him, subtly and ironically, as the New Messiah (the "Son" of God), because it was Layton's mother who had told him that he was born circumcised (Flynn 10) as a sign of his divinity (which Cameron thinks was a genital defect called minor hypospadias [467, 7n]) – a conceit that Layton retroactively extended when he explicitly and ironically characterized himself as Messianic in his 1985 memoir *Waiting for the Messiah*.

7 Layton's decision to associate himself with Nietzsche, who was by then unfairly associated with Nazi ideology, is surprising because Layton was a Jew. His decision attests to his determined appreciation for the good in Nietzsche's ideas and suggests that he was thinking of using controversy for self-promotion at an

early stage in his career, as the following chapter about his television and radio appearances also suggests.

8 Kaja Silverman, in her chapter on the films of Rainer Werner Fassbinder in *Male Subjectivity at the Margins* (1992), "differentiate[s] the gaze from the look, and hence from masculinity" (125). According to Silverman, the gaze is phallic, but the phallus is a symbolic power that women can also have; in contrast, the look is merely the use of the eyes in seeing. Although Layton's poem refers explicitly only to "the eyes / of old women," the women emasculate (and age) the poet and therefore direct the gaze; they are both looking and gazing. More specifically, in their eyes the poet sees his own reflection, which suggests the irony and self-deprecation here.

9 Layton implies that poets outside of England are not respected but are teased and stereotyped by their audiences. Brian Trehearne paraphrases Layton's "Poets: The Conscience of Mankind" (1963): "in the United States and Canada poetry is rewarded with public reputation because it is considered a harmless and irrelevant art form by which the mass sensibility cannot be stirred" (143). Although the speaker himself does not seem "harmless" in "Poetic Fame," his audience certainly has no concerns about his poetry.

10 The central image of the stilts is allusive. On one hand, the stilts seem to refer to William Butler Yeats's "The Circus Animals' Desertion" (1939) (Mandel, *Irving* 26), which equates poetry with circus performances. The speaker in "The Circus Animals' Desertion" associates the circus with his youth and with the boys on stilts who performed in its troupe; for Yeats, innovative poetry comes from youth, because in "old age" (782) the poet is restricted to "old themes" (783). He longs to return to performance. The circus animals, absent from the poem except in the title, have deserted the poet. They are not only the beasts that circus performers use to accentuate their shows but also the only spectators who remain after the human audiences have left. Zarathustra experienced the same failure in not really attracting a human audience, though his animal audience seemed to like him. The image of stilts also refers to Zarathustra, who ironically considered wearing stilts so that people would overlook his long legs (Nietzsche 139); he hoped to seem normal by exaggerating his abnormality, his circus-freakishness. In both Yeats and Nietzsche, the stilts are performative crutches that help to separate the figure of the misfit artist from an absent audience associated with age and death.

11 The absence of the final stanza from the poem's first publication in the *Canadian Forum* is evidence that Layton could not easily believe his own optimistic claims at the end of the poem.

12 Indeed, in Donald Winkler's NFB film *A Tall Man Executes a Jig by Irving Layton* (1986), "he, the man, me, [and] I" are the pronouns that Layton uses to

talk about the tall man. Although that is not enough to prove that the poem is self-referential, the use of the first person indicates a more personal, psychological imagining of the tall man. The fact that Layton decided against the first person suggests that he wanted an epic poem that would be open to many interpretations, which is also implied by the fact that he gives the tall man no other name.

13 Layton later compared these two women directly, in "No Cause for Jealousy" (1963), which claims that Aviva has the more attractive body and the more impressive husband.

14 Donald Winkler's main NFB film about Layton, *Poet: Irving Layton Observed* (1986), suggests that Layton was recognized in Greece in the 1980s, and in "Irving Layton in Italy" (1993), Alfredo Rizzardi claims that Layton enjoyed "the kind of reception usually reserved for rock stars" (42) when he visited Sardinia in 1992 – both much later than the publication of "The Day Aviva Came to Paris." Rizzardi's claim might simply be flattery.

15 In *The Shattered Plinths* in 1968, Layton published another conspicuous elegy for a writer: "Dorothy Parker (1893–1967)." In Faye Hammill's *Women, Celebrity, & Literary Culture between the Wars* (2007), Parker is the only female poet to be considered as a celebrity; she is a rare example of a star poet among female writers, who tend to become recognized for their novels.

16 As I explained in an earlier note, the gaze, in contrast with the look, is phallic (Silverman 125). The thought of being blinded might have been especially frightening for Layton; in the film *Poet: Irving Layton Observed*, he says, "I'm a very visual poet ... My strongest sense is the sense of sight." Unconsciously, his fear of being blinded might be associated with a fear of being castrated, which Layton also implied in "Whatever Else Poetry Is Freedom," as I explained midway through this chapter.

17 Although I agree with Skelton, I would also note – in case it is not yet obvious – that Layton's overemphasis on his "personality" is a result not only of his "egocentricity" but also of the metaphor of celebrity and its effect on his poetry and performances.

18 He was later nominated for the Nobel Prize by Alfredo Rizzardi, whose name Elspeth Cameron mistakenly spells "Rizziardi" (Cameron 442), but despite Rizzardi's enthusiastic claims about the "tumultuous applause" and "whistling and hollering" that greeted Layton in Italy, this reception was by Rizzardi's own admission a "resounding tribute" (42); I suspect that it was more honorific than the attention that celebrities tend to receive, but that distinction is presently beyond the scope of my research.

19 See also the earlier reference to "[i]mmortal fame" in "Prizes."

4 *Fighting Words*: Layton on Radio and Television

1 No one in the debate could name the source of the quotation; it was, according to Cohen, Simone de Beauvoir.

2 The opportunity to define *intellectual* was lost, but Waddington implied, perhaps in response to an elitism that can seem cold in addition to condescending, that intellectuals show compassion and do not attempt to belittle others.

3 At the aforementioned 1955 Canadian Writers' Conference, Robert Weaver – who was perhaps the most influential promoter of Canadian literature on radio, because of his *Anthology* show – said that "[m]ost writers would like to have a sizable and intelligent public" but that it seems "pretty mythical" (103). Nevertheless, his show and other CBC programming contributed – and still do – to the education of the Canadian public.

5 Recognition, Anonymity, and Leonard Cohen's Stranger Music

1 In *Stranger Music,* the woman in "Chelsea Hotel #2" is referred to as "baby," but Cohen almost always sings "babe." Another difference is that "#2" is not in the title of the transcribed lyrics in the book, but it is on the album.

6 "I like that line because it's got my name in it": Masochistic Stardom in Cohen's Poetry

1 This chapter remains focused on masochism, though it includes sadomasochism, simply because my interest is less in the power of the public or of celebrity and more in the poet's representations of being dominated by that power, even if such domination did not occur in reality, or did not occur as it is represented.

2 For a summary of the debate among Desmond Pacey, Linda Hutcheon, Stephen Scobie, and Dennis Lee about Cohen's selves, see Winfried Siemerling's "Hailed by Koan" in *Discoveries of the Other* (1994).

3 In *Male Subjectivity at the Margins* (1992), Kaja Silverman argues that T.E. Lawrence – whose celebrity is considered in chapter 10 – submitted to "feminine masochism, and ... it is only through an examination of this shift that we can explain his subsequent retreat from leadership" (10). Her remark about "leadership" is similar to a remark in P. David Marshall's *Celebrity and Power: Fame in Contemporary Culture* (1997), which examines celebrity with a Weberian focus on the "prophet[ic]" and "charismatic leader" (20); my argument about Cohen's symbolic abdication of his role as a leading star poet – and some of its associated masculinity and religiosity – is partly indebted to both Silverman and Marshall.

4 My article "Celebrity and the Poetic Dialogue of Irving Layton and Leonard Cohen" (2009) deals with the majority of the poems that they wrote for and about each other. In that poetic dialogue, they demonstrated reciprocal influence and debated which of them was freer.

5 He confirmed his interest in actual religious roles by becoming a Buddhist monk in the late 1990s (Eder par. 10).

6 A likely counterargument is that Cohen's metaphor of celebrity as slavery is no more obvious than his definition of freedom. I argue later in this chapter that his ability to be free requires him not to define freedom. There is no such restriction on his implicit definition of slavery. In a different context in *After Theory* (2003), Terry Eagleton states: "To define [freedom] is to destroy it" (195).

7 Scobie's argument more accurately describes Cohen's thinking about selfhood in the late 1970s. See my analysis of *Death of a Lady's Man* near the end of this chapter.

8 Erotogenic masochism is "pleasure ... derived from pain" (Finke 6). Freud and others revised his theory of erotogenic masochism by acknowledging that pain is not actually pleasant (Baumeister 64–5).

9 In Cohen's work, the most prominent martyrs are women – Catherine Tekakwitha in his novel *Beautiful Losers* (1966) and Joan of Arc on his album *Songs of Love and Hate* (1971) – who are admired by male narrators and speakers. Such admiration of women's pain can be interpreted as sadistic and misogynistic, but it also suggests that Cohen was thinking in gendered terms about celebrity and the sadomasochism it potentially elicits. By also portraying himself as a martyr and masochist, he suggests that celebrity dominated and emasculated him – in contrast with what often appears to be his easy manipulation of celebrity and, possibly, women.

10 Baumeister admits that sadomasochism is an "open question" (25) but also claims that most sadists have had masochistic experiences, but not *vice versa,* and not many masochists become sadists. Baumeister's argument is that masochists relinquish control according to predetermined arrangements, thereby helping them to deconstruct the self (30) and ease the "burden of selfhood" (88) associated with work-related demands, responsibilities, and failures. Baumeister also states that "masochism appeals selectively to the most powerful and responsible men" (78) because their work is so demanding; they need to escape into fantasy – and, ironically, they escape into slavery. Star poets might be such "men," even though their representations of themselves suggest that they are hardly "powerful." Instead, their public personas are powerful. Celebrities are both agents of the audience (and, to some extent, representatives of their industry) and people who want relief from that power.

11 In the *Globe and Mail* on 29 March 1977, Scott Symons stated that Cohen was "a distant, if glamorous man (and making millions for it)" (qtd. in French, "Female" 14). Cohen's implicit masochism was an aspect of what his fans were buying; it was worth money.

12 Cohen had, in fact, on one strange occasion actually rehearsed such grandstanding with Layton as the (ironically) bigger man. In late 1957 and early 1958, Layton was blundering through a series of marital problems. In all, Layton had five wives, but the transition from Betty Sutherland to Aviva Cantor was particularly troublesome for him. According to his biographer Elspeth Cameron, "Layton would not ask Betty for a divorce, but he agreed to buy Aviva a wedding ring" (276). They went to a boutique in Montreal with Cohen, "who was to be the 'best man' on this lark" (Cameron 276). As the accounts by Cameron and Layton's son David suggest, Cohen was symbolically much more than the best man: he became a substitute for his friend and mentor. In both accounts, Layton finds a bracelet for Betty and leaves the store, and Cohen placates Aviva by buying her a ring and declaring her married. By putting the ring on Aviva's finger, Cohen substitutes himself for the priest *and* for the intended groom. Cohen's fascination with the priesthood and with similar roles, such as sainthood and monkhood, was important almost from the beginning of his career, but this anecdote suggests that his sense of himself as a replacement for Layton began even before Layton "attained full stature 'officially' as a major Canadian poet" (Cameron 279) with the publication of *A Red Carpet for the Sun.* At its most extreme, by becoming Layton's surrogate as Aviva's symbolic husband, Cohen engaged in grandstanding; he was standing in for Layton (who was already a celebrity), helping to establish his own persona, and insinuating himself into the position of a star. He was also rehearsing the separation and fusion of a celebrity's selves; in effect, he ensured that he and Layton were married to each other, in the sense of "[a]n intimate union; a merging or blending of two things" (*OED*). This impromptu ceremony was also the one and only celebrity wedding in the history of Canadian poetry.

13 On at least one occasion in the late 1950s, Cohen also appeared on television – a program called *Doubletalk*, which generated interest in Cohen's late-night performances of poetry with jazz accompaniment (Cahill 7).

14 Thomas P. Balázs, referring to the "masochistic cuckoldry" of Leopold Bloom in James Joyce's *Ulysses* (1922), says that Bloom indulges in "hyperbolic rationalization" (173) to comfort himself after being cuckolded. Cohen's persona does the same by stating, "I like that line because it's got my name in it."

15 Mailer and Trocchi knew each other (Waters 12), which suggests that cliques of literary celebrities were small, even in the United States. Notably, besides Layton, the other celebrities to whom Cohen refers are non-Canadian, which is evidence of his ambition to broaden his appeal outside of Canada. Layton, Ondaatje, and Gwendolyn MacEwen were similarly attracted to non-Canadian celebrities.

16 The speaker also seems sadistic when he wonders about his apathy (which Deleuze associates with sadism, as I stated previously): "Maybe he doesn't mean a thing to me anymore but I think he was like me" (66).

17 On the topic of secrets, Cohen said in the *Globe and Mail*, around the time that this poem was published, "I think what's happening is that people have now decided to share their secrets. In the recent past, they've kept their secrets" (qtd. in Lawson 13). He is probably referring to confessional poetry even as he is commenting on his emerging celebrity and the public's desire to learn about his private life. After the peak of his literary celebrity several years later, in 1973, he returned to the topic of secrets in an interview: "Everything I do from now on will be completely secret. Whatever motors or furnaces are working within me refuse exhibition of any kind" (qtd. in Martin 15). Asked if he would therefore withdraw into privacy, Cohen responded: "I never left my private life. Whatever adventures I had were to satisfy the demands of my private life at the time, not to abandon it" (qtd. in Martin 15). Despite evidence of identity confusion in his poetry, Cohen insisted that he could recognize his private life as different from the "adventures" he had in public.

18 Jim Devlin states that Cohen's "first acknowledged 'bona fide' appearance into the 'racket' (as he himself often called it) of musical performance in front of a paying audience" (24) involved only one of his songs: "Suzanne." The occasion was a Judy Collins concert that was protesting the war in Vietnam on 30 April 1967 (Devlin 24).

19 See the "Leonard Cohen discography" article on Wikipedia for the peak chart positions of Cohen's studio albums; see also the "Music Recording Sales Certification" article for various figures related to gold albums; finally, see also Wikipedia's "Songs of Leonard Cohen" article, which claims that Cohen's first album did not go gold in the United States (with 500,000 sales) until 1989. Referring to this album, Bruce Eder at Allmusic.com states that "Cohen's music quickly found a small but dedicated following. College students by the thousands bought it; in its second year of release, the record sold over 100,000 copies. *The Songs of Leonard Cohen* was as close as Cohen ever got to mass audience success" (par. 7). If Eder and Wikipedia are correct, Cohen's *Selected Poems* was more popular than his first album, at least until 1978 when Barbara Amiel's article appeared in *Maclean's*.

20 The final instance of his celebrity on film in the era of celebrity in Canadian poetry was Harry Rasky's *Song of Leonard Cohen* (1980), which a letter to the editor of the *Globe and Mail* on 13 September 1980, described as "curiously ignored by [the] press" (Warren 7). Cohen had recently been ignored as a poet – *Death of a Lady's Man* had attracted little attention – and his recent album produced by Phil Spector (*Death of a Ladies' Man*) was, in my opinion, the worst of his career. The

media's lack of attention to *Song of Leonard Cohen* indicated that Cohen's career was in a proverbial slump.

21 Tobin argues that the masochistic women (various Miss Xs) studied by Richard von Krafft-Ebing in *Psychopathia Sexualis* (1886) "have, at the very least, gilded their cages, making a source of pleasure out of the societal structures and restrictions (at least the medical ones) into which they were born. More importantly, the X-women have attained a new identity, by accepting the power of medical discourse and using that power to gain satisfaction" (38). Tobin's remark can also partly explain the motivation of the speaker in "the 15-year old girls." This poem might be his private persona's wishful thinking, a fantasy associated with his implicit masochism that helps him to "gild the cage" of his celebrity. My application of Tobin's quotation about women to my argument about a man is cautious. There might not be any truth to Cohen's suggestion that celebrity dominated him and pushed him to the brink of suicide. Furthermore, an emasculated, feminine, or passive man might still have more power than a woman who partly subverts a system that dominates her.

22 Buddhism shares with celebrity the principle that the self can be negated; the difference is that Buddhists tend to seek that negation, whereas celebrities tend to promote but not negate themselves, though negation of the private self can be the result. Cohen's attempt to deconstruct himself through performances of masochism (seemingly motivated by his celebrity) could be attempted again through the practice of Buddhism.

7 Celebrity, Sexuality, and the Uncanny in Michael Ondaatje's *The Collected Works of Billy the Kid*

1 Ondaatje has, for example, twice refused to grant me access to his archives at the National Library; however, he supported the publication of this book by granting permission to reproduce one poem in full and various block quotations.

2 Following Denisoff, I use the term *homosocial desire* as Eve Kosofsky Sedgwick does in *Between Men* (1985); "Sedgwick's purpose in joining 'homosocial' and 'desire' is [to suggest that homosociality is] 'potentially erotic'" (Denisoff 68n). Of course, homosociality is not always erotic.

3 The Western genre is also known for its male characters who represent self-reliance and independence, and, in *Masculine Migrations* (1998), Daniel Coleman argues that, in *Running in the Family* (1982), Ondaatje is critical of "the myth of self-sustaining masculine independence" (106). This criticism is arguably part of Ondaatje's broader, subtle critique of heterosexual masculinity in texts such as *The Collected Works of Billy the Kid*.

4 One might argue, of course, that Garrett "reconfigur[es]" Billy simply by killing him and thereby transforming him into a ghost – a comparatively marginal figure.

Nevertheless, if Billy is indeed a ghost, and is to some extent responsible for the uncanniness of his book, then he has an authority that Garrett could not have anticipated.

5 In *Discoveries of the Other: Alterity in the Work of Leonard Cohen, Hubert Aquin, Michael Ondaatje, and Nicole Brossard* (1994), Winfried Siemerling examines these ideas in the context of Ondaatje's prose fiction.

6 Cooley's article, while not about celebrity, shows how one of aspect of *The Collected Works of Billy the Kid* is its textual approximation of various techniques of film, which was the twentieth century's dominant medium of celebrity. Ondaatje said, "With *Billy the Kid* I was trying to make the film I couldn't afford to shoot, in the form of a book" (qtd. in Rae 113). He could not have conceived of his book without thinking of celebrity.

7 Most critics who have written about *The Collected Works of Billy the Kid* have opinions about the significance of the blank "picture of Billy," but I will not attempt to summarize them all. In suggesting that Billy is "represented" here as a ghost, I am agreeing with the general view that Billy's subjectivity is tactically not easy to represent.

8 In "The Collected Photographs of Billy the Kid" (1980), Perry Nodelman also associates the gun with the camera. Quoting the text, Nodelman observes that both tools "eliminate much" (75).

9 If the blank photograph can be interpreted as a mirror, Dennis Denisoff's argument about Billy being a vampire (55) gains credibility because vampires are often thought to be invisible in mirrors; however, as much as I like the implication that we could join Billy as vampires looking at our non-images, vampirism is not really Denisoff's focus, and the mirror relevant to this part of my argument is the rather figurative mirror in psychoanalysis.

10 The operative word here is "coincidence." In the recent Vintage Canada edition (2008) of the text, the pagination is different from that of the previous Anansi editions, and the second narration of Billy's death does not begin with the sound of his thinking. That edition raises the question of which text is authoritative, but I am willing to risk an acknowledged assumption about the relevance of an inconsistent element of the text, especially given the metatextual aspects of *The Collected Works of Billy the Kid* that I have been considering.

8 "A Razor in the Body": Ondaatje's *Rat Jelly* and *Secular Love*

1 I am thinking, for example, of the *Tomb Raider* video games, which introduced the popular character Lara Croft and later became a couple of films featuring a digitally altered movie star, Angelina Jolie.

2 Similarly, though not in the context of celebrity, in Ondaatje's *In the Skin of a Lion* (1987) the thief Caravaggio "recognizes the importance of effacing his body

to survive, and actually makes his body invisible" (Overbye 7) through painted camouflage. Although Karen Overbye argues that in this 1987 novel "Ondaatje focuses attention on the bodies of men that are not perceived as being historically important, men whose bodies have no individual market value" (par. 2), he had previously focused on the bodies of stars – namely Billy the Kid and Buddy Bolden – whose "individual market value" was high (and still is, in some historical and cultural contexts).

3 *The Collected Works of Billy the Kid* actually won in 1971 (Barbour 3) in a specially created "Prose and Poetry" (Harvey and Berg 313) category because, in addition to nationality, it was difficult to classify by form.

4 Francis Barker suggests that modernity (beginning in the seventeenth century but arguably continuing until recently if not until today) is defined partly by a distinction between "the public and the private spheres" (vi). The fusion of those spheres, at least for celebrities, would then seem to be a postmodern condition, though these spheres were also supposedly indistinct in the premodern world long before stardom. Here, Ondaatje is coincidentally implying that the various effects of the postmodern condition of globalism or globalization on the body (from "globe" to "town" to "room" to "body") should not be ignored.

5 The emphasis on "the sun" and "imagin[ation]" is Laytonic, but other details point toward Cohen, another potential father-figure. Ondaatje seems to allude to Cohen by declaring "celebrity a razor in the body" (53). Although I cannot be sure of the timing because the poems in *Rat Jelly* were written "between 1966 ... and the summer of 1972" (see the unnumbered final page), the image of the razor might have been borrowed from Cohen's *The Energy of Slaves* (1972), which has a small razor icon at the beginning of every poem – and Sam Solecki hears echoes of *The Energy of Slaves* elsewhere in *Rat Jelly* ("Nets" 106). In *The Annotated Bibliography of Canada's Major Authors* (1985), Judith Brady notes that "Heron Rex" was first published in the journal *White Pelican* (1973) (142). Unless there was a previous publication of "Heron Rex" not recorded in the bibliography, Cohen's *The Energy of Slaves* seems to have preceded that poem.

6 *Rat Jelly* also has a less remarkable poem called "White Room," in which sex is the crash of an aircraft into a desert of flesh described both as "cool fruit" and "sand"; pleasure and pain meet in the private "collapse" (22) of two people. Another crash in a desert happens much later, in *The English Patient* (1992).

7 For a consideration of celebrity in the context of superheroes and their various masks or personas, see also my article in *The Journal of Popular Culture*, which should appear in print around or shortly after the publication of this book.

8 I began this work with an article on the racial geography and urban (rather than domestic) spaces of the New Orleans of *Coming through Slaughter*, published in 2008 in *The American Review of Canadian Studies*.

9 *Running in the Family* is the "centre of the rumour" (64) about the Faulknerian downfall of his family. It begins with his relatives making up one of "the best known and wealthiest" (172) dynasties in Ceylon and ends with his parents toiling among the working class. *Running in the Family* goes beyond using artist-figures such as Billy the Kid and Buddy Bolden and claims celebrity for Ondaatje's actual lineage and, by extension, for himself. Asked years later if he had ever had any "'celebrity' experiences," Ondaatje said, "At an airport a guy looked at my name and said, 'Oh, Mr. Ondondangie, I'm your biggest fan.' That's now a running joke in my family" (qtd. in Schneller R5) – but even in 1981, celebrity was "running" in his "family." To publish a book about the celebrity of one's own family – or to publish any autobiographical book, really – an author (and a publisher) must believe that the degree of his or her own celebrity will be enough to intrigue readers and other buyers; otherwise, the author must make the content especially appealing or sensational. *Running in the Family* does both. It relies partly on the recognizability of Ondaatje's own name and partly on a mythic tale based on adventures associated with his father's alcoholism. By extending the theme of alcoholism related to the celebrity of Pat Garrett in *The Collected Works of Billy the Kid* and Buddy Bolden (who might also have been alcoholic) in *Coming through Slaughter*, Ondaatje makes the self-destructive aspect of celebrity into an aspect of his own private life.

10 Annick Hillger writes about Ondaatje's poetry in the context of a related separation germane to modernity: that of mind and body. According to Hillger, Ondaatje deals with the "crisis of self" and "quest for identity" (21) by creating a "literature of silence" (*passim*) that transcends language and, paradoxically, literature. The purported silence of his poetry offers us another way to think about his focus on the body.

11 He did not, in fact, write *Tin Roof* "for" Bogart; he dedicated it to Phyllis Webb.

12 Ondaatje might have seen *Trapeze* in the theatres, but he must have seen *Casablanca* on television – probably in the late 1950s or 1960s.

13 His transparency or invisibility and his implied desire for it make him similar to Billy the Kid, who achieved invisibility through death. The use of the third person – which at first seems contrary to his usual phenomenological emphasis on first-person, embodied perspectives – reinforces this intertextual connection by suggesting an out-of-body experience akin to that of a ghost looking upon his body, as Billy arguably does, from a disembodied perspective. During moments of fusion, when privacy is publicity, the public's focus on images drives the star out of his body, though this fatal transformation also grants him invisibility and escape. See also Jonathan Goldman's work on Oscar Wilde, who in his later life "reject[ed] the image as a bearer of the subject" (12).

14 Ondaatje had reflected on this tension between self-reflection and outreach to the audience in the introduction to *The Long Poem Anthology* (1979), which he edited.

He wrote: "Something did happen in the 70's that has gone unrecognized by most academic readers of poetry. Some writers became public personalities; but at the same time some poets – from the generation of [Raymond] Souster's *New Wave Canada* – turned inward, away from the individual occasional poem, to explore, to take a longer look at themselves and their landscape, to hold onto something frail – whether the memory or discovery of a place, or a way of speaking" (12). Ondaatje seemingly wanted to "tur[n] inward" while imagining a more "outward" life – even in his long poems, such as *The Collected Works of Billy the Kid*.

9 The Magician and His Public in the Poetry of Gwendolyn MacEwen

1 Akhenaton "is a king who is, quite literally, blinded by the sun" (Bartley 25). For MacEwen, the sun is a symbol of celebrity (among other things) that she uses, as Layton did, to represent not only spirituality (the sun-god) but also megalomaniacal egotism. Arguably, Ondaatje's sun often represents the scrutiny of the public upon the private life of the celebrity; because Julian the magician is similarly "blinded" by his public, I agree with Bartley that the magician is a general equivalent of the king. Unlike the magician, however, the king appears as a symbol of celebrity in one of her novels without also appearing as such in a poem.

2 Implicitly, MacEwen is asking her readers to believe in her as a pseudo-religious figure of the magician, too; Atwood argues that "MacEwen specializes in magician as artist as Christ" ("Canadian" 110).

3 None of my sources is entirely clear about who was involved with the tour, and perhaps more than one tour happened. A full-page story in the *Woman's Globe and Mail* in 1965 on MacEwen, Gotlieb, Cecile Cloutier, and Miriam Waddington ambiguously suggested that these women were on tour together. Linda Munk's preface to the story states: "Last Fall, a Toronto publisher arranged a poetry tour ... four poets reading their latest work at Canadian universities. The tour created a controversy ... some critics called it a *circus* ... others described it as a show of the artistic ego. In the following interviews, four of Canada's leading women poets talk about their work, the poetry tour and discuss the current literary scene" (W1, my emphasis). Five years later, Ondaatje also called the tour that featured Cohen a "circus" (35), which suggests that he had read Munk or that he and Munk had heard the same "critics" referring to the tour that featured Cohen. Munk implies, however, by interviewing MacEwen, Gotlieb, Cloutier, and Waddington that *these* four poets were on tour; perhaps Munk intended to promote only three alternative poets (only three because Gotlieb certainly was on tour with Layton, Cohen, and Birney). Sullivan might have read this story in MacEwen's archives, where I found it in Box 32 OVS, and she might have assumed that MacEwen had toured with Cohen. MacEwen did mention him and Layton: "The tour was

frightening, it was too much. Either ... Layton or Leonard alone could have drawn the audience. I think they should each have had individual readings" (qtd. in Munk W1). If MacEwen was describing her participation with them on the tour, she also seems to be suggesting that she was intimidated by their higher degree of celebrity; however, she might have been describing the tour from an outsider's perspective.

4 An actual escape artist named Mario Manzini had been active in the United States since as early as 1974 (Walljasper), though there is no evidence, besides this poem, that MacEwen knew of him in 1966 or afterward.

5 For further distinctions between these three tropes, see Lodge 75–7 or Ricoeur, *Rule* 55–9.

10 Passing and Celebrity in MacEwen's *The T.E. Lawrence Poems*

1 This chapter has been published elsewhere in a slightly different form. See Deshaye, "Celebrity and Passing." My thanks go to the editors and peer reviewers at the *Journal of Commonwealth Literature*.

2 Some men, such as Robert Weaver of CBC Radio and *Tamarack Review*, very supportively helped to publicize MacEwen's writing (Sullivan 191, 324), so her implicit criticism appears more general than personal in this case.

3 See, for example, Brent Wood, who shows that Rosemary Sullivan and Liza Potvin both "wonder[ed]" ("From *The Rising Fire*" 40) about MacEwen's death. He then implies, through a quotation from Samuel Taylor Coleridge, that MacEwen's death had a somehow spiritual logic – an implication that also reinforces the religiosity of celebrity.

4 The poems that have no underlining in MacEwen's annotated copy in the archives are "Water," "The Legitimate Prince," "My Half-Sisters," "Janet," "The Water-Bearer," "The Story of a Stone," "A Farewell to Carcemish," "The Mirage," "Solar Wind," "On the Day of Resurrection" (which is listed as a found poem but contains no underlining), "Their Deaths," "Horses" (which has a marginal note by MacEwen indicating a source in Lawrence's translation of *The Odyssey*, though nothing is actually underlined), "A Photograph from Carcemish," "Tall Tales," and "Notes from the Dead Land."

5 Another source for this poem – specifically its line about "posterity" – is a letter from Lawrence to Mrs. Lionel Curtis, dated 1 August 1933, which is printed in David Garnett's *The Letters of T.E. Lawrence* (1938) (771–2).

6 Wood summarizes these numerous critics: "Potvin, for example, saw [MacEwen's] work as an emblem of 'female spiritual desire'; Penn Kemp wrote of feeling MacEwen's spirit visiting her after her death, and of joining Anima, the energy of inspiration (Kemp 1988). Thomas Gerry sees her as inheriting a tradition of

mystical poetry dating back to eighteenth century Baptist and Quaker leaders and writers Henry Alline and David Willson (Gerry 1991). Jan Bartley (1983) sees MacEwen as a mystic explorer, and Gillian Harding-Russell locates her as a maker of 'creative myth' (1984, 1988)" ("From *The Rising Fire*" 67). I would add that Davey claims MacEwen had a "belief in transcendence" (*Canadian* 13) and that some of her work is "within the tradition of the mystic quest" (*Surviving* 48). I agree with Wood that mysticism seems to be MacEwen's main interest in religion, as her focus on being "empty" (29) in "Apologies" suggests. I use "emptiness" and "transcendence" as synonyms; both terms suggest, to me, the absence of desire for attachments and identifications that involve one's identity in the social world.

7 The phrase "Death's little silver cock," which is not among those in "Tafas" that were previously Lawrence's, is partly an accident. In MacEwen's annotated and corrected copy of *The T.E. Lawrence Poems*, she drew a square around "little" and noted in the margin: "accidental misprint. leave in." MacEwen's editorial decision here is a perfect example of her intervention – exploiting, in this case, someone else's contribution, intentional or otherwise – in the text as an author whose decisions are political. She belittles not only "Death" but also Lawrence, a soldier who causes death, to criticize masculinity for its traditionally direct involvement in war.

Conclusion: Public, Nation, Now

1 Morton was in her sixties before she began to publish her work and gain publicity for it; Bök was much younger when he published *Eunoia*. If an equally intelligent, presentable, charming, but younger woman were to begin her poetic career today through corporate marketing not only in relatively established media but also on the Internet (a technology that Morton has not, to my surprise, used much for promotion), the potential for her celebrity could be very great. Like Layton, Morton probably achieved celebrity at too old an age to sustain it for long. One must usually begin young, as Cohen did; the ageism that I have not often remarked upon should be mentioned along with the sexism of the culture of poetic celebrity that I considered in previous chapters.

2 Brooke Pratt's scholarship on literary tourism (e.g., her address at the ACCUTE 2012 conference) suggests that celebrity is one prerequisite of the history making, heritage building, and canonizing that extend the cultural memory of authors.

3 Price acknowledges MacEwen's "Manzini" in his epigraphs and elsewhere in *Anatomy of Keys*.

References

Primary Texts: Books

Cohen, Leonard. *Beautiful Losers*. Toronto: McClelland, 1966. Print.

Cohen, Leonard. *Death of a Lady's Man*. Toronto: McClelland, 1978. Print.

Cohen, Leonard. *The Energy of Slaves*. Toronto: McClelland, 1972. Print.

Cohen, Leonard. *Flowers for Hitler*. Toronto: McClelland, 1964. Print.

Cohen, Leonard. *Let Us Compare Mythologies*. Toronto: McClelland, 1956. Print.

Cohen, Leonard. *Parasites of Heaven*. Toronto: McClelland, 1966. Print.

Cohen, Leonard. *Selected Poems: 1956–1968*. Toronto: McClelland, 1968. Print.

Cohen, Leonard. *The Spice-box of Earth*. Toronto: McClelland, 1961. Print.

Layton, Irving. *Balls for a One-armed Juggler*. Toronto: McClelland, 1963. Print.

Layton, Irving. *The Black Huntsmen*. Montreal: n.p., 1951. Print.

Layton, Irving. *The Cold Green Element*. Toronto: Contact, 1955. Print.

Layton, Irving. *Here and Now*. Montreal: First Statement, 1945. Print.

Layton, Irving. *The Laughing Rooster*. Toronto: McClelland, 1964. Print.

Layton, Irving. *A Laughter in the Mind*. Highlands: J. Williams, 1958. Print.

Layton, Irving. *The Long Pea-shooter*. Montreal: Laocoon, 1954. Print.

Layton, Irving. *Lovers and Lesser Men*. Toronto: McClelland, 1973. Print.

Layton, Irving. *In the Midst of My Fever*. Palma de Mallorca: Divers Press, 1954. Print.

Layton, Irving. *Nail Polish*. Toronto: McClelland, 1971. Print.

Layton, Irving. *Now Is the Place*. Montreal: First Statement, 1948. Print.

Layton, Irving. *A Red Carpet for the Sun*. Toronto: McClelland, 1959. Print.

Layton, Irving. *The Swinging Flesh*. Toronto: McClelland, 1961. Print.

Layton, Irving. *Wild Gooseberries: The Selected Letters of Irving Layton*. Ed. Francis Mansbridge. Toronto: Macmillan, 1989. Print.

Layton, Irving and David O'Rourke. *Waiting for the Messiah: A Memoir*. Toronto: McClelland, 1985. Print.

MacEwen, Gwendolyn. *Armies of the Moon*. Toronto: Macmillan, 1972. Print.
MacEwen, Gwendolyn. *A Breakfast for Barbarians*. Toronto: Ryerson, 1966. Print.
MacEwen, Gwendolyn. *The Fire-eaters*. Ottawa: Oberon, 1976. Print.
MacEwen, Gwendolyn. *The Honey Drum*. Oakville: Mosaic, 1983. Print.
MacEwen, Gwendolyn. *Julian the Magician*. Toronto: Macmillan, 1962. Print.
MacEwen, Gwendolyn. *Noman*. Ottawa: Oberon, 1972. Print.
MacEwen, Gwendolyn. *The Rising Fire*. Toronto: Contact, 1963. Print.
MacEwen, Gwendolyn. *The Shadow-maker*. Toronto: Macmillan, 1969. Print.
MacEwen, Gwendolyn. *The T.E. Lawrence Poems*. Oakville: Mosaic, 1982. Print.
Ondaatje, Michael. *The Cinnamon Peeler: Selected Poems*. Toronto: McClelland, 1992. Print.
Ondaatje, Michael. *The Collected Works of Billy the Kid: Left Handed Poems*. Toronto: Anansi, 1970. Print.
Ondaatje, Michael. *Coming through Slaughter*. Toronto: Anansi, 1976. Print.
Ondaatje, Michael. *The Dainty Monsters*. Toronto: Coach House, 1967. Print.
Ondaatje, Michael. *The English Patient*. New York: Knopf, 1992. Print.
Ondaatje, Michael. *In the Skin of a Lion*. 1987. Toronto: Penguin, 1988. Print.
Ondaatje, Michael. *Leonard Cohen*. Toronto: McClelland, 1970. Print.
Ondaatje, Michael. *Rat Jelly*. Toronto: Coach House, 1973. Print.
Ondaatje, Michael. *Running in the Family*. Toronto: McClelland, 1982. Print.
Ondaatje, Michael. *Secular Love*. Toronto: Coach House, 1984. Print.
Ondaatje, Michael. *There's a Trick with a Knife I'm Learning to Do: Poems 1963–1978*. Toronto: McClelland, 1979. Print.
Ondaatje, Michael. "What Is in the Pot." *The Long Poem Anthology*. Ed. Ondaatje. Toronto: Coach House, 1979. 11–18. Print.

Primary Texts: Recorded Music

Cohen, Leonard. *Death of a Ladies' Man*. 1977. Sony, 1990. CD.
Cohen, Leonard. *I'm Your Man*. 1988. Sony, 1990. CD.
Cohen, Leonard. *New Skin for the Old Ceremony*. 1974. Sony, 1994. CD.
Cohen, Leonard. *Songs from a Room*. 1969. Sony, 2007. CD.
Cohen, Leonard. *Songs of Leonard Cohen*. 1967. Sony, 2007. CD.
Cohen, Leonard. *Songs of Love and Hate*. 1971. Sony, 2007. CD.
Cohen, Leonard. *Various Positions*. 1984. SBME, 2008. CD.

Secondary Texts

Abraham, Michael Q. "Neurotic Affiliations: Klein, Layton, Cohen, and the Properties of Influence." *Canadian Poetry* 38 (1996): 88–129. Print.

Alberoni, Francesco. "The Powerless Elite: Theory and Sociological Research on the Phenomenon of the Stars." *Sociology of Mass Communications*. Ed. Denis McQuail. London: Penguin, 1972. 75–98. Print.

Aldington, Richard. *Lawrence of Arabia: A Biographical Enquiry*. London: Collins, 1955. Print.

Allan, Blaine. *CBC Television Series: 1952 to 1982*. Ed. Blaine Allan and Derek Redmond. U of Queens, 4 Dec. 1996. Web. 15 Feb. 2007. <http://www.film.queensu.ca/CBC/Fab.html>

Al Purdy: "A Sensitive Man." Dir. Donald Winkler. National Film Board of Canada, 1988. Film.

Amiel, Barbara. "Leonard Cohen Says That to All the Girls." *Maclean's* 18 Sept. 1978: 55–9. Print.

Amiel, Barbara. "Poetry: Time Capsules on Canada." *Maclean's* 15 Jan. 1979: 49–50. Print.

Anderson, Benedict. *Imagined Communities: Reflections on the Origin and Spread of Nationalism*. London: Verso, 1983. Print.

Anthology. CBC. 21 Dec. 1968. Radio.

Atwood, Margaret. "Canadian Monsters: Some Aspects of the Supernatural in Canadian Fiction." *The Canadian Imagination: Dimensions of a Literary Culture*. Ed. David Staines. Cambridge: Harvard UP, 1977. 97–122. Print.

Atwood, Margaret. "Introduction." *The New Oxford Book of Canadian Verse*. Toronto: Oxford UP, 1982. xxvii– xxxix. Print.

Atwood, Margaret. "MacEwen's Muse." *Canadian Literature* 45 (1970): 24–32.

Balázs, Thomas P. "Recognizing Masochism: Psychoanalysis and the Politics of Sexual Submission in *Ulysses*." *Joyce Studies Annual* 13.1 (2002): 160–91. Print. http://dx.doi.org/10.1353/joy.2002.0003

Banks, Russell, Michael Ondaatje, and David Young, eds. *Brushes with Greatness: An Anthology of Chance Encounters with Celebrities*. Toronto: Coach House, 1989. Print.

Barbour, Douglas. *Michael Ondaatje*. New York: Twayne, 1993. Print.

Barker, Francis. *The Tremulous Private Body*. Ann Arbor: U of Michigan P, 1995. Print.

Barthes, Roland. "The Death of the Author." 1977. *The Book History Reader*. Ed. David Finkelstein and Alistair McCleery. London: Routledge, 2002. 221–4. Print.

Barthes, Roland. *The Pleasure of the Text*. 1973. Trans. Richard Miller. New York: Hill and Wang, 1975. Print.

Bartley, Jan. *Invocations: The Poetry and Prose of Gwendolyn MacEwen*. Vancouver: U of British Columbia P, 1983. Print.

Baudrillard, Jean. *Simulacra and Simulation*. 1981. Trans. Sheila Faria Glaser. Ann Arbor: Michigan UP, 1994. Print.

Baumeister, Roy F. *Masochism and the Self*. Hillsdale: Lawrence Erlbaum, 1989. Print.

Bentley, D.M.R. *The Confederation Group of Canadian Poets, 1880–1897*. Toronto: U of Toronto P, 2004. Print.

Berlin, Isaiah. "Two Concepts of Liberty." 1958. *Four Essays on Liberty*. 1969. London: Oxford UP, 2002. Print. http://dx.doi.org/10.1093/019924989X.001.0001

Bloom, Harold. *The Anxiety of Influence: A Theory of Poetry*. New York: Oxford UP, 1973. Print.

Boorstin, Daniel J. *The Image: A Guide to Pseudo-events in America*. 1961. New York: Atheneum, 1977. Print.

Bouchard, Gilbert A. "He Came to Edmonton a Private Person and Left Famous." *Globe and Mail* 23 July 2008: R3. Print.

Bourdieu, Pierre. *Distinction: A Social Critique of the Judgement of Taste*. 1979. Trans. Richard Nice. Cambridge: Harvard UP, 1984. Print.

Brady, Judith. "Michael Ondaatje: An Annotated Bibliography." *The Annotated Bibliography of Canada's Major Authors*. Ed. Robert Lecker and Jack David. Vol. 6. Toronto: ECW, 1985. Print.

Braid, Kate. *A Well-mannered Storm: The Glenn Gould Poems*. Halfmoon Bay: Caitlin, 2008. Print.

Braudy, Leo. *The Frenzy of Renown: Fame and Its History*. New York: Oxford UP, 1986. Print.

Bristol, Michael D. *Big Time Shakespeare*. London: Routledge, 1996. Print.

Broten, Delores. *The Lumber Jack Report: English Canadian Literary Trade Book Publishers' Sales 1963–1972*. Toronto: Canlit, 1975. Print.

Butler, Judith. *Gender Trouble: Feminism and the Subversion of Identity*. New York: Routledge, 1990. Print.

Cahill, Brian. "Exotic Poetry, Jazz in the Cultural Temple." *Globe and Mail* 8 Mar. 1958: 7. Print.

"Calgary Poet Hits U.K. Bestseller List." *CBC News*. CBC, 5 Jan. 2009. Web. 20 Nov. 2011. <http://www.cbc.ca/news/world/story/2009/01/05/eunoia-poet.html>.

Callwood, June. "The Lusty Laureate from the Slums." *Irving Layton: The Poet and His Critics*. Toronto: McGraw-Hill, 1978. 107–16. Print.

Cameron, Elspeth. *Irving Layton: A Portrait*. Toronto: Stoddart, 1985. Print.

Camlot, Jason. "'I am their mouth': Listening to the Layton Archive." Layton Out Loud. Concordia University, Loyola Campus. 1 Oct. 2009. Address.

"Canadian Broadcasting Corporation: The Advent of Television." *The Canadian Encyclopedia*. Historica-Dominion, 4 May 2009. Web. 2 Apr. 2012. <http://www.thecanadianencyclopedia.com>.

Casablanca. Dir. Michael Curtiz. Warner Bros. Pictures, 1943. Film.

Cashmore, Ellis. *Celebrity / Culture*. New York: Routledge, 2006. Print.

Cherry, Zena. "Poet Layton Marries Movie Publicist." *Globe and Mail* 24 Nov. 1978: 11. Print.

"Christian Bök." Griffin Trust for Excellence in Poetry, n.d. Web. 5 Sept. 2012. <http://www.griffinpoetryprize.com/awards-and-poets/shortlists/2002-shortlist/christian-bok/>.

Citizens' Forum. CBC. 12 Dec. 1956. Radio.

Cohen, Leonard. Interview by Jian Ghomeshi. "Leonard Cohen: In Three Acts." *Q*. CBC Radio. 88.5 FM, Montreal, 16 Apr. 2009. Radio.

Cohen, Ted. "Metaphor and the Cultivation of Intimacy." *Critical Inquiry* 5.1 (1978): 3–12. Print. http://dx.doi.org/10.1086/447969

Cohen, Ted. *Thinking of Others: On the Talent for Metaphor*. Princeton: Princeton UP, 2008. Print.

Coleman, Daniel. *Masculine Migrations: Reading the Postcolonial Male in "New Canadian" Narratives*. Toronto: U of Toronto P, 1998. Print.

Cooke, Nathalie. *Margaret Atwood: A Biography*. Toronto: ECW, 1998. Print.

Cooley, Dennis. "'I Am Here on the Edge': Modern Hero / Postmodern Poetics in *The Collected Works of Billy the Kid*." *Spider Blues: Essays on Michael Ondaatje*. Ed. Sam Solecki. Montreal: Véhicule, 1985. 211–39. Print.

Cowen, Tyler. *What Price Fame?* Cambridge: Harvard UP, 2000. Print.

Crocker, J. Christopher. "The Social Functions of Rhetorical Forms." *The Social Use of Metaphor: Essays on the Anthropology of Rhetoric*. Ed. J. David Sapir and J. Christopher Crocker. Philadelphia: U of Pennsylvania P, 1977. 33–66. Print.

Cuordileone, K.A. *Manhood and American Political Culture in the Cold War*. New York: Routledge, 2005. Print.

Currie, Robert A. "Don't Blame This on Bliss." 1954. *The Making of Modern Poetry in Canada*. Eds. Louis Dudek and Michael Gnarowski. Toronto: Ryerson, 1967. 149–51. Print.

Davey, Frank. *Canadian Literary Power*. Edmonton: NeWest, 1994. Print.

Davey, Frank. *Surviving the Paraphrase: Eleven Essays on Canadian Literature*. Winnipeg: Turnstone, 1983. Print.

Davidson, Donald. "What Metaphors Mean." *Critical Inquiry* 5.1 (1978): 31–47. Print.

Davidson, Michael. *Guys Like Us: Citing Masculinity in Cold War Poetics*. Chicago: Chicago UP, 2004. Print.

Debord, Guy. *The Society of the Spectacle*. 1967. Trans. Donald Nicholson-Smith. New York: Zone, 1995. Print.

Del Caro, Adrian, and Robert B. Pippin, eds. *Thus Spoke Zarathustra*. 1883–5. Cambridge: Cambridge UP, 2006. Print.

Deleuze, Gilles. "Coldness and Cruelty." 1971. *Masochism*. New York: Zone, 1989. Print.

Denisoff, Dennis. "Homosocial Desire and the Artificial Man in Michael Ondaatje's *The Collected Works of Billy the Kid*." *Essays on Canadian Writing* 53 (1994): 51–70. Print.

Derrida, Jacques. *Psyche: Inventions of the Other*. 1987. Stanford: Stanford UP, 2007. Print.

Deshaye, Joel. "Celebrity and Passing in Gwendolyn MacEwen's *The T.E. Lawrence Poems*." *Journal of Commonwealth Literature* 46.3 (2011): 531–50. Print. http://dx.doi.org/10.1177/0021989411409810

Deshaye, Joel. "Celebrity and the Poetic Dialogue of Irving Layton and Leonard Cohen." *Studies in Canadian Literature / Études en littérature canadienne* 34.2 (2009): 77–105. Print.

Deshaye, Joel. "Parading the Underworld of New Orleans in Ondaatje's *Coming through Slaughter*." *American Review of Canadian Studies* 38.4 (2008): 473–94. Print. http://dx.doi.org/10.1080/02722010809481725

Devlin, Jim. *In Every Style of Passion: The Works of Leonard Cohen*. London: Omnibus, 1996. Print.

Dudek, Louis. Interview. "Committed to Excellence." *Books in Canada* Nov. 1993: 7–12. Print.

Dudek, Louis. "Layton on the Carpet." 1959. *Irving Layton: The Poet and His Critics*. Ed. Seymour Mayne. Toronto: McGraw-Hill, 1978. 88–92. Print.

Dudek, Louis. "Poetry in English [The Writing of the Decade]." *Canadian Literature* Summer 1969: 111–20. Print.

Dudek, Louis. "The State of Canadian Poetry: 1954." *Canadian Forum* 34 (1954): 153–5. Print.

Dudek, Louis and Michael Gnarowski, eds. "Poetry Finds a Public." *The Making of Modern Poetry in Canada*. Toronto: Ryerson, 1967. 231–3. Print.

Dyer, Richard. *Stars*. London: BFI, 1998. Print.

Eagleton, Terry. *After Theory*. London: Penguin, 2003. Print.

Eder, Bruce. "Leonard Cohen: Biography." *Allmusic.com*. Rovi, 16 Oct. 2011. Web. <http://www.allmusic.com/artist/leonard-cohen-p1948/biography>.

Eliot, T.S. "What Is Minor Poetry?" 1944. *On Poets and Poetry*. London: Faber, 1957. Print.

Elliott, Robert C. *The Literary Persona*. Chicago: U of Chicago P, 1982. Print.

Engel, Marian. "The Greek Light Suits Him." Rev. of *Lovers and Lesser Men*, by Irving Layton. *Globe and Mail* 10 Mar. 1973: 11. Print.

English, James F., and John Frow. "Literary Authorship and Celebrity Culture." *A Concise Companion to Contemporary British Fiction*. Ed. English. Malden: Blackwell, 2006. 39–57. Print. http://dx.doi.org/10.1002/9780470757673

Faludi, Susan. *Stiffed: The Betrayal of the American Man*. New York: Perennial, 2000. Print.

Fighting Words. CBC. 28 Jan. 1958. Radio.

Fighting Words. CBC. 11 Nov. 1958. Radio.

Fighting Words. CBC. 28 January 1958. Radio.

Fighting Words. CBC. 6 Dec. 1956. Television.

Fighting Words. CBC. 31 Jan. 1960. Television.

Fighting Words. CBC. 19 June 1960. Television.

Filip, Raymond. "The Only Montreal Poet Who Doesn't Know Leonard Cohen." *Take This Waltz: A Celebration of Leonard Cohen*. Ed. Michael Fournier and Ken Norris. Ste Anne de Bellevue: Muses' Co. 1994. 71–80. Print.

Finke, Michael C. "An Introduction." *One Hundred Years of Masochism: Literary Texts, Social and Cultural Contexts*. Ed. Michael C. Finke and Carl Niekerk. Amsterdam: Rodopi, 2000. 1–14. Print.

Flynn, Kevin. "Balanced on Wooden Stilts and Dancing: What Irving Layton Taught Me about Leonard Cohen." *Essays on Canadian Writing* 69 (1999): 9–11. Print.

Francis, Wynne. "Adjusting the Sights: Gnarowski's Binoculars." *Raging Like a Fire: A Celebration of Irving Layton*. Ed. Henry Beissel and Joy Bennett. Montreal: Véhicule, 1993. 78–90. Print.

Francis, Wynne. *Irving Layton and His Works*. Toronto: ECW, 1984. Print.

Francis, Wynne. "Layton and Nietzsche." *Canadian Literature* 67 (1976): 39–52. Print.

Fraser, Nancy. "Rethinking the Public Sphere: A Contribution to the Critique of Actually Existing Democracy." *Habermas and the Public Sphere*. Ed. Craig Calhoun. Cambridge: MIT, 1992. 109–42. Print.

French, William. "Female Authors Mauled in Pan of Engel's Bear." *Globe and Mail* 29 Mar. 1977: 14. Print.

Freud, Sigmund. "The Uncanny." 1919. *The Uncanny*. Trans. David McLintock. London: Penguin, 2003. 121–62. Print.

Frow, John. "Is Elvis a God?" *International Journal of Cultural Studies* 1.2 (1998): 197–210. Print.

Frye, Northrop. "The Motive for Metaphor." 1963. *The Educated Imagination*. Toronto: Anansi, 2002. 1–11. Print.

Fuss, Diana. *Identification Papers*. New York: Routledge, 1995. Print.

Gaar, Gillian G. "Joplin, Janis." *Encyclopaedia Britannica Online*. Encyclopaedia Britannica, 24 July 2009. Web. <http://www.search.eb.com/eb/article-9105269>.

Geddes, Gary. "An Imperfect Devotion." *Raging Like a Fire: A Celebration of Irving Layton*. Ed. Henry Beissel and Joy Bennett. Montreal: Véhicule, 1993. 20–4. Print.

Glass, Loren. *Authors Inc.: Literary Celebrity in the Modern United States, 1880–1980*. New York: New York UP, 2004. Print.

"Globe and Mail." *The Canadian Encyclopedia*. Historica-Dominion, 13 Jan. 2010. Web. <http://www.thecanadianencyclopedia.com>.

The Globe and Mail: Canada's Heritage from 1844. 2002. Web. 15 June 2009. <http://heritage.theglobeandmail.com/Default.asp>.http://www.thecanadianen cyclopedia.com/

Goldman, Jonathan. *Modernism Is the Literature of Celebrity*. Austin: U of Texas P, 2011. Print.

Goldman, Marlene. *Rewriting Apocalypse in Canadian Fiction*. Montreal: McGill-Queen's UP, 2005. Print.

Goldman, Marlene, and Joanne Saul. "Talking with Ghosts: Haunting in Canadian Cultural Production." *University of Toronto Quarterly* 75.2 (2006): 645–55. Print.

Grant, Douglas. "Critic." *Writing in Canada: Proceedings of the Canadian Writers' Conference, Queen's University, 28–31 July, 1955*. Ed. George Whalley. Toronto: Macmillan, 1956. 32–40. Print.

"Grisham Ranks as Top-selling Author of Decade." *CNN.com*. Cable News Network, n.d. Web. 23 Mar. 2009. <http://archives.cnn.com/1999/books/news/12/31/1990. sellers/index.html>.

Hamilton, Edith. *Mythology*. Boston: Little, Brown, 1942. Print.

Hammill, Faye. *Women, Celebrity, & Literary Culture between the Wars*. Austin: U of Texas P, 2007. Print.

Harries, Karsten. "Metaphor and Transcendence." *Critical Inquiry* 5.1 (1978): 73–90. Print. http://dx.doi.org/10.1086/447973

Harris, Michael. "Leonard Cohen: The Poet as Hero: Cohen by Himself." *Saturday Night* 84.6 (June 1969): 26–30. Print.

Harvey, Jocelyn, and Katherine Berg. "Governor General's Literary Awards." *The Oxford Companion to Canadian Literature*. Ed. William Toye. Toronto: Oxford UP, 1983. 309–14. Print.

Hedley, Jane. *Power in Verse: Metaphor and Metonymy in the Renaissance Lyric*. University Park: Pennsylvania State UP, 1988. Print.

Heinricks, Geoff. "From *A Fool and Forty Acres*." *The Al Purdy A-frame Anthology*. Ed. Paul Vermeersch. Madeira Park: Harbour, 2009. 66–72. Print.

Hillger, Annick. *Not Needing All the Words: Michael Ondaatje's Literature of Silence*. Montreal: McGill-Queen's UP, 2006. Print.

Hochbruck, Wolfgang. "Metafictional Biography: Michael Ondaatje's *Coming through Slaughter* and *The Collected Works of Billy the Kid*." *Historiographic Metafiction in Modern American and Canadian Literature*. Ed. Bernd Engler and Kurt Müller. Zurich: Ferdinand Schöningh, 1994. 447–63. Print.

Holmes, Su, and Sean Redmond, eds. *Framing Celebrity: New Directions in Celebrity Culture*. London: Routledge, 2006. Print.

Hope, A.D. Rev. of *A Red Carpet for the Sun*, by Irving Layton. 1960. *Irving Layton: The Poet and His Critics*. Ed. Seymour Mayne. Toronto: McGraw-Hill, 1978. 101–4. Print.

Hošek, Chaviva. “Poetry in English 1950 to 1982.” *The Oxford Companion to Canadian Literature*. Ed. Eugene Benson and William Toye. 2nd ed. Toronto: Oxford UP, 1997. 933–41. Print.

Hostert, Anna Camaiti. *Passing: A Strategy to Dissolve Identities and Remap Differences*. 1996. Trans. Christine Marciasini. Madison: Fairleigh Dickinson UP, 2007. Print.

Huggan, Graham. *The Postcolonial Exotic: Marketing the Margins*. London: Routledge, 2001. Print. http://dx.doi.org/10.4324/9780203420102

Hutcheon, Linda. “Leonard Cohen and His Works.” *Canadian Writers and Their Works*. [Fiction Series]. Ed. Robert Lecker, Jack David, Ellen Quigley, et al. Toronto: ECW, 1989. 25–65. Print.

Hutcheon, Linda. “Leonard Cohen and His Works.” *Canadian Writers and Their Works*. [Poetry Series]. Ed. Robert Lecker, Jack David, Ellen Quigley, et al. Toronto: ECW, 1992. 21–65. Print.

Jackson, Marni. “Saving a Purdy A-frame – and Other Cultural Edifices.” *Globe and Mail* 6 Sep. 2012. Web. 30 March 2013. <http://www.theglobeandmail.com/commentary/saving-a-purdy-a-frame — and-other-cultural-edifices/article4097919/>.

Jaffe, Aaron. *Modernism and the Culture of Celebrity*. Cambridge: Cambridge UP, 2005. Print.

Jenson, Joli. “Fandom as Pathology: The Consequences of Characterization.” *The Adoring Audience: Fan Culture and Popular Media*. Ed. Lisa A. Lewis. London: Routledge, 1992. 9–29. Print.

Jewinski, Ed. *Michael Ondaatje: Express Yourself Beautifully*. Toronto: ECW, 1994. Print.

Kamboureli, Smaro. “The Culture of Celebrity and National Pedagogy.” *Home-work: Postcolonialism, Pedagogy & Canadian Literature*. Ed. Cynthia Sugars. Ottawa: U of Ottawa P, 2004. 35–56. Print.

Kamboureli, Smaro. “Outlawed Narrative: Michael Ondaatje’s *The Collected Works of Billy the Kid*.” *Sagetrieb: A Journal Devoted to Poets in the Imagist / Objectivist Tradition* 7.1 (1988): 115–29. Print.

Kane, Thomas H. “The Deaths of the Authors: Literary Celebrity and Automortography in Acker, Barthelme, Bukowski, and Carver’s Last Acts.” *Lit: Literature Interpretation Theory* 15.4 (2004): 409–43. Print.http://dx.doi.org/10.1080/10436920490534389.

Krugman, Paul. “Block Those Metaphors.” *New York Times* 10 Dec. 2010. Web. 3 Jan. 2011. <http://www.nytimes.com/2010/12/13/opinion/13krugman.html>.

Lacan, Jacques. *Écrits: A Selection*. 1966. Trans. Bruce Fink. New York: Norton, 2002. Print.

Lacan, Jacques. *The Four Fundamental Concepts of Psychoanalysis*. 1973. Ed. Jacques-Alain Miller. Trans. Alan Sheridan. New York: Norton, 1981. Print.

Ladies and Gentlemen... Mr. Leonard Cohen. Dir. Donald Brittain and Don Owen. National Film Board of Canada, 1965. Film.

Lakoff, George, and Mark Turner. *More than Cool Reason: A Field Guide to Poetic Metaphor*. Chicago: U of Chicago P, 1989. Print.

Latham, Sean. *Am I a Snob?: Modernism and the Novel*. Ithaca: Cornell UP, 2003. Print.

Lawrence, T.E. *The Letters of T.E. Lawrence*. Ed. David Garnett. London: J. Cape, 1938. Print.

Lawrence, T.E. *The Mint: A Day-book of the RAF Depot between August and December 1922*. London: J. Cape, 1955. Print.

Lawrence, T.E. *Seven Pillars of Wisdom: A Triumph*. 1935. London: Penguin, 2000. Print.

Lawson, Bruce. "A New Religious Age for Leonard Cohen." *Globe and Mail* 23 July 1966: 13. Print.

Layton, David. *Motion Sickness: A Memoir*. Toronto: Macfarlane, 1999. Print.

Lecker, Robert. *Keepers of the Code: English-Canadian Literary Anthologies and the Representation of Nation*. Toronto: U of Toronto P, 2013. Print.

Lecker, Robert. *Making It Real: The Canonization of English-Canadian Literature*. Toronto: Anansi, 1995. Print.

Lecker, Robert. "Privacy, Publicity, and the Discourse of Canadian Criticism." *Essays on Canadian Writing* 51–2 (1993): 32–82. Print.

Lee, Dennis. "The Collected Works of Billy the Kid." *Savage Fields: An Essay in Literature and Cosmology*. Toronto: Anansi, 1977. 15–44. Print.

"Leonard Cohen Discography." *Wikipedia*. Wikimedia Foundation, 4 Oct. 2011. Web. 15 Oct. 2011. <http://en.wikipedia.org/wiki/Leonard_Cohen_discography>.

Lewis, Joanne. "Irving's Women: A Feminist Critique of the Love Poems of Irving Layton." *Studies in Canadian Literature / Études en Littérature Canadienne* 13.2 (1988): 142–56. Print.

Lodge, David. *The Modes of Modern Writing: Metaphor, Metonymy, and the Typology of Modern Literature*. Ithaca: Cornell UP, 1977. Print.

Lynch, Gerald. "Star-stricken." Rev. of *Literary Celebrity in Canada*, by Lorraine York. *Canadian Poetry* 62 (2008): 87–91. Print.

Maggs, Randall. *Night Work: The Sawchuk Poems*. London: Brick, 2008. Print.

Mandel, Eli. "Cohen's Life as a Slave." *Brave New Wave*. Ed. Jack David. Windsor: Black Moss, 1978. 209–26. Print.

Mandel, Eli. *From Room to Room: The Poetry of Eli Mandel*. Ed. Peter Webb. Waterloo: Wilfrid Laurier UP, 2011. Print.

Mandel, Eli. *Irving Layton*. Toronto: Forum House, 1969. Print.

Marchand, Philip. “The Year in Books.” *Star.com*. Toronto Star Newspapers, 30 Dec. 2007. Web. 3 Apr. 2013. <http://www.thestar.com/entertainment/books/article/289559>.

Marshall, P. David. *Celebrity and Power: Fame in Contemporary Culture*. Minneapolis: Minnesota UP, 1997. Print.

Martin, Robert. “Cohen Extremely Private Despite Displays of Emotion.” *Globe and Mail* 29 June 1973: 15. Print.

McCutcheon, Lynn E., et al. *Celebrity Worshippers: Inside the Minds of Stargazers*. Baltimore: PublishAmerica, 2004. Print.

McKay, R. Bruce. “The CBC and the Public: Management Decision Making in the English Television Service of the Canadian Broadcasting Corporation, 1970–1974.” Diss. Stanford U., 1976. Print.

McLuhan, Marshall. *Understanding Media: The Extensions of Man*. New York: McGraw-Hill, 1965. Print.

Mead, George Herbert. *Mind, Self and Society*. Ed. Charles W. Morris. Chicago: U of Chicago P, 1934. Print.

Merleau-Ponty, Maurice. *Phenomenology of Perception*. 1945. Trans. Colin Smith. London: Routledge, 1962. Print.

Messenger, Cynthia. “Poetry in English 1983 to 1996.” *The Oxford Companion to Canadian Literature*. Ed. Eugene Benson and William Toye. 2nd ed. Toronto: Oxford UP, 1997. 941–8. Print.

Mole, Tom. *Byron’s Romantic Celebrity: Industrial Culture and the Hermeneutic of Intimacy*. Basingstoke: Palgrave Macmillan, 2007. Print. http://dx.doi.org/10.1057/9780230288386

Moran, Joe. *Star Authors: Literary Celebrity in America*. London: Pluto, 2000. Print.

Morton, Wendy. *Six Impossible Things before Breakfast: Taking Poetry Public across Canada*. Victoria: Emdash, 2006. Print.

Moynihan, Sinéad. “History Repeating Itself: Passing, *Pudd’nhead Wilson*, and *The President’s Daughter*.” *Callaloo* 32.3 (2009): 809–21. Print. http://dx.doi.org/10.1353/cal.0.0475

Munk, Linda. “Four Women Poets.” *Woman’s Globe and Mail* 28 Jan. 1965: W1. Print. http://dx.doi.org/10.1093/screen/39.1.22

“Music Recording Sales Certification.” *Wikipedia*. Wikimedia Foundation,8 Sep. 2011. Web. 15 Oct. 2011 <http://en.wikipedia.org/wiki/Gold_album>.

Nadel, Ira. *Various Positions: A Life of Leonard Cohen*. Toronto: Random House, 1996. Print.

Nash, Knowlton. *The Microphone Wars: A History of Triumph and Betrayal at the CBC*. Toronto: McClelland, 1994. Print.

Nietzsche, Friedrich. *Thus Spoke Zarathustra*. 1883–5. Trans. Adrian Del Caro. Ed. Adrian Del Caro and Robert B. Pippin. Cambridge: Cambridge UP, 2006. Print.

Nodelman, Perry M. "The Collected Photographs of Billy the Kid." *Canadian Literature* 87 (1980): 68–79. Print.

Osborne, Stephen. "Banker Poet." *Geist* 81 (2011): 10–13.

Overbye, Karen. "Re-membering the Body: Constructing the Self as Hero in *In the Skin of a Lion*." *Studies in Canadian Literature / Études en littérature canadienne* 17.2 (1992): n.p. Web. 13 Sept. 2011. <http://journals.hil.unb.ca/index.php/SCL/article/view/8161/9218>.

Owens, Judith. "'I Send You a Picture': Ondaatje's Portrait of Billy the Kid." *Studies in Canadian Literature* 8.1 (1983): 117–39. Print.

Pacey, Desmond. Rev. of *The Swinging Flesh*, by Irving Layton. *Irving Layton: The Poet and His Critics*. Ed. Seymour Mayne. Toronto: McGraw-Hill, 1978. 119–21. Print.

Pacey, Desmond. "The Writer and His Public: 1920–1960." *Literary History of Canada*. Toronto: U of Toronto P, 1965. 477–95. Print.

Paul, Annie Murphy. "Your Brain on Fiction." *New York Times* 17 Mar. 2012. Web. 20 Sept. 2012. <http://www.nytimes.com/2012/03/18/opinion/sunday/the-neuroscience-of-your-brain-on-fiction.html?pagewanted=all>.

Pirrie, Alastair. "Cohen Regrets." *New Musical Express* 10 Mar. 1973: 66. Print.

"Poet Al Purdy's home to become writer's residence." CBC News 29 Oct. 2012. Web. 30 March 2013. http://www.cbc.ca/news/canada/ottawa/story/2012/10/29/ottawa-al-purdy-aframe-home-to-become-writer-residence.html.

Poet: Irving Layton Observed. Dir. Donald Winkler. National Film Board of Canada, 1986. Film.

Potvin, Liza. "Gwendolyn MacEwen and Female Spiritual Desire." *Canadian Poetry* 28 (1991): 18–39. Print.

Pratt, Brooke. "Celebrity with a Cause: The Al Purdy A-frame Trust." Association of Canadian College and University Teachers of English Conference. Wilfrid Laurier University and the University of Waterloo. 28 May 2012. Address.

Price, Steven. *Anatomy of Keys*. London: Brick, 2006. Print.

Punter, David. *Metaphor*. London: Routledge, 2007. Print.

Purdy, Al. *The Al Purdy A-frame Anthology*. Ed. Paul Vermeersch. Madeira Park: Harbour, 2009. Print.

Purdy, Al. *Reaching for the Beaufort Sea: The Autobiography of Al Purdy*. Madeira Park: Harbour, 1993. Print.

Queyras, Sina. "Public Poet, Private Life: On the Dream of a Communal Self" [a title that she also referred to as "20 Riffs, Provocations, Asides, Assertions, and One Statement"]. Public Poetics Conference. Mount Allison University. 21 Sept. 2012. Address.

Rae, Ian. *From Cohen to Carson: The Poet's Novel in Canada*. Montreal: McGill-Queen's UP, 2008. Print.

Ravvin, Norman. “Making It Mainstream: Montreal and the Canadian Jewish Poetic Tradition.” *Literature & Theology* 24.2 (2010): 121–36. Print. http://dx.doi.org/10.1093/litthe/frq020

Reid, Mary. “‘This Is the World as We Have Made It’: Gwendolyn MacEwen’s Poetics of History.” *Canadian Poetry* 58 (2006): 36–54. Print.

Richler, Mordecai. *The Incomparable Atuk*. Toronto: McClelland, 1963. Print.

Ricoeur, Paul. “The Metaphorical Process as Cognition, Imagination, and Feeling.” *Critical Inquiry* 5.1 (1978): 143–59. Print. http://dx.doi.org/10.1086/447977

Ricoeur, Paul. *Oneself as Another*. Trans. Kathleen Blamey. Chicago: U of Chicago P, 1992. Print.

Ricoeur, Paul. *The Rule of Metaphor: The Creation of Meaning in Language*. 1975. Trans. Robert Czerny with Kathleen McLaughlin and John Costello, SJ. London: Routledge, 1977. Print.

Ricou, Laurie. “Poetry.” *Literary History of Canada: Canadian Literature in English*. Vol. 4. Ed. W.H. New. 2nd ed. Toronto: U of Toronto P, 1990. 3–45. Print.

Rio Bravo. 1959. Dir. Howard Hawks. Perf. John Wayne, Dean Martin, Ricky Nelson, and Angie Dickinson. Warner, 2007. DVD.

Rizzardi, Alfredo. “Irving Layton in Italy.” *Raging Like a Fire: A Celebration of Irving Layton*. Ed. Henry Beissel and Joy Bennett. Montreal: Véhicule, 1993. 39–42. Print.

Roberts, Gillian. *Prizing Literature: The Celebration and Circulation of National Culture*. Toronto: U of Toronto P, 2011. Print.

Rojek, Chris. *Celebrity*. London: Reaktion, 2001. Print.

Rosengren, Karl Erik. “Time and Literary Fame.” *Poetics* 14.1–2 (1985): 157–72. Print. http://dx.doi.org/10.1016/0304-422X(85)90009-9

Ross, Alexander. “The Man Who Copyrighted Passion.” *Maclean’s* 15 Nov. 1965: 22, 45–9. Print.

Royle, Nicholas. *The Uncanny*. New York: Routledge, 2003. Print.

Ruddy, John. “Is the World (or Anybody) Ready for Leonard Cohen?” *Maclean’s* 1 Oct. 1966:18–19, 33–4. Print.

Samei, Maija Bell. *Gendered Persona and Poetic Voice: The Abandoned Woman in Early Chinese Song Lyrics*. Lanham: Lexington, 2004. Print.

Schmid, David. “Idols of Destruction: Celebrity and the Serial Killer.” *Framing Celebrity: New Directions in Celebrity Culture*. Ed. Su Holmes and Sean Redmond. London: Routledge, 2006. 295–310. Print.

Schneller, Johanna. “Writing ‘Always Gets Harder’ for Michael Ondaatje.” *Globe and Mail* 14 Apr. 2007. Web. 18 May 2008. <http://www.theglobeandmail.com>.

Scobie, Stephen, ed. *Intricate Preparations*. Toronto: ECW, 2000. 100–16. Print.

Scobie, Stephen. *Leonard Cohen*. Vancouver: Douglas, 1978. Print.

Scobie, Stephen. "Two Authors in Search of a Character: bp Nichol and Michael Ondaatje." 1972. *Spider Blues: Essays on Michael Ondaatje*. Ed. Sam Solecki. Montreal: Véhicule, 1985. 185–210. Print.

Scott, Andrew Murray. *Alexander Trocchi: The Making of the Monster*. Edinburgh: Polygon, 1991. Print.

Sedgwick, Eve Kosofsky. *Between Men: English Literature and Male Homosocial Desire*. New York: Columbia UP, 1985. Print.

Siemerling, Winfried. *Discoveries of the Other: Alterity in the Work of Leonard Cohen, Hubert Aquin, Michael Ondaatje, and Nicole Brossard*. Toronto: U of Toronto P, 1994. Print.

Silverman, Kaja. *Male Subjectivity at the Margins*. New York: Routledge, 1992. Print.

Skelton, Robin. "The Personal Heresy." *Canadian Literature* 23 (1965): 63–5. Print.

Slonim, Leon. "Exoticism in Modern Canadian Poetry." *Essays on Canadian Writing* 1 (1974): 21–7. Print.

Smith, Patricia Keeney. "Irving Layton and the Theme of Death." 1971. *Irving Layton: The Poet and His Critics*. Ed. Seymour Mayne. Toronto: McGraw-Hill, 1978. 189–98. Print.

Solecki, Sam. "Coming Through: A Review of Secular Love." *Spider Blues: Essays on Michael Ondaatje*. Ed. Sam Solecki. Montreal: Véhicule, 1985. 125–31. Print.

Solecki, Sam. "Introduction." *A Wild Peculiar Joy*. By Irving Layton. Toronto: McClelland, 2004. 15–27. Print.

Solecki, Sam. *The Last Canadian Poet: An Essay on Al Purdy*. Toronto: U of Toronto P, 1999. Print.

Solecki, Sam. "Nets and Chaos: The Poetry of Michael Ondaatje." *Spider Blues: Essays on Michael Ondaatje*. Ed. Sam Solecki. Montreal: Véhicule, 1985. 93–110. Print.

Solecki, Sam. *Ragas of Longing: The Poetry of Michael Ondaatje*. Toronto: U of Toronto P, 2003. Print.

Solway, David. "Framing Layton." *Raging Like a Fire: A Celebration of Irving Layton*. Ed. Henry Beissel and Joy Bennett. Montreal: Véhicule, 1993. 212–26. Print.

Song of Leonard Cohen. Dir. Harry Rasky. Canadian Broadcasting Corporation, 1980. Film.

"Songs of Leonard Cohen." *Wikipedia*. Wikimedia Foundation,16 Sep. 2011. Web. 15 Oct. 2011 <http://en.wikipedia.org/wiki/Songs_of_Leonard_Cohen>.

Spinks, Lee. "Sense and Singularity: Reading Ondaatje's *The Collected Works of Billy the Kid*." *Canadian Literature* 197 (2008): 62–77. Print.

Staines, David. Foreword. *The Journals of Susanna Moodie*. By Margaret Atwood. 1970. Toronto: Macfarlane, 1997. ix–xv. Print.

Starnino, Carmine. “Vowel Movements: Pointless Toil and Empty Productivity.” *A Lover’s Quarrel: Essays and Reviews*. Erin: Porcupine’s Quill, 2004. 129–36. Print.

Stelter, Brian. “Upending Anonymity, These Days the Web Unmasks Everyone.” *New York Times* 20 June 2011. Web. 10 July 2011. <http://www.nytimes.com/2011/06/21/us/21anonymity.html>.

Stewart, Susan. *On Longing: Narratives of the Miniature, the Gigantic, the Souvenir, the Collection*. Baltimore: Johns Hopkins UP, 1984. Print.

Stromberg-Stein, Susan. *Louis Dudek: A Biographical Introduction to His Work*. Ottawa: Golden Dog, 1983. Print.

Sullivan, Rosemary. *Shadow Maker: The Life of Gwendolyn MacEwen*. 1995. Toronto: HarperPerennial, 1996. Print.

A Tall Man Executes a Jig by Irving Layton. Dir. Donald Winkler. National Film Board of Canada, 1986. Film.

“Television Programming.” *Canadian Encyclopedia*. Historica-Dominion, n.d. Web. 4 May 2009. <http://www.thecanadianencyclopedia.com>.

Thomas, Alan M. “Audience, Market and Public—an Evaluation of Canadian Broadcasting.” *Canadian Communications* 1.1 (1960): 16–47. Print.

Tobin, Robert. “Masochism and Identity.” *One Hundred Years of Masochism: Literary Texts, Social and Cultural Contexts*. Ed. Michael C. Finke and Carl Niekerk. Amsterdam: Rodopi, 2000. 33-52. Print.

Tompkins, Jane. *West of Everything: The Inner Life of Westerns*. Oxford: Oxford UP, 1992. Print.

Trehearne, Brian. *The Montreal Forties: Modernist Poetry in Transition*. Toronto: Toronto UP, 1999. Print.

Trehearne, Brian. “‘Scanned and Scorned’: Freedom and Fame in Layton.” *Inside the Poem: Essays and Poems in Honour of Donald Stephens*. Toronto: Oxford, 1992. 139–50. Print.

Turner, Graeme. *Understanding Celebrity*. London: SAGE, 2004. Print.

Underhill, Evelyn. *Mysticism: A Study in the Nature and Development of Spiritual Consciousness*. 1911. Mineola: Dover, 2002. Print.

Vermeersch, Paul, ed. *The Al Purdy A-frame Anthology*. Madeira Park: Harbour, 2009.

Walljasper, Joe. “1 Pool, 30 Seconds, 12 Pairs of Cuffs and 1 Elvis Impersonator.” *Columbia Daily Tribune* 28 Oct. 2008. Web. 17 Nov. 2008. <http://columbiatribune.com/2008/oct/20081028Spor004.asp>.

Warner, Michael. *Publics and Counterpublics*. Brooklyn: Zone, 2002. Print.

Warren, C. Letter. “Film on Leonard Cohen Curiously Ignored by Press.” *Globe and Mail* 13 Sept. 1980: 7. Print.

Waters, Colin. “Taking a Trip Downstream.” *Sunday Herald* 5 May 2002: 12. Print.

Weaver, Robert. "Broadcasting." *Writing in Canada: Proceedings of the Canadian Writers' Conference, Queen's University, 28–31 July, 1955*. Ed. George Whalley. Toronto: Macmillan, 1956. 103–14. Print.

"Wendy Morton: Honours and Sponsorships." *Canadian Poetry Online*. U of Toronto Libraries, n.d. Web. 5 Sept. 2012. <http://www.library.utoronto.ca/canpoetry/morton/awards.htm>.

"White Dwarf Star." *Encyclopædia Britannica Online*. Encyclopædia Britannica, n.d. Web. 11 Mar. 2010. <http://www.britannica.com/>.

Witten, Mark. "Billy, Buddy, and Michael: The Collected Writings of Michael Ondaatje Are a Composite Portrait of the Artist as a Private 'I.'" *Books in Canada* June–July 1997: 9–10, 12–13. Print.

Wood, Brent. "From *The Rising Fire* to *Afterworlds*: The Visionary Circle in the Poetry of Gwendolyn MacEwen." *Canadian Poetry* 47 (2000): 40–69. Print.

Wood, Brent. "No-man's Land: Mythic Crisis in Gwendolyn MacEwen's *The T. E. Lawrence Poems*." *Studies in Canadian Literature / Études en Littérature Canadienne* 29.2 (2004): 141–62. Print.

Woodcock, George. "Poetry." *Literary History of Canada: Canadian Literature in English*. Vol. 3. 2nd ed. Toronto: U of Toronto P, 1976. 284–317. Print.

Yeats, William Butler. "The Circus Animals' Desertion." 1939. *The Norton Anthology of Poetry, Shorter*. Ed. Margaret Ferguson, Mary Jo Salter, and Jon Stallworthy. 5th ed. New York: Norton, 1997. 782–4. Print.

York, Lorraine. *Literary Celebrity in Canada*. Toronto: U of Toronto P, 2007. Print.

York, Lorraine. *Margaret Atwood and the Labour of Literary Celebrity*. Toronto: U of Toronto P, 2013. Print.

York, Lorraine. "Viticultural Verse: Advertising, Poetry, and the Niagara Wine Industry." *Canadian Poetry* 69 (2011): 59–74. Print.

Index